CW00924352

"A refreshing read on the future of leadership! *The Language of Transition in Leadership* will not only teach you the nuances of great management style, but also the decisiveness, team building and empathy you need to get the best out of your team and organization. A must read!"

—**Dr. Marshall Goldsmith** is the Thinkers50 #1 Executive Coach and New York Times bestselling author of The Earned Life, Triggers, and What Got You Here Won't Get You There.

"Perhaps the most challenging task for the leader is to remain inspired when everything around them is changing. My son Tariq was killed by 14-year-old Tony at the age of 20. To return to the full joy of my life and thrive, I had to take the path of forgiveness. It is no different: leaders only grow to their full power, impact and results when they dare to face the deepest pain in their lives and make it a source of inspiration. Jakob, Riet and Leo superbly guide you to manifest that and land on higher ground. A must read for every leader!"

—**Azim Khamisa**, founder and director of the Tariq Khamisa Foundation, USA.

"Humans evolved and flourished by focusing on and avoiding danger. But for most of us today, that hard-wired approach no longer works. Focusing on opportunity, on the positive, is the surest way to flourish. This guide is full of practical and inspiring insights on how to learn from 'negative' experience and rewrite our stories and forge new paths to growth – individually, as teams or as organisations. We honor the past, as the authors write, but focus on the future that asks to be made possible."

—**Audrey Clegg**, Chief Talent Officer, Sanofi

"This book has become a compass for my leadership journey. Arriving at a point where I was allowed to make the transition from the leader of a local religious community of monks to the leader of all the communities of the same religious institute worldwide, this book brought me back to the importance of my calling as a human being, a Christian and a monk. Calling as a secure base. The Language of Transition in Leadership is a treasured travel guide for my leadership journey but also helps the religious institute on its journey through history, present and future. It continues to inspire me!"

—**Dom Bernardus Peeters OCSO**, Abbot General of the Order of the Cistercians of the Strict Observance (Trappists)

"The Language of Transition in Leadership offers a bold vision, and a deep one, built on the premise that we cannot know how to foster or navigate organizational change without intimate knowledge of our own life transitions, how we have been unconsciously shaped by them, and what we can learn from them. Just as the title implies, this requires a new language of understanding that pierces through our conventional wisdom to reach

the heart of the matter: *how we lead begins with who we are, and extends to what we do.* In chapter after chapter readers will encounter surprising new insights into themselves, their work, and their personal relationships, prompted by fresh conceptualizations of familiar problems, practical tools for self-reflection, relatable real-life illustrations, and unshakable belief in the capacity of every leader to find in every ending the seeds of new beginnings."

—**Robert A. Neimeyer, PhD**, Director of the Portland Institute for
Loss and Transition and editor of *New Techniques
in Grief Therapy: Bereavement and Beyond*

"First we must learn self-leadership before we lead others effectively. This book challenges us to deeply reflect on ourselves, what has shaped us, what makes us tick, what are our triggers, what are our deepest motivators, to help refine our leadership practice. As a young leader growing up in South Africa, I was fortunate to have worked directly for Nelson Mandela. A man who overcame considerable adversity including years of imprisonment, and yet emerged as a giver of hope, as the icon of unity. He had a powerful presence radiating both a compelling vision for the future, and personal warmth to all those he met, whatever their station. His example challenges us to grow beyond our circumstances, to continually practice leadership through deep self-knowledge, reflection, and discipline."

—**Viv McMenamin**, CEO South Africa, Mondi

"This book is phenomenal. I now enjoy conflict and the way I handle tense dialogue, which has helped me at work, but even more so at home. It's all-encompassing leadership vision and exceptionally effective methods allow any organisation to remain perfectly sane and inspired during the toughest of transformations. It is so powerful, that we designed our own multi-year leadership programme around it, and rolled it out throughout our entire organisation. It has changed the way we communicate, think and lead. We wouldn't be the same company without it. Read it with an open mind, it might change your life."

—**Rik van der Woerdt**, CEO Amsterdam Data Collective

"This book provides a novel exploration of the path to effective leadership. The authors adeptly shift between the leader's inward reflective journey and the outward expression of leadership that extends from a place of conscious choice and intentionality. The direct and positive approaches identified in the text uniquely identify change, loss and transition as potentially transformative experiences that can be built upon to enhance everyday life. I know of no other written works for leaders that cover this ground in such depth, and in such a powerfully positive way. This is a must read for anyone who wishes to lead from the heart."

—**Darcy Harris, PhD**, Professor of Thanatology,
King's University College at Western Ontario

"I think you become a leader by never ceasing to find new answers to questions in a context that is constantly changing. In doing so, leadership begins with the person of the leader himself, but moves toward the other. This book is very special. The case histories drawn from the real, sometimes so unruly practice of the leader hit the mark. So do the questions to work with. To shape transition is above all to enter into dialogue with yourself and the people around you. With this book in hand, you will learn how AND gain the confidence to succeed."

—**Maurice Unck**, CEO of RET, the public transport operator of the Rotterdam Region

"This book is a must-read for every leader navigating transition. It offers guidance, reflection questions, and practical examples on understanding one's calling as a leader and leading a team through change. The authors wisely state, "You cannot take your employees further than you are prepared to go yourself." I invite all readers to use this book as a tool for personal growth and to push beyond their current limitations."

—**Dr. Judith Konermann**, Head of Leadership, Culture and Inclusion, Coca-Cola HBC

The Language of Transition in Leadership is a book that should be in every leader's library. This is a fresh look at leadership and the complex challenges leaders face in all kinds of organizations. Drawing on the authors deep understanding of attachment, loss, and self-awareness, this book helps us understand our personal evolution as leaders and leads us to a deeper understanding of our own calling."

—**Stephen R Connor, PhD**, Executive Director, Worldwide Hospice Palliative Care Alliance

"I am in transition. You are in transition. We are all in transition if we are open and honest about our lives. The north star to our constant state of transition is our calling. 30 years ago, I spent 18 months determining my calling. Had there been the benefit of *The Language of Transition in Leadership: Your Calling as a Leader in a World of Change* it's quite possible my discovery would have been quicker. The authors provide a powerful road map guiding one to the discovery of why you are here!"

—**Ed Chaffin**, PCC – Author - #1 Best Seller *UnCommon Leadership for the New Reality: 3 Principles That Drive Greater Awareness, Engagement and Psychological Safety*

"In a world burdened by conflict and environmental degradation, leadership from the inside out is more important than ever. In many organizations, including in education and governance, psychological conflicts are determining outcomes and are the source of untold suffering. This book shares vignettes and principles of leadership that intend to promote self-awareness and make sustainable leadership possible. This is an excellent resource to begin the deeper conversations about what it means to evolve and accompany others in freeing themselves to lead with compassion and clarity."

—**Reinekke Lengelle, PhD**, associate professor of writing for transformation in Canada and The Netherlands and award-winning author of *Writing the Self in Bereavement*.

"*The Language of Transition in Leadership* is a must-read travel guide for every person who wants to grow as a leader while being an inspiration to the people around them. The methods and insights provided for facilitating change are effective and instantly applicable. Discovering and understanding your calling as a leader and determining your person effect is an intense and reflective journey and a guideline for personal growth and increasing impact."

—**Jean-Paul van Haarlem**, CEO, ONVZ, The Netherlands

"Having studied grief for many years, its impact on our lives is undeniable. But until I read *The Language of Transition in Leadership*, I had never considered how grief impacts leadership. This book teaches us how we can use what is known about attachment to become better leaders and serve as the secure base from which our teams can grow and succeed."

—**Mary-Frances O'Connor, PhD**, author of *The Grieving Brain*: *The Surprising Science of How We Learn from Love and Loss*

"Leadership is a topic with a huge literature base, and so any book that is going to make a difference has to be distinctive in order to stand out from the crowd. This text is one such book. It is well conceived, well written and innovative in a number of ways. It is a breath of fresh air."

—**Dr. Neil Thompson** is a visiting professor at the Open University and the author of *The Managing People Practice Manual*

"Jakob, Riet, and Leo are geniuses. I am recommending this book to everyone I know! This is a unique, insightful, practical take on inspiring, transition based leadership for these challenging times of disruption and uncertainty. This isn't just a collection of tips and strategies, it's a whole new way of thinking. This book is a gift. Get it. Read it. Use it."

—**Terry Small**, president of the Terry Small Learning Corporation

"Some books stay with you for a long time, this is one of them. *The Language of Transition in Leadership* has shaped me as a leader and pushed me to make different choices in my career. I brought that same language to an international environment, and even though there are large cultural differences, the aspects of secure base and bonding; but also the need for conflict and rituals have been welcomed by all. It has equipped us with the right tools to grow and work together in these times of change."

—**Ankie van Wersch**, CEO Enviu

"*The Language of Transition in Leadership* is not only a practical and concrete guide but it mostly is an inspirational piece enabling leaders to continuously develop themselves. This book enhances the discovery of your calling and consequently the understanding of what you would like to move forward or mobilize during your leadership journey. I recommend every leader to read this book as it allows for growth during times of constant change and challenges."

— **Ingrid Uppelschoten-Snelderwaard**, Chief DE&I officer and Head of People - People and Finance function at A.P. Møller-Maersk.

"Being a compassionate and inspirational leader has become ever more challenging in an increasingly complex world filled with moral dilemmas and ethical quandaries. Leaders are often pulled in all directions while being thrusted into situations that require prudent judgement and equitable decision making. It is fair too common for leaders to feel loss in the midst of transition and change. This book provides readers with fresh and invigorating perspectives for navigating through such complexities by offering opportunities for deep reflections, self-understanding, and rediscovery of our true calling. A valuable addition to any leader's library."

— **Dr. Andy Hau Yan Ho**, Head and Associate Professor of Psychology, Nanyang Technological University, Singapore; President of the Association for Death Education and Counseling (ADEC)

"Jakob, Riet and Leo have an uncanny ability to simplify complex concepts and make them not just easy to understand but also to implement. Their views on leadership are especially timely in today's current climate and I would highly recommend everyone reads The Language of Transition in Leadership."

— **Candice Mama**, co-CEO AIME, Vogue Paris' Most Inspiring Woman 2020

The Language of Transition in Leadership

In this book, the authors utilize their decades of experience in leadership and coaching for change to help leaders develop the necessary skills to lead people and organizations in transition. Combining a scientific and practice-based approach, they show readers how to develop and maintain their own impactful leadership style while creating psychological safety in their teams.

Leadership that achieves sustainable results comes from connecting past, present and future. Describing leadership as a journey, the book invites the reader to discover their calling and realize the importance of examining the roots of their leadership, before thinking about its destination. It gives leaders access to a new dimension of unprecedented growth and demonstrates the ways these lessons and skills can transform change into lasting transitions.

Accessible and written in a lively style, *The Language of Transition in Leadership* is an important book for leaders and executives. It will also be of interest to coaches, organizational advisers, management consultants, students of leadership and those transitioning into the workforce.

Jakob van Wielink is an international leadership coach and trainer. He is a partner at The School for Transition and an affiliate of the Portland Institute for Loss and Transition.

Riet Fiddelaers-Jaspers, Ph.D., is a trainer and grief therapist. She is a pioneering author in the field of attachment, loss and grief and an affiliate of the Expertise Centre for Coping with Loss.

Leo Wilhelm is an executive in the Dutch central government and an affiliate of The School for Transition.

The Language of Transition in Leadership

Your Calling as a Leader in a World of Change

Jakob van Wielink, Riet Fiddelaers-Jaspers and Leo Wilhelm

Routledge
Taylor & Francis Group

LONDON AND NEW YORK

Designed cover image: © Tonny Teuwisse

First published in English 2023
by Routledge
4 Park Square, Milton Park, Abingdon, Oxon OX14 4RN

and by Routledge
605 Third Avenue, New York, NY 10158

Routledge is an imprint of the Taylor & Francis Group, an informa business

© 2024 Circle Publishing, an imprint of In de Wolken

Translated by James Campbell. James can be found at www.thelastword.eu

The right of Jakob van Wielink, Riet Fiddelaers-Jaspers and Leo Wilhelm to be identified as authors of this work has been asserted in accordance with sections 77 and 78 of the Copyright, Designs and Patents Act 1988.

All rights reserved. No part of this book may be reprinted or reproduced or utilised in any form or by any electronic, mechanical, or other means, now known or hereafter invented, including photocopying and recording, or in any information storage or retrieval system, without permission in writing from the publishers.

Trademark notice: Product or corporate names may be trademarks or registered trademarks, and are used only for identification and explanation without intent to infringe.

Published in Dutch by Circle Publishing, an imprint of In de Wolken, 2020

British Library Cataloguing-in-Publication Data
A catalogue record for this book is available from the British Library

Library of Congress Cataloging-in-Publication Data
Names: Wielink, Jakob van, author. | Fiddelaers-Jaspers, Riet, 1953– author. | Wilhelm, Leo, author.
Title: The language of transition in leadership : your calling as a leader in a world of change / Jakob van Wielink, Riet Fiddelaers-Jaspers and Leo Wilhelm.
Description: Abingdon, Oxon ; New York, NY : Routledge, 2023. | Includes bibliographical references and index.
Identifiers: LCCN 2023007624 (print) | LCCN 2023007625 (ebook) | ISBN 9781032530505 (hardback) | ISBN 9781032530499 (paperback) | ISBN 9781003409922 (ebook)
Subjects: LCSH: Leadership. | Organizational change.
Classification: LCC HM1261 .W54 2023 (print) | LCC HM1261 (ebook) | DDC 303.3/4—dc23/eng/20230307
LC record available at https://lccn.loc.gov/2023007624
LC ebook record available at https://lccn.loc.gov/2023007625

ISBN: 978-1-032-53050-5 (hbk)
ISBN: 978-1-032-53049-9 (pbk)
ISBN: 978-1-003-40992-2 (ebk)

DOI: 10.4324/9781003409922

Typeset in Optima
by Apex CoVantage, LLC

Contents

Foreword: You Always Have a Choice   *xiv*
EDITH EVA EGER

Foreword: Welcome to The World of Transition   *xvii*
NICK CRAIG

**1   Welcome to The Language of Transition:
      About Change, but Different**   1

2   Route Planner: The Transition Cycle   7
Learning to speak the Language of Transition   7
It begins and ends with your calling   7
On the nature and meaning of the Transition Cycle   7
The roots of your leadership: the lifeline   11
Not available separately   13
Setting a course   13

**3   Every Change Begins with an Ending:
      The Importance of Transition**   15
On the importance of transition   15
Leadership is shaping transition   20
Leading transition   23
Important insights to take away   30
Questions for self-reflection   31
*Questions for you to ask of the people around you – your
      person effect   31*

**4   From Kitchen Table to Conference Room:
      Contact and Welcome**   33
About contact and welcome   33
Leadership and organizational systems   36

Breaking through behavioral patterns   43
Psychological safety and team performance   46
Important insights to take away   50
Questions for self-reflection   50
Questions for you to ask of the people around you – your
    person effect   51

5   In Your Vulnerability Lies Your Strength:
    Attachment and Resilience   52
About attachment and resilience   52
Attachment and attachment styles   52
Attachment and secure base   57
Attachment and the brain   62
Attachment: the basis for life and work   68
The emotional language of transition and the power of
    words   71
Neuroplasticity   74
The calm brain and resilience   75
Mindset   78
Important insights to take away   79
Questions for self-reflection   79
Questions for you to ask of the people around you – your
    person effect   80

6   First Bond, Then Lead: Bonding and Intimacy   82
About bonding and intimacy   82
Vulnerability   84
Needs   86
Delay judgment – express compassion   88
Dialogue and the four keystones of bonding   90
Four leadership approaches   99
Important insights to take away   105
Questions for self-reflection   105
Questions for you to ask of the people around you – your
    person effect   106

7   To Welcome is to Learn to Let Go: Loss and Separation   108
About loss and separation   108
Embracing by letting go   109
Leaving in the context of organizations   112
Saying goodbye professionally   113
The effect of hidden grief on leadership   114

Saying goodbye: shaping a continuing bond   120
The necessity and power of rituals   126
There is no sustainable way to bypass discomfort   131
Resistance   132
Important insights to take away   133
Questions for self-reflection   134
Questions for you to ask of the people around you – your
person effect   134

8   First the Pain Then the Gain: Grief and Integration   136
About grief and integration   136
Grieving in the context of work   137
Grief and attachment   139
The myth of resistance to change   144
Grief and transition   145
Avoiding painful feelings   147
Mental health through integration   157
The gift of forgiving   161
Important insights to take away   163
Questions for self-reflection   164
Questions for you to ask of the people around you – your
person effect   165

9   The Key to Real Change is in Your Pocket: Meaning and Calling   166
About meaning and calling   166
Meaning   167
Let's talk about your calling   172
The relationship between meaning and calling   175
Calling as the journey to the second mountain   178
Finding and formulating your calling   179
The calling of an organization   184
Important insights to take away   186
Questions for self-reflection   187
Questions to ask of the people around you – your person
effect   188

Behind the Names   189
The Shoulders On Which We Stand   198
Notes   201
Index   220

Foreword: You Always Have a Choice

> *We do not choose what happens to us,*
> *but we can always choose*
> *how we respond to it.*

Foreword by Edith Eva Eger

This amazing book you now hold in your hands is an invitation to discover your full potential and to invite others to do so too. Accepting this invitation has become the most important and fulfilling journey of my life. And that journey began in the most unlikely place imaginable. In Auschwitz, when I was just sixteen years old.

I will never forget how I waved to my father on the platform, after the men and women were separated, not realizing that this would be the last time I would see him. Or the moment of the first selection, when I stood in line with my mother and my sister Magda and watched Doctor Mengele who, with a simple hand gesture, decided the fate of each new arrival. I did not realize the implication of being pointed left or right and believed him when he said, "Your mother is going to take a shower now, you will see her again soon". The grief over the loss of my parents, the trauma inside me as a result of the horrors I faced, and the guilt of having survived while millions of others had perished, were so strong that, for decades after I was released from the camp, I tried to run from the past.

I had a family together with my husband, emigrated to America and overcame many of the hurdles that come with the life of an immigrant. I left the past behind, or at least I thought I did. But I was not truly free. From the outside my life seemed to be in order: I learned the English language, studied psychology, finished my studies *cum laude*, and received my doctorate.

My mother always told me, "It's a good thing you've got brains, because you don't have looks", and I took this message seriously. I devoted all my attention to studying, gaining qualifications and providing opportunities for my children. But it was the effort I made, to close myself off from my past and my pain, that kept me trapped. Even though I was further away from my prison than I had ever been, I was actually more trapped psychologically than at any time: my feelings were numb, I was stuck in unprocessed grief, and I was paralyzed by perfectionism and fear. When I finally made the choice to face and heal my past – a story I share in my first book, *The Choice* – I began to see that growth and freedom come when we embrace our whole, imperfect self. That we can never be fully ourselves when parts of us remain hidden or denied. That the potential of our unique diamond lies in harnessing everything in our lives – even the darkest, most frightening and painful aspects – to discover our power and *purpose*.

I began to see that Auschwitz had given me the opportunity to develop inner resources that I might never have discovered otherwise: the wonderful bonds, with my sister and fellow prisoners, that helped us survive by allowing us to attach to something greater than ourselves.

The words my mother said to me in the dark cattle car as the train sped toward Auschwitz, "*We don't know where we are going. We don't know what's going to happen. But no one can take your thoughts away from you*". The way I learned to build an inner sacred space, even in that hell. To keep hope alive, I told myself, "If I survive today, I will be free tomorrow". I learned that everything is temporary. That much in our lives is beyond our control. We don't choose what happens to us, but we can always choose how we respond to it. You, as a leader, also have a choice, no matter the circumstances. Do you choose to be a prisoner of yourself or do you choose to use the key you carry in your pocket? Are you willing to look at your own story and the fault lines in your own life, those of your employees, your team and your organization? Are you willing to take risks, even with the pain that they might bring, with all the effort it takes? I challenge you as a leader to embrace the reality that people don't do what you say – they do what you do.

In May 2019, together with my daughter Audrey, I was invited by The School for Transition and the Expertise Center for Coping with Loss to come to the Netherlands and give a master class on how everything in your life can be a source of inspiration and growth. It was an experience I will never forget: a renewed contact with Jakob, a fulfilling acquaintance with Riet and Leo and many other special people, and a breathtaking encounter with my past. In Theater Carré I saw Igone de Jongh perform a ballet based on my first night in Auschwitz, when I was forced to dance for Dr. Mengele. What a rewarding and healing moment it was, witnessing her portrayal of resilience – of the hope, beauty and potential that shines in each of us, even in hell.

Your strength lies in the freedom to choose what you do in the here and now. It is your calling.

Be free. If I can do it, so can you!

Dr. Edith Eva Eger

Dr. Edith Eva Eger is a leading psychologist and Holocaust survivor. She has worked with veterans, military personnel and victims of physical and psychological trauma. She lives in La Jolla, California and is the author of the award-winning international bestseller, *The Choice. Embrace the Possible*. Her second book, *The Gift,* was published in 2020.

Foreword: Welcome to The World of Transition

Foreword by Nick Craig

Welcome to the world of transition with meaning, purpose, and the gift of your deeper calling.

Jakob, Riet, and Leo are offering you a life-altering journey. Beware, for this path is not one for those who are faint of heart. The road to wisdom is one that can only be traveled by digging deep into our unique triumphs and humbling challenges in life.

This book is about how we face the most significant transitions in our lives and how to become the leaders and the individuals we are meant to be. The path they take you on will leverage insights from Aristotle to many of the best thinkers of our day. I am reminded of a quote from one of the first leadership books in the western world, *The Emperor's Mediations*, by Marcus Aurelius Emperor of Rome in 180 AD.

"People who labor all their lives but have no purpose, are wasting their time – even when hard at work".

My hope is as you read this quote, it offers you a true challenge. Do you really know your calling? Are you *leading a life* of great meaning or are you attempting to keep up with your digital calendar and all the to-do's that never end.

It turns out, most of us face this overwhelming reality and may add a glass of wine, a good movie, or send out a few text messages/emails and start over the next day. This is what Marcus Aurelius was talking about as laboring all our lives.

Yet, for some reason, here you are. Some part of you knows it's time to do the work you have been waiting for all your life. The funny part for me having been on this journey of meaning, purpose and calling, as with many transitions, it's not a path you ever step down from. It is about opening a portal to a way of seeing and interacting with the world, which over time, gives you the courage to do the hard right over the easy wrong. Thus, becoming the leader that not only others need, but becoming who you truly are.

Change happens around us continuously without our asking. Transition is about our internal journey of how we make sense of, adopt, integrate, and if you really work it, you can transform it.

The good and sometimes the bad news is, we are always in transition in some aspect of our life. How we deal with it is key, and this is what this book is about.

For all of us, when Covid-19 happened our worlds changed dramatically. Yet, the transition occurred over time as we needed to make sense of our fragile new world. Endless Zoom calls, daily Covid-19 reports, shortages of toilet paper, and an attempt to go the grocery store and not get anything filled my days. I did too much trying to take care of everyone else, as did many during this time. I was fine. Yet, in reality I wasn't fine. I needed just as much love and support as everyone else. I needed a safe place to share what I was scared about and what doubts I had about the future. Turns out applying your calling to everyone else only takes you so far. It's how you apply your calling to yourself that is key to being really alive and fulfilled. I smile as I realize this book would have been perfect for me at that time!

Fortunately, Jakob, Riet and Leo can now help you discover the unconscious patterns that get in the way and provide insight to what really works. For myself, it was about being vulnerable and creating a safe place to share what was really happening as I attempted to lead a global organization to help everyone else live from purpose. Once I did, and what turns out to be in this book, I was literally able to relax in a way I couldn't before. I was so much more present to those I supported. The situation hadn't changed, but I had finally found a place of peace to lead from in a crazy world.

Allow yourself to be taken care of for once. Bring both your great and challenging adventures in your life as well as the current challenges that seem to have no compelling solution.

Enjoy,

Nick Craig

Nick Craig is the President and Founder of the Core Leadership Institute (CLI), a global development firm committed to waking up those who will wake up the many.

Nick is also the co-author of *Harvard Business Review* article "From Purpose to Impact" with Scott Snook, Senior Lecturer at the Harvard Business School.

His insights from working with these organizations are captured in his book *Leading from Purpose. Clarity and confidence to act when it matters*.

1 Welcome to The Language of Transition

About Change, but Different

For many months you have known that you will have to say goodbye to a colleague. Results, despite clear agreements, support and guidance, are steadily lagging behind target and contribution to the team is below par. But you hesitate, because you have let this go on too long. He's a nice guy and things aren't going so well for him at home at the moment. Can he really deliver what he promises? You are also apprehensive about the potential impact on the team, as many colleagues have strong ties with him. The last thing you need right now is more conflict. There is a lot of change planned in the organization and you have a clear vision of where you want to go. Meanwhile, one of your most loyal team members is growing impatient. She accuses you of "fearful procrastination". You get defensive, and this makes you irritable. Things are not any better at home for you either. Your partner and your children react to your increased irritability. You register this somewhere, but you don't do anything with it yet. And, sometimes, on the way to the office, doubts come flooding in. Why did you start this job in the first place? You notice that you are out of the house more often, going to the tennis club and lingering at the bar. That's not really helping. When, after talking to a good friend, you finally decide to confront your colleague, the tension has already risen considerably. Of course, he's not stupid: he's also realized that things are not going well. It's not a pleasant conversation, but you find a way through it together. There is clarity and relief. For your colleague, for yourself and for the team. You should have done this earlier.

Do you recognize anything in this story? The search for the right decision, at the right time, in the right context? Do you see yourself as a capable leader who would like to take that extra step towards more effectiveness and success in managing their organization, department or team? Do you sometimes get feedback that you could pay more attention to bonding, and are you curious how you could grow, in an emotional sense, in your job?[1] Do you also find – like the vast majority of leaders worldwide – that leading change is a challenging task which asks you to balance on the tightrope of "hard on

DOI: 10.4324/9781003409922-1

the results, soft on the relationship".[2] Are you ever faced with really difficult conversations that you would rather put off?[3] Do you have the idea that in personal relationships and situations there is (much) more in you than you sometimes show? Are you, in short, curious about the untapped potential in you and in those to whom you are bonded?

Welcome to *Language of Transition*. A book about change, but a very different book. Because, through it you will experience the power that transition brings to change. Shaping transition means making the future more important than the past, and being prepared to do what is necessary to achieve that. This means making (sometimes tough) personal and business choices, at crucial moments, with a lot of emotion, to make that future really possible.

Speaking about transition requires a subtly different language than the everyday phrases we are used to saying – especially in the language of work. It requires expanding our arsenal of words, learning new words that go both beyond and deeper than everyday business language. Let's compare it to a wine-tasting course. In the beginning you are confident that you know the difference between white and red wine, and whether or not you like a particular wine. As you taste and compare, you discover more and more nuances. The scent of blackberries, wood, vanilla. You taste apple; a salty taste or acidic aftertaste. You never knew there were so many nuances in wine and you carry on noticing more and more. It's the same with words. The themes of this book demand other words, which are there but are often deeply hidden under everyday speech. In this book we make it easier and easier for you to find this language when you need it.

Leadership is always an act of trust. From your vision of the future, you inspire and awaken hope. You have the faith and conviction that achieving challenging goals is possible, because your own life bears witness to that. The love for what you do and the people you work with make achieving those goals possible. When change happens, it is always in a context where people have the key roles. And the success of the change, that the leader and his organization desire and strive for, rests wholly in the hands of these same people.[4]

Over decades of working with leaders in many situations, in the Netherlands and worldwide, there is one fundamental of any change process that touches us again and again: the challenge to give authentic meaning to the many and different roles that you fulfill in your life. Personal roles such as mother or father, professional roles in your chosen work, organizational roles as leaders and social roles in associations, boards, foundations. For example, how do you combine parenting at home with leadership at work? How do these roles relate to each other and who **are** you really in all these roles? The themes that we explore in this book are the underlying issues that you will always encounter: the repetitive, cyclical patterns of entering and exiting relationships, professionally and personally. You will discover that leadership is a path from origin to destination. We will travel with you for a while: you have to do it yourself, but you do not have to do it alone.

In our work with leaders during the crisis of the Covid-19 pandemic, we discovered that many of them, forced to a standstill by circumstance, are struggling more than ever with questions about their roles. As a result of the profound changes, people are trying to get a grip on what they are now supposed or expected to do. Consciously and unconsciously, many have been challenged by the questions, *"Who am I really, and what can I do? How bonded am I to the people and the world around me, and where am I going?"*

These fundamental questions, about who you are in the roles you play and what you want to achieve in the world, are questions about your calling.[5] Becoming aware of your calling and starting to live it, and leading your organization from this inner place, requires you to walk the path of transition. To go beyond a nostalgic longing "for the past", beyond the sigh of *"if only I (still) had . . .".* By becoming aware of your calling and starting to live it, you will discover that a crisis is always an opportunity.[6]

Transition is always a tough job; it is like the hero's journey, along the sheer edge of the ravine, navigating the fault lines of his own history and that of the organization. A journey that invariably takes much longer than expected or desired, that tests one's resilience to the extreme. The leader must walk the path, looking into the abyss, eyes wide open, anchored by his secure bases. The ravine has a bridge and, when you're standing at one end, looking across, it takes trust and surrender to step out across the bridge, to the other side and into the unknown. The task of the leader in any organization is not to cross the bridge and shout back that it is safe, but to lead her people across showing precisely the movements needed to get safely and successfully to the other side.

All three of this book's authors are inspired by the example of the conductor of a choir or orchestra. How is it possible that with the same choir or orchestra, but with a different conductor, you hear such a different performance? Conducting is more than just waving a baton. Leading is more than saying how you want it done. Conducting and leadership have in common that they require the willingness and ability to follow and listen. When both are available, the ultimate outcome is bonding and dialogue, a safe place for everyone to give their own unique input, let their own sound be heard, their unique sound.[7]

When everyone takes their proper place, as in a choir or an orchestra, harmony is created. Harmony, however, does not arise without conflict. The leader who is willing to live his calling by walking the path of the fault lines of his personal life story will encounter conflict, it's unavoidable. Conflict, however, doesn't need an 'other'. It can arise, for example, in the tension between who you want to be and what you can do, between various personal and professional roles, or from the search for justice or forgiveness.[8]

The paradox is that leaders who avoid conflict will never achieve the lasting harmony they long for and will not fully experience the joy and success that lies in bringing their talents to fruition in their life. The leader who is, with his heart open, willing to enter into conflict not because he enjoys it, but because he sees the necessity of it for joint growth, *will* experience harmony, joy, success. Engaging constructively with conflict requires intimacy and a willingness to keep the heart open. With a closed heart, the leader will find himself pulled into the conflict, the bitter and destructive expressing of unresolved enmity and differences.[9] Transition is therefore also about always accepting the journey back to the place you once left; where you lost or won and then moved on. Not to stay there, but to finally leave behind what must be left behind in order to leave again, but fully this time. You cannot solve anything in the past, but the path from understanding and meaning into the future is always open to you.

The leader who through this journey has discovered the pleasure, playfulness and joy of developing his own talents, cannot help but want to bring out the best in others.[10] The joy that arises when everything comes together and there is flow. However, the leader who starts living his calling will be tested. In fact, his life will not get easier. Your calling challenges you to make happiness right now, less important than the reward of joy later.[11] Living your calling requires the will and courage to make decisions and the willpower to persevere. Willpower that must be trained, as an athlete trains her muscles through regular practice.[12] Living the calling requires a *grit factor:* the discipline to stay on the right path. And it requires support and encouragement from secure bases.[13] When you consider that the origin of *discipline* is *disciple*, surely leadership is first and foremost about being curious, wanting to learn. Not about telling what you already know, but about heading out into the unknown. Daring to step into the desert, for forty years, if that's what it takes.

In this book we want to help you bond with your secure bases and with your primal sources, where you were first welcomed into the world and from where you took your first steps. For this purpose we will use experiences from your personal life as well as from your professional and business contexts. After all, you don't leave your human beingness behind when you leave home to go to work. Perhaps, sometimes, you do want to distinguish between who you are at home and what you experience there, and who you are at work and what happens there. Inevitably, however, your experiences at home and at work are in constant interplay with each other.

We also want to bond you to your calling: everything that happens on the journey between your origin and your destination. Your origin will always have some mystery in it; you can try to go back to your origin, yet you will never be able to reach it completely. Your destination is uncertain but, guided by your calling, you can travel confidently. In this respect, your calling is magical but, as we will show you in this book, it is far from mysterious. In fact, it is as concrete as it gets.

In all the case histories (drawn from our practice) you'll see examples of how people have experienced the major themes of leadership, that we represent via the Transition Cycle: *Contact and Welcome; Attachment and Resilience; Bonding and Intimacy; Loss and Separation; Grief and Integration;*

Meaning and Calling. How people in the case histories probed and practiced, fell and got up again: they learned simply through trial and error. For the sake of privacy, we have changed much, including names, genders, places and specific circumstances. Reader recognition of case histories is on the one hand possible, based on chance; on the other hand, these stories are unique and at the same time universal.

We find, working internationally, that your culture influences who you are, what you do and especially how you do it.[14] Cultural differences are an incredible source of inspiration.[15] Working with different cultures and spiritual traditions is a wonderful exercise of your resilience, adaptability and curiosity.[16] The sheer 'otherness' of the other, in which he and his culture act as a mirror for you, challenges you to think about who you really are and what your roots are and make you. The deeper your roots reach, the higher you can grow. At the same time, in our international work, we see many similarities. The longing to come 'home', to experience bonding, to learn, to develop and to grow. A developmental journey that begins – no matter where in the world – with a father or mother (present or absent)[17] and the impact of your attachment history on your leadership journey.[18] You come up against these themes everywhere, and in this book we explore them at length. Invariably, they can be a potential source of strength or lurk in the shadows, unseen obstacles to progress.

In the words of thanks at the end of this book, we will reflect on the shoulders on which we stand and on which this book partly sits. At this point we would like to give a particular mention to Edith Eva Eger who is especially significant to us and who, in her own remarkable way, has added color to our lives and to this book. She also opens this book with a very personal foreword.

As a Holocaust survivor, Edith showed how knowing she had a choice liberated her.[19] She made Auschwitz her classroom; the lessons she learned there, she shared with the world. Our meetings with her changed our lives forever.[20]

We can hardly put into words the impact of Edith's message. That regardless of what happens, on your lifepath, no matter how great your losses, you can always use grief as a source of strength: for personal growth and to enable you to experience true joy again. The significance that Edith has in our lives and work contributed greatly to bringing soul into our work.

We would also like to specifically mention Nick Craig here, who kindly wrote our second foreword. Nick's wise and inspirational work around purpose in leadership brought an additional focus and a new layer of depth to our work. The importance of purpose when attributing meaning to your life, finding your calling, and transcending different roles in life, cannot be overstated, especially when dealing with loss and grief.

As authors, we learned that even the best leaders struggle and that leadership is often a struggle with one's history. We know all too well the struggles of the leader. We enlarge on that in our personal biographies at the end of the book. We have fallen many times, gotten back up just as many times. We practice our asses off. And we would like to pass on as many of the lessons we learned, working with leaders, in this book. We wish you, on your journey through this book, the curiosity of the uninhibited young mind. The route planner for this book, which you will find immediately after these words of welcome, does provide you with the tools you need for this journey.

2 Route Planner
The Transition Cycle

Learning to speak the Language of Transition

In this book, the next seven chapters take you through the themes of leadership you meet as you move round the Transition Cycle.[1]

Via the route planner, we offer suggestions for how you might navigate the book. For example, we explore:

- Our calling as the umbrella, the overarching theme of the book
- The nature and significance of the Transition Cycle themes
- The meaning we give to *secure base*, *mind's eye* and *excellence*
- How the themes relate to each other
- A way to 'read' the book.

It begins and ends with your calling

We intend this book to be a compass for your leadership journey. While the specific direction of your journey is determined by your calling, the book will help you in the quest to find the qualities you have been given and, through practice, can develop further. Change, in any area, invites transition, and each transition brings you closer to your calling as a leader. Your journey is not without consequences. When you have found your calling, life asks you to acknowledge it and respond personally. This means looking honestly and concretely at the roles you fulfill, through the lens of your calling, and seeking a fruitful balance between these roles.

On the nature and meaning of the Transition Cycle

The Spanish philosopher George Santayana warned us, that when you do not know your past, you are condemned to repeat it.[2] In other words, if you do what you did, you get what you got.

In the way you relate to other people, and to things, you might be able to discern a repeating pattern. Especially when it comes to people with whom you maintain (or would have liked to maintain) meaningful relationships.

DOI: 10.4324/9781003409922-2

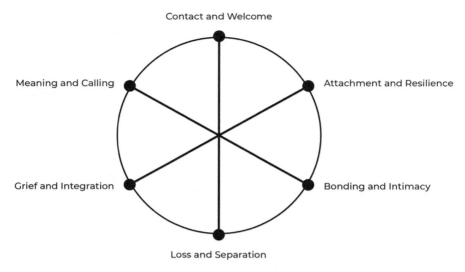

Figure 2.1 Themes on the Transition Cycle.

In every new relationship, themes from previous relationships, personal and professional, are repeated. And in every relationship, your earliest experiences – when you formed your first, most important, relationships – resonate. The themes of the Transition Cycle are inextricably linked to this phenomenon.

Let's look at the themes separately.

Contact and Welcome

Every new contact references your first contact, every welcome references your first welcome. This applies to your life: How welcome were you when you were born? And it applies, for example, to how you were welcomed on your first day at work. How as a leader you welcome your employees to meetings, and so on. Being welcomed, feeling welcome, is the basis for every relationship and therefore every collaboration. Without a welcome there is no contact, without contact no welcome. They are fundamental and inseparable.

Attachment and Resilience

Building on the groundbreaking work of John Bowlby – the founder of attachment theory, whom you'll get to know in more detail later – this theme shows how, as a child, you shape your attachment style based on your experience of the safety and availability of your attachment figures.

Attachment is the natural (instinctive) and *unconscious* behavior by which closeness to an available other is sought. Through attachment, parents offer safety and care to the child for as long as it is dependent. In addition, a good – that is safe – attachment ensures that the child can confidently, step by step, discover her world. Attachment provides a safe starting point – a comfort zone – to explore the world, to investigate and to take risks. Attachment figures that provide this are called *secure bases*.

Secure Base, Mind's Eye and Psychological Safety

A *secure base* is a resource which makes us feel welcome and which inspires and encourages us to face, together, the challenges life presents.

Secure bases are your main sources of inspiration for development and growth. They ensure 100 percent *caring* and 100 percent *daring*. Caring without sufficient daring leads to rescuing behavior: trying to protect the other person from pain. But this hinders growth. Daring without sufficient caring leads to experiences of insecurity, the idea that you have to manage on your own and poor risk assessment.[3]

By focusing on 100 percent caring and 100 percent daring, our *mind's eye* is constantly refocused on the positive; on learning and development. For our purposes, the mind's eye has a specific meaning: it is a selective filter in our brain that determines our focus. By nature, the mind's eye is focused on the negative, on danger and on avoiding fear, shame and pain. In the presence of external secure bases, this preprogrammed tendency of the brain is overridden; ensuring that all emotions – of any kind – are welcome without judgment.

When we bond with our secure bases, and our mind's eye is focused on the positive, we are in a state of mind that we call *psychological safety*. This involves being constantly engaged with questions such as: How can I improve and how can I help you improve? Psychological safety is about breaking free of negative patterns from the past. It disempowers so-called self-fulfilling prophecies. It means that, if together you experience psychological safety, the future will not be simply a repeat of everyone's past negative experiences.[4]

Your attachment needs are a biological necessity and are neurologically anchored. Therefore, the attachment style that you develop as a child forms the fabric from which you weave every new relationship you begin. This occurs irrespective of whether you are in your private or business environment. From birth to grave, at home and at work, in all phases of your life, you need secure bases if you are to perform well.

As your attachment style develops, so does your resilience, your ability to deal with setbacks and disappointments. This affects both the development of your nervous system and how you handle stressors such as drastic changes and failure.

Bonding and Intimacy

Whereas your attachment style is about the unconscious underlayer of your way of shaping relationships, bonding is about your *conscious* desire for closeness with a meaningful other and your choice to *consciously* shape this.

So, this theme is also about the vulnerability which goes hand in hand with searching for and allowing intimacy.

Intimacy is about the ability to bond in the deepest sense. It is about being able to surrender to another and to a goal: being able to follow another, and really allowing the other, and what is different, to be. Allowing yourself to be touched, fed and carried without having to be on the alert. Intimacy is the longing to be touched at the edges. The physical or 'external' boundary, the body, the skin.[5] This might be an encouraging handshake or pat on the back, someone's silent touch when you are hurting, but also eye contact with a colleague as a sign of trust. And then there's the internal boundary. Being touched at the 'internal' boundary means that deeper thoughts, doubts and feelings become visible to the other person with all the vulnerability they are wrapped in.

Intimacy, then, elicits a bonding that takes us back to our experiences with previous rejections, experiences stored in the deeper layers of our brain. Any attempt at bonding or intimacy also touches on the mostly unconscious, but fundamental, fear of rejection. This fear paralyzes the initiative you so desperately need in your organization. Intimacy is needed to truly learn, develop and grow as individuals and as teams.

Loss and Separation

Everything you are attached to and everything you have committed to in this life is finite. Just as you yourself are finite. Loss and separation are part of relationships; they test your ability to bond (again). The loss of secure bases is among the greatest losses of all.

Your behavior, including at work, is – without you consciously knowing – largely determined by your fear of losing someone or something or by previous losses that you had in life. The famous psychiatrist Irvin Yalom shows how losses and traumatic experiences can be turning points, pivots towards a more meaningful life. This is possible if you can find in such experiences the inspiration to shift priorities and take more and more risks on the way to joy, love, health and success. The fear of death – the end of things – is a deep driving force that can only be overcome by no longer trying to avoid it.[6]

Loss and separation can shake our world to the foundations. Acknowledging, recognizing and exploring loss, and saying goodbye properly, are necessary before the next theme can enter the picture.

Grief and Integration

Grief is the set of reactions – feelings, thoughts and behaviors – that result from having to miss someone with whom, or something with which, you maintain or would have liked to maintain a meaningful relationship. Grieving is about the discomfort, pain, difficulty and inconvenience you might experience, after you have said goodbye.

Grief has the duality of orientating towards the past – towards that which has been lost – and orientating towards the future – the unknown.

Grief bounces you back and forth between the two. When you grieve, you experience the break in your attachment and are invited – and challenged – to tap into your resilience. And your resilience can get overwhelmed.

Grief requires integrating the loss into your life and into the life of your organization; finding a new balance. When you integrate grief, *you* put the pieces of the puzzle back in place, as it were. Grief teaches us the essential difference between accepting something or agreeing with something. Integration means accepting what the facts are for you (accepting what is) and no longer fighting them. The principle here is, "I don't agree with this, but I want to move on".

Meaning and Calling

Experiences of loss require rewriting the story of your life or organization. In a way you create, as it were, a new order out of the chaos of the loss. A new order that has meaning for you and your team, for your unique situation, for your unique loss. You give meaning by reshaping your story and the *corporate story*. You continue to honor the past but focus more strongly on the future that asks to be made possible.

Meaning is the pivot point in relating once more to your calling. Relating differently, more deeply, more effectively, more joyfully. Your calling is the question of who you are at the identity level – and what is the *raison d'être* of your organization – what your larger life goals are and how you realize those goals.

Shaping your calling is about how you bond to the roots of your leadership: the themes of your lifeline. Your lifeline allows you to review, and provides an overview of all the impactful events, experiences, periods and changes in your life. Calling is like an arc that spans all the themes on that line. The same themes you encounter in the Transition Cycle.

The roots of your leadership: the lifeline

As you begin your journey through this book, we'd like to invite you to look deeper into the roots of your leadership, by way of your personal lifeline.

The lifeline

The first step: draw a map of your life

Ideally, you take a large sheet of paper. This will make it easier for you to explore and fill out your lifeline. Later, with another person, should you wish.

The first step is to draw a horizontal line starting at your birth and ending at your current age. At the beginning of the line, you draw a vertical line

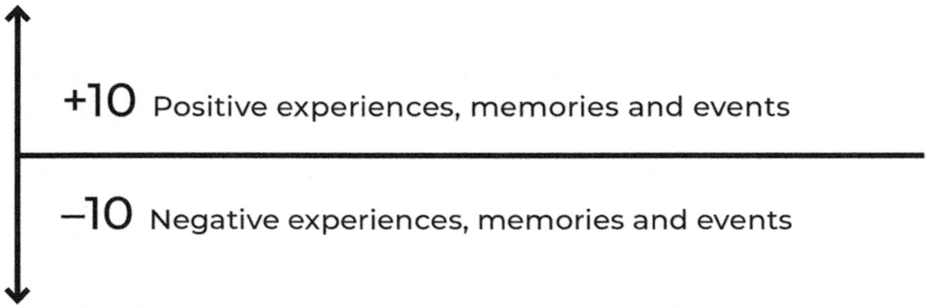

+10 Positive experiences, memories and events

−10 Negative experiences, memories and events

Figure 2.2 The lifeline.

that goes from '+10' to '−10', as a scale for the impact of a particular event. Then you divide the horizontal line into periods. You could call these the *chapters* of your life. Some are a little longer, some a little shorter. Usually, you feel intuitively what these periods are, how long each should be. Then, both above and below the line, you mark – with words, numbers, drawings, whatever – the small and large impactful experiences and events in your life.

Sometimes it can help to draw a line between specific events to bring a sequence into sharper focus.

The second step: explore

Once you have created your lifeline, share it with the people around you. For example, you can do this with your team, inviting team members to create their own lifelines. It is also a powerful way to engage with your father, your mother, your partner and your children. To get to know each other in a whole new way.

In sharing your lifeline with others, the following questions can help you to reflect.

People who shaped you

Describe four people who have had a significant impact on you. At least one should be a person who had a negative impact on you. You might want to name them. Answer the following questions for each person.

- Who was this person in relation to you?
- What did you see him/her do?
- How did he/she bond with you?
- What words did he/she use?
- How has this affected your leadership?

Experiences that have shaped you

Describe four impactful experiences in your life. Include at least one negative experience. Answer the questions for each experience.

- What made this moment or experience matter?
- Was there any struggle or conflict and how did you handle it?
- What choice did you make?
- What quality(s) have you developed as a result?
- How has this affected your leadership?

Not available separately

The lines that segment the Transition Cycle show you two things: that the themes cannot be seen in isolation from each other, and that they constantly refer to each other. The Transition Cycle is not a phase model. It is a window that, chapter by chapter, invites you to discover, for example, how:

- You have to say goodbye before you can welcome again.
- In times of grief your resilience is tested and strengthened.
- A calling only becomes fruitful in the context of your environment.

Setting a course

We have written the book in such a way that we take you step by step along the above themes. We encourage you to follow the order in which we present them and to take your time. You will discover that each chapter gives you powerful and unexpected information about who you are as a leader, how you interact with your environment, how that environment in turn helps shape your leadership and what the impact of your leadership is on your organization. Each chapter offers you new keys on the path to impact, influence and results. Perhaps this book works in a similar way to other contexts, such as a training course you take, conversations you have, the family life you shape. And, as with all of those, the more you put in, the more you get out.

The chapters share a structure. You'll read about the theoretical foundations of transition. These are always linked to a case study from the authors' practice. At the end of each chapter, we present a summary of the core learning. We always conclude with two types of questions. The first type lead you to reflect on your own leadership journey. The second type invite you to enter into a conversation with those around you about the chapter's themes.

The last chapter differs slightly, as it offers you something extra: a concrete exercise to begin the process of giving form, color and texture to your calling.

Leadership, of course, is about walking uncharted paths. By definition, you also will have to make these paths yourself. So, above all, experiment. Maybe you'll begin at a different chapter, because, intuitively, you feel pulled to a particular chapter by a current question or problem in your organization. Go ahead. You can't really get lost, because each chapter points back to previous chapters and forwards to what is yet to come. It helps you to find *your* way in the book. We make extensive use of endnotes in which we refer to (research) literature and sources that you can consult when you want to delve deeper into a specific subject. Finally, the keyword index is always useful if an issue is demanding attention.

Bon voyage!

3 Every Change Begins with an Ending

The Importance of Transition

On the importance of transition

Everything is changing, constantly. What once seemed a progressive approach has, over time, been superceded by new developments bringing new possibilities. If you continue holding on to what was once good or right, you will be overtaken on both sides. You have to let go, sometimes with pain in your heart, of who or what you, perhaps, were so attached to. Only then is development and growth possible. Contradictory as it may sound, your willingness to change is the basis which makes continuity possible. Everything you might prefer to hold on to, that you had to fight for, was the result of change.

In this chapter we will lead you through the themes of change and transition, both at the level of the organization and of you as a leader. We will pay attention to the secure bases you need to shape transition and implement the message of this book: that shaping transition – from your secure bases – leads to living your calling. You find out who you are and what you have to offer to the world, and therefore to do. Transitions lead to real change, rather than repetition of history, and make learning and development possible. Attention to transition and its impact on the undercurrent, on what is hidden, is a crucial factor for success in change.

The family business had been run by their father for thirty years. A man who was held in high esteem by the staff because he was friendly and always ready to support them in their work. He often had arranged things for the employees before they had asked if he would. His son and daughter, who took over the management baton from him, took a different view of leadership and wanted to give the employees more responsibility and autonomy. The atmosphere in the company changed. In the first few years there was a lot of discontent among the employees, especially in those who had worked there the longest. Conflicts arose and several people resigned. New recruits, on the other hand, appeared to really enjoy and appreciate the new regime. They wanted more responsibility and regularly came up with ideas for improvement.

DOI: 10.4324/9781003409922-3

The leader of this family business had for years plotted a safe and steady course, marked by attention, helpfulness and care for his staff; he rarely gave them any personal responsibility or autonomy. The change in management changed the workplace atmosphere from friendly to more businesslike. Autonomy was now expected from the employees. The arrival of the new managers also set in motion a transition that was not without consequences: many of the employees who had been with the company for ten years or more quit and found new work. This did not make it easy for the new leaders; even seemingly minor changes provoked reactions from deep in the undercurrent.

When we talk about leadership in this book, we mean the ability to influence others, to have an impact and to achieve results. Leadership is not so much linked to a role or a function as to who you are. It is, therefore, personal. And the personal nature of leadership is not confined to the workplace, it is also expressed outside of it, such as in parenting, friendships and intimate partnerships. Leadership inspires movement and growth, whereas management is much more about getting things done. Leadership is about giving direction, but without management it is rudderless. A leader must be able to get things organized and managed. At home, at work, at the sports club. But above all, the challenge of the leader is to place himself in a context in which he is nurtured and inspired, so that he, in turn, can nurture and inspire others. It starts with self-leadership.

It is a persistent misconception that leadership is innate and so will arise on its own. There is no such thing as a *self-made leader*. We know from research that only a small part of leadership is connected to hereditary factors or inborn character traits. Ninety-five percent of your talent and leadership is learned.[1] This begins in your earliest years, as a young child, through the examples you receive from your parents and educators. This learning continues at school, in circles of friends, in team sports, in training courses and so on. It is this experience, practice and the following of appropriate examples that make you a leader.

Tim Ferriss is regarded worldwide as an innovative and successful entrepreneur. He is a *New York Times* best-selling author in the field of personal leadership. In his book *Tools of Titans,* he features Austrian-American Arnold Schwarzenegger. Schwarzenegger tells him that, despite all his achievements, he is not a self-made man. Though he grew up in Austria, in a house without plumbing and moved to America with only a gym bag, before becoming a millionaire, Schwarzenegger does not consider himself a self-made man. Like everyone else, he states, he stood on the shoulders of giants before he got to where he is today. He emphasizes the importance of his mother, who made him do his homework, of his father telling him to make himself useful, and of the teachers and coaches in his career. According to Schwarzenegger, it would not only be detracting from every person and every piece of advice that was valuable to him, it would give the wrong impression, namely that you can do it yourself.[2]

Floris van Bommel, creative director of the family business called van Bommel, explains how his father always strived for delayed gratification, through discipline, by thinking carefully before making a decision. This also applied to buying something. His whole childhood, Floris wanted a remote-controlled car for Christmas. At one point he had saved enough to buy it for himself. Then his father told him to wait two or three months, even though Floris had the money. If Floris would still want it after that period, then he could have it. It was one more step towards self-control. The idea, of course, was that Floris would carry this discipline through to his adulthood. But the opposite is true: nowadays Floris buys whatever he wants.[3]

Floris's response to his father's approach is to do the opposite. This is how you develop your leadership: you learn from the other in a positive or negative sense. Consider where and how you learned to let your 'self' be seen, to get things started, to lead? When and with whom did you learn to withdraw, to be afraid, to give up, to avoid?

You can also see your transition as a leader – we'll come back to the term transition in a moment – through the lens of Joseph Campbell, as the *Hero's Journey*.[4] Myths and legends that have existed for thousands of years have this recurring basic pattern. Someone embarks on an arduous journey in search of their identity. The power of these stories lies in their appeal to our shared, or collective, unconscious. They refer to images that are stored in this collective unconscious. For example, although you may not have been a knight, because of the collection of images and stories about a knight, you have an idea or feeling about being a knight. The same is true, for example, of the idea of 'mother'. You form thoughts, feelings and ideas about what a mother is and does, and what she isn't and doesn't. And so, as you share and retell these collective stories, you make them your own in your love of them or your dislike of them.

Your journey, as hero, proceeds in steps and begins with a signal and a call that you, gradually, will learn to hear or see, and to understand.

The leader is renowned for his direct, no-nonsense approach and focus on control. When he suddenly loses his younger brother, his certainty deserts him. The world turns out to be much less controllable than he had always assumed. A deep personal crisis ensues.

Just as a leader has responded in some way to a signal or a longing to lead, to want to take responsibility, so every hero's journey begins with a, usually unexpected, event that functions as a call to embrace the adventure. Your curiosity is aroused, you are called upon, your desire to be responsible is addressed. You are the one chosen to answer this call. If you dare to answer, you can begin the journey and start to adventure. Who chooses who? Does the hero choose the way, or the way choose the hero?

Since you are holding this book in your hand, we suspect that you are driven by a longing that goes deeper than your current leadership. That you want to discover how, from real bonding, you can have more impact as a leader – with yourself and with your environment. How you can move from transacting – getting things done – to transforming.[5] Transformational leadership goes beyond the day-to-day issues, the work that has to be done, the KPIs (key performance indicators) that need to be attained. Transformational leadership puts people first. Perhaps this book will lead you to discover how your journey as a parent – if you have received such a gift – influences your journey as a leader, and vice versa.[6] You might discover parallels between the different roles in your life, that you didn't see so clearly before.

Wanting to answer the call to a journey of adventure is about becoming aware of your calling. A stronger word (for responding to who you might be and what you have to do in life) does not exist. Calling is about feeling precisely when what you are doing is in line with who you really are; learning to understand signals, being able to read signs. You are bonded to a deeper purpose and driven by the desire to make a meaningful contribution to the world.

You are in touch with your intrinsic values and goals. They influence every area of your life.

Upon returning from his brother's funeral, David – manager of a dairy cooperative – receives a great deal of sympathy. He is also pleasantly surprised by the presence of several close colleagues and the condolence card he has received. He is not used to such treatment and begins to wonder how he bonded, in the past, with colleagues facing the loss of a loved one. David sees himself as a man of control. 'Action is the best way to deal with emotions'. He is a bit ashamed to notice that his brother's death clearly shows him who he wants to be, and what he needs to become that person. In recent 360-degree feedback sessions, his rational approach is invariably the point of focus and concern. He employs a coach to examine his need for control. How can he develop into a leader who is attentive to the personal lives of his employees without panicking about losing control?

The invitation is to make your calling visible in every role of your life and work. Your calling, and what it means to you in your life, does not accept a lack of commitment. It brings direction and coherence to every choice you make. It is your compass, unerringly pointing to your path of success.

Leading from one's calling puts people central, in a special way. It is an approach that assumes each person has specific talents and that the leader has a unique role and impact in allowing those talents to develop and in actively drawing them out.[7] Transformations take place when love for people is given form. Where leaders invite others and themselves to go further, to reach deeper, so that they realize their calling in the world and increase their impact. We will see, while navigating this book, that dialogue is a leader's most important tool for creating a learning organization. Dialogues that ignore the border between life and work. Dialogues about old beliefs and new experiences, about dreams fulfilled and ideals lost, about wanting to but not knowing how, about living but sometimes also about dying, about protecting yourself while wanting to learn, about the desire to have fun, about where and why you forgot to play, about the difference between perfectionism and excellence.

Every journey has setbacks, disappointments and resistance along the way, obstacles to overcome. While answering the call and setting out on the road is, itself, often difficult enough, the real challenges begin when you are actually on the road, walking the path of your calling. The setbacks are not just the inevitable challenges of the hero's journey, they are also manifestations of the hero's own uncertainty and doubt about answering his or her calling. Enduring these trials is necessary where the old solutions no longer suffice and new answers must be found. Warren Bennis, the celebrated American leadership thinker, speaks of these trials as *crucibles of leadership*, where leaders are formed through ordeal by fire.[8]

In Chapter 7, we will further discuss calling and meaning, as we follow your journey along the other themes of the Transition Cycle. And, as is the case with cyclical themes, vocation and meaning thus open up a new journey, at a deeper level, along the same themes on our path, again and again.

> *We learn in life not from our experiences,*
> *but from reflecting on our experiences,*
> *bonded with others.*

After the hero has chosen to accept the (invitation of the) journey, she meets a wise counsel who offers magical assistance and protection along the way. This person will guide and safeguard the hero on her journey. Although she must make the journey herself, she does not have to do it alone. Her sources of inspiration and support travel within: they are her *secure bases*.

The hero sets out in the direction of adventure, where he is destined to reach the limits of his capabilities. Confronted with his fear and tested to and, perhaps, beyond the limits of his resilience, he must show courage and the readiness to face danger. If he succeeds, the hero's victory is celebrated. Not only has the danger been averted and a new balance found in this world, but the hero has also found answers to the longing, the desire that compelled him to begin the journey.

And no journey is complete without a return to the old world. While the hero returns as a different person, the old world, however, has not changed with him, not yet. Now comes the hero's final challenge, to truly bring home the new insights he has attained. The hero gained his new experience outside of his comfort zone. But *in* his comfort zone, he learns about his experiences in a dialogue with his secure bases. He reflects on success and failure, on joy and disappointment. In this comfort zone, what he has learned becomes anchored and, in turn, he encourages others who want to walk their particular paths. The hero thus completes his own journey, in which it is not the events themselves that bring about change, but how the hero has worked with them. Transition ensures the successful integration of experience.

Leadership is shaping transition

Changes are about what is objective and visible from the outside.[9] Examples in the personal sphere might include the ceremony where you received your university or college diploma, your wedding day or when your divorce became final, the days your children were born or when they left home, the moment a loved one died or the day on which you were diagnosed with burnout. In the professional sphere, you remember the day you took up a new position, the moment you were given notice to leave or handed in your resignation, or your last week in the office before retirement. In organizations, you come across examples like relocating from one building to another, the merging of teams, introducing a new logo, offshoring a business unit, making a group of employees redundant in order to cope with a crisis. Changes take place in the 'surface current'. It is visible to all that something has changed.

> *Transition is growth at the level of identity,*
> *called forth by change.*

Transition takes place primarily in the 'undercurrent', as a largely emotional process within and between people. In the context of organizational change, it is about the emotions elicited by that change. This often happens outside the leader's field of vision and often outside the conscious perception of the actual people affected. The brain hates losing control and the pain that comes with it. Loss of control, pain and discomfort are inseparable bedfellows and all are magnified when confronted by change. Perhaps the most important job and challenge for any leader is to create an atmosphere of trust and bonding, in which underlying themes can be explored and where vulnerability is given space.[10] "How do I know if the effect I want to have as a leader is being achieved?" This is especially noticeable in the degree to which other people really dare, or not, to let you know how they feel.

When there is no attention specifically to transition, changes are likely to be frustrated or even fail. This is precisely the reason for the failure of so many strategy and culture changes or other, much-needed, change that leaders try to implement. Indeed, John Kotter showed, after extensive research, that *circa* 70 percent of planned change fails: that the change process either takes much longer than planned, coming in way over budget, is met with far more resistance and hassle than was anticipated, or simply fails abjectly.[11] The quick and easy verdict is to conclude that the employees "do not want to change", or "show resistance".

This kind of mindset and perspective creates a powerful new problem. Professors Jean-François Manzoni and Jean-Louis Barsoux talk about the *set-up-to-fail* syndrome.[12] This widely researched phenomenon shows that leaders have a special pair of glasses through which they look at their employees. In short, they tend to divide them into two categories: the good-to-excellent performers and the adequate-to-substandard performers. In both categories, they create strong self-fulfilling prophecies: employees turn out to function exactly as they do because of the way they are seen and approached by their managers. During any kind of change, this becomes even more visible. The employee who doesn't understand, or isn't driven by a desire to be successful, can't prioritize, doesn't accept direction and so on, is soon seen as the employee who doesn't *want* to change. Manzoni and Barsoux's studies show that almost every leader tends to think that they don't have such a lens. *The others are to blame.* It turns out that they are not. Looking at change in a different way requires putting on the glasses of transition. For example, what might you encounter behind behaviors that you label as resistance? You are about to see this in detail.

In your early leadership roles, it's not long before you find that much of your time is not spent on the content of your work and the goals of the team, but on people's everyday problems. Worries about home, future and relationships in and out of the office. This is where you will feel challenged, provoked, touched and sometimes desperate. Here, the leader has to take a wider perspective, beyond the issues of the day, and this helps him see how things are connected. It is essential that you know about basic, human emotional and mental processes and the dynamics that occur between people and in groups. This is fundamental to successfully leading transition. The leader does not have to be a psychologist but, by being fully present and willing to go that little bit further in the dialogue, he does have a psychological effect.[13]

Change is saying goodbye

American leadership thinker William Bridges was one of the first to make clear how changes in organizations begin with an ending and end with a new beginning.[14] You, too, might be more inclined to think that change, in and of itself, heralds a new beginning. However, it means that first, and unavoidably, you have to say goodbye.

Saying goodbye challenges you more than almost anything else. Saying goodbye to people, to particular positions and places, to attachments, partnerships, liaisons. Your brain is constantly monitoring your surroundings and trying to keep you safe. "Will you eat me or will I eat you?", your reptilian brain muses. While you as a human being are constantly changing in all sorts of ways, at the level of the brain you experience a deep aversion to the pain that accompanies these changes.

The change plan, the new objectives, the new mission, vision and strategy fit neatly into the need for social engineering within an organization. However, the discomfort that change can evoke eludes the leadership paradigm of control and mastery. Transition asks you to pay attention to the undercurrent of emotions that, inevitably, arise with separation.

Stages of transition

William Bridges shows transition occurring in three stages, with those stages happening interdependently and in parallel, rather than one after the other. We have already written that change begins with an ending. The first stage is characterized by the closure of the old situation. Alongside this, overlapping in time, is a phase between the ending and the new beginning. The old has not yet ended for everyone, the new has not yet arrived for everyone. This neutral zone is, on the one hand, a kind of in-between stage, a no-man's-land in which not everything that is new is fully known and clear. On the other hand, the old no longer works in this neutral zone. This interim period is fundamental to finally arriving at the new beginning, the last stage, in which the transition takes its final shape.

> *A renowned lawyer, Lisanne, ran a large law firm. She was regularly invited to speak on talk shows and received many invitations to networking events. Then, due to some health issues, she had to slow down considerably. She had to hand over leadership of the firm to a partner, which made her feel less respected. After a while the invitations for her expert opinion and to dinners and parties also diminished. This she experienced as an almost greater loss.*

Layers of transition – change never comes alone

Each change builds on the previous one. Whether consciously or unconsciously, intentionally or unintentionally, it raises old pain in the organization. Pain about how previous changes went, about losses that were suffered earlier. Losses that perhaps were not recognized by the organization or by yourself. The emotions associated with that experience have often gone underground, to a deeper layer; one you can no longer access easily. Complications arise when the new change evokes old emotions, which can manifest again, often powerfully. Connecting these 'new' feelings with the pain of the previous change doesn't happen that quickly. It can only happen when you look back at your own lifeline and that of the organization. When 'digging up' previous losses in the organization, you come across old layers of 'solidified grief'.

> *Juliette has worked for years as a manager of a good team. Now she has been asked to be a manager of another team. After much deliberation, she has accepted the challenge. But it starts to bug her and she has no idea why. She discusses this with a fellow manager. When he asks her if she has experienced this previously – having to make choices and feeling conflicts of loyalty – at first she is silent. "At home", she then says. Her mother died in childbirth and, quite soon, her father remarried. Several more children were born. There was always hassle between the first wife's children and those of the second wife. She felt like she was caught in the middle. She got along well with her 'new' sister, but her full siblings did not like her at all. Through her colleague's questions she was able to make a connection to her work situation.*

Leading transition

As a leader, it is up to you to visibly lead the transition, to let the truth of what's happening inside you and your personal involvement in the change be seen. How am I dealing with the change myself, what have I lost and what am I finding difficult about saying goodbye? There are no ready-made answers to these 'slow questions'; they take time. But, by pausing at this juncture, you can establish a bond with the other person that is essential to shaping the transition well.

As a leader you want to explore what it takes for others to join you in a movement of change. Experience shows that you really get them on board when you lead by sharing your personal journey; revealing the fault lines of your own life and leadership. Along those fault lines of achievements and setbacks, of succeeding and failing, of profit and loss, are the impactful experiences of your leadership. It is from those experiences that you learned, consciously or unconsciously, to deal with emotions: yours and others. There you learned about showing or suppressing emotions and how this affects yourself and those in your environment.

Since 1734, nine generations of van Bommels have been making shoes in the Netherlands. Reynier van Bommel is the oldest brother to Floris. Reynier tells of his struggle as a director of the family business, due to growing pains because of expansion. He becomes increasingly married to the company, and finds it hard to develop intimate personal relationships. At management meetings, he would be banging his fist on the table, with tears in his eyes, saying that if something does not change now, he would be quitting and selling his shares. And somewhere in those days he manages to calmly explain what was not going well. The next day his brother Floris comes to him with flowers, telling Reynier that the way he did it yesterday, that's the way a director should do it. To Reynier that was a beautiful moment. To have his brother say to him that he performed extraordinarily well in his role. Though they did not really talk about it, but Floris could see what that meant to Reynier.[15]

The oldest van Bommel brother gives a wonderful example of, above all, personal fault lines and moments to celebrate; when he opens up to them as a director, he is completely transparent. If you really want to bond as a leader, the key is to recognize such meaningful moments and then to engage in conversation with others present. These personal experiences have an impact on performance, especially at transition moments. When you have the willingness to discuss this with each other and explore this impact, there can be a real meeting, an encounter beyond the everyday. To be true to this, you cannot avoid the need to examine how your experiences in your family of origin have shaped you. To think deeply about how those experiences are reflected in how you bond with people and with goals.

The person effect

The way you bond with yourself and others, and the way you deal with (potential) separation, disappointment and pain in that bond, is what forms your identity in the most profound way. And these 'identity' experiences also, to a large degree, form your *person effect*. Your person effect is the unique way, both positive and negative, in which you come across to people and bond with others.[16]

> *Martin is a seasoned finance professional. He has worked for fifteen years in senior roles at the country's second largest insurer. A man who knows his files and folders like the back of his hand. Colleagues describe him as a rock; calm and reliable. But Martin is far from satisfied, he tells his best friend at tennis. He aspires to be a CFO, but doesn't seem to be able to make that step. The recurring feedback he gets is that he isn't inspiring enough and doesn't know how to get people to buy into a vision. He is quite despondent about this, because he can't see why that's an issue. He sees colleagues with demonstrably less knowledge and experience moving up to CFO-level roles. What's the problem?*

Martin receives candid feedback on his person effect, for the first time, in a training he is taking with 'strangers' from other companies. For leaders, the person effect is deeply connected to being able to have real influence and lasting impact. Having a calling without knowing about your person effect leads irrevocably to feeling like a voice crying in the wilderness. In his inspirational book *Throw the Helm*, former US Navy submarine captain David Marquet shows that leaders always have to bridge the gap between the leader they want to be and the person they actually are.

One of the major barriers to growth as a leader is the belief that you already know exactly who you are, and how you are received.[17]

Elements of the person effect include status, authority, gender, nationality and culture, age, physical appearance, mode of dress, energy level, perfectionism, optimism versus pessimism, words and language, reputation and so on.

The person effect is caused by what neuroscientists call 'brain triggers', which mostly take place in the unconscious. These triggers cause numerous physical and emotional reactions such as the *amygdala hijack*, which we will discuss in Chapter 5.[18] James Lynch published a groundbreaking book in which he shows the enormous positive and negative impacts on the heart of human contact.[19] So, alongside appropriate expertise, the degree that a nurse or physician truly cares for the patient can enhance survival rates after invasive (surgical) procedures. For example, during the Covid crisis, a patient told the media that he had already said goodbye to life, while in intensive care, but that the caring touch of his nurse made sure he did not give up.[20] People who go through life alone are more likely to die of heart failure than those who live together.[21] Lynch also discovered the effects of syntax, tone and rate of speech on blood pressure and heart rate.

Why is the person effect so important to you as a leader, to your calling and the way you lead transition? Primarily because there is nothing that more determines your level of effective bonding with others. Positive people attract others.[22] Someone who radiates negativity and cynicism – without perhaps being aware of it – repels people. You cannot inspire people from a negative state of mind. We all know people who are extremely positive or negative. Yet the person effect often involves subtler and more-nuanced issues. The triggers that the person effect causes, and the signals that it sends, come through words, gestures and how you use your voice. We will return to this in Chapter 5 when we discuss right-brain communication.

Chantal is head of communications at a large hospital and is attending a week-long leadership training course. During the week, participants are invited to give feedback on each other's person effect. Some participants remark that while her words are inspiring, her hand and head gestures distract from the message. They say she tilts her head, waves her arms and her voice breaks. It is not easy for Chantal to hear this. Yes, she thinks, that's exactly how I am. If leadership is about having to use tricks to come across differently, then I'll pass. It's more important to me that I am authentic! She speaks, holding back her anger. Because of the safety in the group and the constructive way in which the feedback is given, she manages, bit by bit, to practice using different body language and tones of voice. At the end of the week a participant says: "Sometimes I almost wanted to give up, but now I see you standing here like a different woman. You radiate from head to toe. You inspire me. At the beginning of the week I didn't think this was possible".

Being aware of your person effect means knowing your impact on others and the subtlety of the impact others can have on you. There is probably no more powerful key to increasing your impact as a leader!

You discover your person effect by watching and listening to how you speak: the words you choose, the tone you use, the story your body tells while you are speaking.

At some time, you have, probably, walked into someone's office when you're wired, angry, agitated, about to let them know precisely what's on your mind. You feel your heart beating in your throat, your hands tingle, your cheeks are blushing. And you probably have also had the experience that, when the other person remains calm, gives you space and listens, that you feel yourself relaxing. Your heart rate drops and you breathe easier. In a similar way, unfortunately, you might also have experienced a leader who talks too much. You could almost fall asleep. Appealing as the content might be you simply can't stay present.

It's sad but true. As leaders move up in organizations, their ability to listen often declines proportionally. They simply try to convey too much. Endless monologues and, if things are not going their way, the seemingly endless PowerPoint, which are even more boring. One of the most frequent evaluations after a leadership training is: "I also don't receive enough feedback". It is a consequence of transference, which we will talk about later, but which increases as you take on more-senior roles. The higher up in the hierarchy, the less feedback leaders receive and the more important it becomes to actively solicit it, especially about your person effect.[23]

The person effect has a major impact on the focus and behavior of others. If your person effect is threatening, patronizing or uninvolved, others around you will be more likely to focus on the negative. This, in turn, will trigger defensive reactions in them and even lead to behavior that you perceive as untrustworthy.

> *Patrick was obviously a committed executive. He knew 'his people' inside out. They only had to sigh and he already knew what was going on. Or so Patrick thought. His team members grew tired of his patronizing manner; some called him Papa Patrick behind his back. "It's as if everything gets covered in a warm clammy blanket". After the organization had to deal with a major fraud case that had been in the news almost daily, the team, including Patrick, received coaching, over a number of sessions, with the goal of reestablishing the bonds between them. Over many years, an atmosphere of mutual concealment and avoidance had developed, contributing to the eventual fraud. Together with the coach they looked at the existing dynamics. Patrick heard, for the first time, direct feedback about his person effect. But also, Patrick was able for the first time to say how disappointed he was, because he had felt for a long time that something was going on and that there had been a lack of courage to address him directly. "I don't want to*

hide behind it. It hurts to hear it, but it also brings some relief. I've been sleeping badly for months".

If your person effect is positive, employees will feel empowered, inspired and challenged. They will thus become much more effective at being able to give honest and sometimes painful feedback without the other person feeling the need to defend themselves. As a leader, you simply have to be able to give painful feedback in a way that contributes to growth and development. That is because you're giving the feedback from a basic attitude of *caring,* and the employee experiences receiving your positive focus which carries the possibility of learning and development. Many leaders are deeply convinced that caring – and with it the capacity for empathy – cannot be taught. "That's just the way you are". Nothing could be further from the truth.

In this book you will encounter extensive explorations about the workings of the brain in leadership. Plasticity is a feature of your brain; it is changing all the time. Every leader can be caring, if he puts his mind to it.[24] Simply put, this means lots of practice at putting yourself in the shoes of others. Your brain helps you do that. Our brain is built to mirror. That is to say that by mirroring – the way your brain responds to and simulates the emotions of others – you really understand what other people are feeling.[25]

> *Anita works as an HR director in the city fish market. During lunch with her CEO, with whom she has a good bond, she starts talking about her relationship and tells an anecdote about an event that has had more effect on her than she would like. Six months ago, her partner, Erik, came home and, rather triumphantly, told her about a good conversation he had had with a friend. The friend had advised him to get a personal trainer. Erik was convinced that this was the best advice he could get. "I couldn't believe what I was hearing. We had talked about this many times – Erik is just too fat – and I had repeatedly suggested that he consider employing a personal trainer. When I confronted him, he said", "Yes, you did, but you've also always criticized how I look. You just don't find me attractive anymore. So should I trust you when you try to get me to start working out more?" Anita explains that this is a pattern. He feels attacked by her but, when someone else gives him advice, he accepts it. The fact that people don't readily accept anything from her is a recurring theme at her work. She finds it difficult to build up sufficient trust. When her CEO asks her what she thinks about this, she realizes that it's mainly because of the critical way in which she approaches employees. She doesn't mean it to be critical, but that's how she comes across. Her CEO suggests that she works on this with a coach.*

A positive person effect contributes to increased employee engagement, while a negative person effect contributes to discouragement and employees 'switching off', to people experiencing that they are not important enough. The degree that people feel motivated is also inextricably linked to the person effect.

What is your person effect as a leader? Perhaps this first of the seven chapters about your leadership journey, the beginning of your journey, is a good place to start asking this question of colleagues, team members, your own boss, your partner, your children and close friends. It is one of the most influential resources for your learning and development.

The person effect is positively influenced by such things as empathy, authenticity, respect, curiosity, transparency, concreteness, willingness to confront, strength, readiness and competence to engage in dialogue, approachability and availability, warmth, honesty and directness.

So, the person effect is the way your mood, mindset, emotions and behavior come across to another or a group, and can be positive or negative. It takes courage and willingness to look very closely and critically at those behaviors to which you usually don't pay attention – your own. Just think about your smile: how often, how warm, how honest. Your facial expressions, whether you make eye contact when greeting, during conversations and when saying goodbye, your use of voice (volume, pitch, tone) and so on.

You saw earlier that one of the main reasons leaders fail is that they don't lead (enough) from their calling. They fulfill a role, do a job, but are not deeply bonded to who they are. Other reasons why, all over the world, leaders fail are that they do not bond well enough, take too few risks, are conflict-averse, and do not sufficiently or courageously lead transition. It is a paradox, as it were. The most successful leaders will quickly recognize that it was not they who did the job, but the team, the collective, the organization. But that same team, collective and organization will say that at critical moments the leader did something, said something, made something possible, displayed understanding or patience, provided space. In that zone of tension, the person of the leader materializes in a very special way.

In this fast-changing world of complexity and uncertainty, you are challenged to relate to those changes.[26] It is important to check to what extent you are able, as a leader, to relate to change. You cannot take your employees any further than you are prepared to go yourself. Shaping transition is largely about your ability as a leader to bond at an ever-deeper level with questions about where you come from and where you are going. Your journey from origin to destination. This is the question of your calling. It might send you out in search of themes of vulnerability that arise within yourself in your encounters with others and the world around you. How do you step forward as a leader when things get stressful?

The themes of this book call you to examine your personal arena, the place where you are visible and where you struggle, and the stories you tell about this arena. Is it for you a source of inspiration, or a pool of cynicism and sourness? Are you able to take your losses, separations, disappointments and failures, and translate them into sources of strength for a recalibrated vision of a possible future. Or are they proof for you that people and organizations are bad and untrustworthy? Will what you didn't achieve become your burnout or depression, or will you pull yourself out of the swamp by your hair like Baron von Münchhausen?[27]

Transition in the organization always circles around your transition as a leader. Most of the people in the team, the department and the organization will – whether you like it or not – wait until they see and experience their leaders' transitions. They will not do what they are told to do, but what they see their leaders doing.

To assist you in your growth as a leader, via reflection and feedback on your person effect, we conclude each subsequent chapter with reflection questions and questions for dialogue with the people around you, both in your personal and professional life. This last category of questions is always implicitly or explicitly about your person effect.

Transition and learning

Marcel, for five years a director at a business services company, has a real heart for the business. In the first meeting with his mentor, he speaks freely and with no little embarrassment: "It irritates me that all the employees stay so stuck. I feel that they think they are working in a bubble and that everything will continue as it has been for years. And that's just not the case. Our market share has been shrinking for years; competition is incredibly strong. In recent years we invested heavily in results-oriented leadership, but it doesn't really work. I find it hard to admit, but I'm still pretty frustrated. My employees really need to be taken out of their comfort zone".

Transition takes you to the edges of your comfort zone, where your desire for a comfortable life is tested. Where your first reaction is often that the other person must step out of their comfort zone first, and then you (might) follow. The paradox is that you have to go outside the comfort zone for new experiments and risks. Outside the comfort zone, your experiments take place, you take healthy risks, you practice new behaviors, and you experience *achievement*: getting results and accomplishing goals. But the learning from those findings only really takes place in and on the edges of your comfort zone. Real movement and growth take place from an awareness of the comfort zone and from a *sense of belonging*. So you know there is a place where, with bonding and in dialogue, you can reflect on the experiences you had. Then, in your brain, the anchoring of that learning can take place, fueling further growth. Celebrating successes and marking transitions with rituals also take place in the comfort zone. This is what the secure base is and does: allows belonging to be experienced. Achievement to be realized and felt.

We have experienced significant growth in the past year, especially in our own executive team. Together we have been able to conduct increasingly frank, open-hearted dialogues. About why we do what we do, how we have learned to deal with mistakes and disappointments and, even more, whether we really can talk with each other about anything and everything. I had not dared to hope that we would take these steps together. I had reservations about the approach, thinking it might be too soft. But to my delight and surprise it has had a strong impact in the organization. It has certainly brought tension at times, but we are already getting feedback that there is more 'air', more openness and, above all, more fun.

By consciously pushing the boundaries of your comfort zone and always consciously returning to it, you can develop behaviors that better fit your calling. The opportunity to practice and to apply your talent is conditional for success. This does involve conscious practice.[28] Without hours of practice, talent will not flourish. Improving yourself structurally requires intense focus, a willingness to move beyond your assumed limits and try something beyond your current capabilities. To succeed at this, feedback is indispensable.

Important insights to take away

Leadership is always personal and requires exemplary behavior from out of your calling, from the deeper realization of who you are and what you are here to do in the world.

- Change begins with an end and ends with a new beginning. In between, you travel through a neutral zone, in which the old is not quite over and the new has not yet arrived.
- Change is about the visible outer side, and takes place in the surface current.
- Transition is growth at the identity level, summoned by change. Transition takes place in the undercurrent, where there is difficulty in saying goodbye and dealing with the loss caused by the change.
- The person effect – the unique way you come across to people and bond with others – is a strong determinant of your leadership success.
- Secure bases support you within your comfort zone – *belonging* – through which you can reflect on and learn from your experiences. At the same time, secure bases challenge you to experiment with new behaviors, at the boundaries of your comfort zone, in order to realize sustainable change – *achievement*.
- Shaping transition requires the willingness and ability to dialogue on all the themes of the Transition Cycle.

Questions for self-reflection

1. Who is an inspiring leader for you? What does this leader show you? What impact has this leader had, including on you?
2. How inspiring do you experience yourself to be? Do you see yourself as someone that others like to be around?
3. How would you describe your calling at this time? What is it like, would it be like, to speak it out loud, to share it with others?
4. What large and small changes have you experienced, both personally and professionally? When you create your lifeline – see the Route Planner – what common thread runs through what you learned from changes?
5. What transition is currently playing out in your life or what transition is getting closer? Are you looking forward to it, or are you apprehensive about it?
6. What transition is currently playing out in your team or organization? How are you preparing for it?
7. What loss has had a significant impact on you? How did it shape you as a leader?
8. In your leadership, are you primarily transactional (getting things done) or transformational (talent development)? How do you think your employees see you in this regard?
9. What is your person effect? What feedback do you get on this from others? From whom can you ask for feedback about this?
10. How do you deal with (painful) feedback? How do you think your partner, colleagues, team members and your supervisor would experience your reactions to feedback?
11. Which emotions are permissible for you at work, which are not? Where does the difference come from in you?
12. Which emotional challenges do you tend to take on, and which do you avoid?
13. Do you experience your relationship as a source of inspiration right now? Regardless of the answer to your question, how does it impact how you go to work each day?
14. Do you have friends who know everything about you, who you can turn to, without hesitation, with anything? How does this affect who you are?
15. Are you a friend? How does that show itself? How would others answer this question about you?

Questions for you to ask of the people around you – your person effect

1. How do you experience me bonding with you, positively as well as negatively?
2. What do you see as a strong leadership quality of mine? What is its effect on you?

3. Do you experience me as inspiring? If yes, why? If no, what are you missing?
4. Do you feel that you are using your talents? Do you experience me as supportive and encouraging in that?
5. How emotionally involved do you find me? Would you describe me as empathetic?
6. How do you handle feedback? What is a common thread that returns often in the positive and negative feedback you get in your life and work to date?
7. How do you feel about me giving you feedback? Do you experience it as focused on your growth and development? How could I do this better?
8. What inspires you in your life? Are you inspired by the work that you do? Do you experience the team as inspiring?

4 From Kitchen Table to Conference Room
Contact and Welcome

About contact and welcome

Your first welcome

You don't come into the world as a tabula rasa. At birth you not only receive the genes of your parents, you also receive their past history. It is a gift (of sorts). Although you have no influence on your past history, that history influences you through your upbringing, the messages you receive from your parents and educators and the energy of the (family) systems in which you grow up.

Your family of origin has an impact on how you shape your leadership. Your place at the family dining table is something you encounter repeatedly, even at the conference table. Gaining insight into this helps to understand the communication, emotions and conflicts that occur in every team. And also puts flesh on the bones of your own emotions, irritations, likes and dislikes. That is why we repeatedly, in this chapter, make the connection between the family system and the organizational system.

Much depends on your earliest contact, on how you are received into your family of origin. How you experience your first welcome forms the blueprint for later relationships. Are you welcomed with open arms? Are you the long-awaited child, or do you arrive into a family that, in a way, was already complete? Did your father's company go bankrupt just before you were born? Did your mother lose her father unexpectedly while she was pregnant? Did your parents find it difficult to give you enough attention because they were busy working in their own businesses? How your parents related to you, shapes how you learn to relate to others and the world around you.

Because your parents have such a significant influence on who you are as a leader, in this chapter we take a closer look at the influence of parents and the family system in which you grew up. We do so because, in your work, you regularly encounter the internalized image you have of your father and mother, sometimes also of your grandparents, and the place you occupied in the family. It is helpful to have insight into those influences and your (unconscious) reaction to them.

DOI: 10.4324/9781003409922-4

As a child, you can internalize an (unintended) message from your parents and start to live it. You chain yourself, as it were, to your parent and come to some point where you have to escape these chains in order to lead your own life. Because, before you know it, you'll be transmitting your parent's message to your family, your team members; perhaps appropriately but often inappropriately. In that sense, you have to honor what your parents impart to you and, at the same time, find your own voice. But it's not just your parents who influence your leadership; your siblings, for example, can also affect who you become.

> *There is a new young employee in the department, just graduated and full of zeal. He has many questions and sometimes gives feedback on the way things are going with youthful hubris. The leader notices his own increasing irritation. What is the kid doing, he is still wet behind the ears. When he talks to a colleague about this, he realizes that he is bumping into his younger brother in the employee, the brother who always had the last word at the table and commented on everything. He realizes that he is not doing the new employee justice and resolves to have an open discussion with him to get to know him better.*

The influence of circumstances begins in the womb. Epigenetic research is increasingly clear about how challenging circumstances during pregnancy can cause genes to be turned on or off, with consequences for the baby's development. The uterine environment can change the expression of genes.[1]

During the Hunger Winter (the Dutch World War II famine of 1944–1945), specific genes in pregnant women switched on, to ensure they took in a lot of food: it was an autonomic survival mechanism. When their children were born, there was no longer a famine, but the genes for survival were still switched on. They therefore have a higher risk of diseases such as diabetes and obesity, because of the adaptation to survival in times of famine.[2] Another study showed that babies, of the pregnant partners of men who had been deployed to war zones, showed an elevated heart rate even after twenty-five years.

But there is also research on less intense conditions. For example, it was found that babies of anxious mothers showed a stronger response to a repeated sound. They continued to respond even though the sound contained no new information. These children show increased alertness and are always 'on'.[3]

Epigenetics goes further. Your thinking, feeling and choice of words have an impact on your genetic expression. With every thought you have, genes are switched on and off, and every thought you have is a response to the way you see and interpret your life experiences.[4] Your parents and educators consciously and unconsciously pass on the messages they themselves received from their own upbringing. Also, as a leader, you'll have encountered these internalized messages. Perhaps for you it's *"Do your best"*, *"Don't fail"*, *"Make sure you win"*, *"Take others into account"* and so on. Even when parents consciously want their parenting to be different from their own parents, it remains difficult for them to escape that influence. Parenting remains human work, and even with the best of intentions, it is an impossible task for parents to exactly match the needs of their children. Perfect parenting does not exist. For children, "good enough" parents are perfect enough. According to Ed Tronick, a leading researcher on attachment, even good parents manage to tune in and adapt to their children's needs only a third of the time. Tronick states that a natural cycle of breakup and repair in relationships is more important for secure attachment than attunement alone.[5]

It is important to intuitively feel if there was a "yes" to the following questions at your birth:

- **Am I welcome**? The desired answer is: Yes, whoever you may want to be in your life. For the child, a problem arises when the answer is: *yes, provided . . .*, or *yes, if . . .*, or *yes, but . . .*, or *yes, as long as . . .* Problems also arise when there is a clear 'No'. No, I don't want this child, it is not the right time, it is one child too many. It hinges on the question: May I belong here or not?
- **Will I be loved**? If the answer to the first question is a resounding yes, then it is almost always a yes here as well.
- **Am I safe**? Can my parents provide a safe environment in which I can grow up?

Despite a yes to the two previous questions, despite the best intentions of the parents, it is not a given that there will be a yes to the third question.[6]

A poignant story about being welcome in a family and in the world can be found in the book *The Choice* by Edith Eva Eger, born in Hungary.[7] She writes in the preface to this book that, as the youngest in a family of three daughters, she is told by her mother, "I'm glad you have a brain, because then you don't have to depend on your looks". Her mother is not happy about Eger's relationship with her father. "Did you know that I wished you were a boy?" her father asks Eger, "I was so angry that I got another daughter. But now you're the only one I can talk to". Her parents' attention is precious to Eger, but unreliable. She feels like she gets their love not so much because she is worthy of it, but because her parents are both lonely in their own ways. As if her identity is not about who she is, but merely a measure of what her parents lack. Only in ballet dancing can she be herself.

Parent-child alignment is about parents responding appropriately to the children's signals. It is about being sensitive to the signals and needs of the child (sensitive) and being able to respond appropriately. It is important that parents are sufficiently available, both emotionally and in terms of time and attention. Because young children do not yet have language at their disposal and do need to make their needs known, they may have to deal with reactions from parents that do not fit well with their needs. This is where you begin to develop your first survival behaviors. You may suffer emotional scratches or injuries. These partly form the initial foundation on which you build your expectations of the outside world and formulate your answer to the question: *Am I valued?* This contributes to your self-image, where the pain experienced and the effort you make to mask this pain are the basis on which you will enter into relationships with others.

Leadership and organizational systems

An organization is very similar to a family system in a number of aspects: your sense of belonging or not, your place in the hierarchy, and the balance between giving and receiving. Every system strives for completeness. When you are aware of this, and take it into account, the organization benefits.[8]

Siets Bakker and Leanne Steeghs found that when people, functions, products or events are excluded or not recognized, it has a weakening effect on the whole organization or system. When you watch carefully, you can see this reflected in all manner of symptoms that are expressed in the surface current: gossip, reduced commitment, self-justification or negativity in the form of complaining. But these symptoms in the surface current are still only a reflection of the deeper disturbances in the undercurrent.[9] A complication is that many of these processes take place in the undercurrent and exert their influence from this unconscious layer, which is often inaccessible through words. We explain these aspects further below.

Belonging

The question "Am I welcome?" also raises the question of "Do I belong?" Am I wanted, or am I excluded? The same question plays out in organizations. An important beginning is the welcome. How was your application interview? In what way did you receive information prior to your first day of work? How are you addressed in that communication? And how and by whom are you welcomed on the first day? Or are you just assigned your workspace and told to shout if you need anything? At that point, a lot of information has already been given between the lines: whether you should adopt a formal or informal attitude, whether you can ask for help in this organization, how rules are handled, how you address each other. Whether you should always work just a little longer than contracted in order to fit in, or how you should dress. In particular when you are new, it is tangible what you have to do and not do in order to belong, what the dos and don'ts are.

> *Els came as an HR consultant from an organization where there was always gossip going on behind people's backs. She had switched to a new employer to take on a more strategic role. When her manager gave her a tour of the department and Els made a slightly negative comment in the hallway about what she had seen a colleague do, she immediately noticed that it did not go down well with him. Without saying a word, he showed her that people here treat each other with respect. She was upset, but this particular 'new' rule was clear to her.*

This requires that you set an example by including everyone. If the boundaries of the system are rigid and offer little room for variation, you can relax them by ensuring nobody falls out of the boat. Exclusion can lead to loneliness in the workplace and even to bullying. That's why it's important as a leader to regularly check that everyone does belong and no one is being excluded: the intern, employees who have been out of the labor market for some time, but also the colleague who does not participate in gossip and teasing, or cannot talk about soccer, or has a different dress style. So it's not just about the welcome when someone joins the company, but every day you are welcoming the team. Inclusion requires an active focus and attention to a balanced distribution of your attention.

> *From the get go in her previous organization she hadn't felt comfortable. Something just wasn't right. On the first day of work she had to take a compulsory day off because there was no time to train her. In her mind she was already 1–0 down. There was a big difference between the director and the staff; he put himself outside and above the team and didn't bond. When she fell ill after a year, she was soon told that her contract would not be renewed. Despite the economic crisis, she managed to get a 32-hour job in a small organization. Because of the Covid-19 crisis, this company also had too little capacity to train her properly. Therefore, she was told to come to the office only when the person training her was there. However, she did not have to take compulsory days off and was paid her full salary. From day one she felt: I belong here, people are treated with care.*

Ordering

In a family, everyone has their own place. As a child you occupy a different place from your parents and there is also an order among the children: an order based on age. The order has a number of unwritten rights and duties, privileges and responsibilities. The oldest child usually has to deal with the strictest rules, born of the worries new parents usually have. The oldest child often takes on more responsibility than the younger children. They are usually given a little more leeway, with the youngest usually allowed the most freedom.

> *Reynier van Bommel, the oldest son of the Dutch shoemaking family, always wanted to be the boss, being the first to do everything. The youngest brother Pepijn was allowed everything, according to Reynier, and the other brothers nothing. Pepijn admits to getting pampered a bit more. If he coughed in the morning, their mother would keep him home from school for a day. Going on vacation with the caravan, one of the brothers was allowed to sit in the middle and that would always be Pepijn. He could choose. Pepijn remembers getting off scot-free in the end, when there were fights in the back seat, though often he would be one who started it.*[10]

For example, you can grow up with brothers and sisters in the same family and still have to deal with different implicit or explicit rules. Different messages are passed on, depending on a child's place.

> *As the oldest child of a young couple, Peter had to deal with the strictest rules. Going to bed on time, coming home on time, always letting people know where he was if he hung out with a friend after school. The younger children experienced more freedom in their upbringing, because Peter had already fought most of the battles with his parents and had paved the way for his younger brothers and sisters. For Peter, it had become natural to take the lead in everything. He combined a great sense of loyalty with an equally great sense of justice, traits which made his men like and appreciate him in his military career as a non-commissioned officer. Among his superiors, these qualities brought him appreciation but also conflict.*

What is important is that a parent takes a parent's place and a child takes a child's place. What applies to families also applies to organizations. As a leader, are you taking the leader's place, and accepting everything that comes with it? And as an employee, are you taking your right place? Or do you, as a newcomer, assume privileges that belong to experienced employees? Order creates clarity in an organization. If everyone is in the right place, the organization functions the best. In doing so, all functions are equally needed for the whole, whether they are strategic functions such as management, or core functions or support functions. The absence of the janitor in an educational institution can be just as disruptive as the absence of the director.

> *Martin, principal of a secondary school, tended to receive very nice feedback from his assistant principals. "But they also found it exciting*

because I was the boss". These are colleagues who are older and more experienced than me. But that's what hierarchy does. When I reflect on it, I sometimes experience an inconsistency between my formal role as director and how I feel emotionally. I'm a youngest child, always struggling with who I am, what I want and with the feeling of having to compete with others and the older people around me. So I assume that others also see me in this way and, therefore, not as the 'principal'. I realize that this probably applies to many leaders. That, over the years, their awareness of their impact does not grow in line with their actual impact".

The identity of organizations and family systems is characterized by patterns. Unconscious family patterns are brought into the organization – like the position of the youngest child who was never listened to, or the child whose place in the line of children wasn't clear. The order can be disturbed when two families become one, and the oldest is suddenly no longer the oldest, or the youngest is now the middle child.

Jesse had been hired on an interim basis as an organizational consultant. He soon found that he was reluctant to go to work. He was assigned a small office. From there he saw how the regular employees drank coffee together during the break, but nobody invited him to join them. There was almost no reaction to his consultancy advice. Jesse knew this position well from his extended family, where he was not listened to and his stepbrothers excluded him from playing. While in his family of origin he was the oldest, he had lost that position in the stepfamily. And also here, in this organization, he had no place. Jesse was tolerated, no more than that.

As a result of changes, shifts in the ordering can take place. In a family system, children can change places in the original ordering that was based on age. If your oldest brother dies, you could suddenly be first in line. New births displace the previously youngest child from her place. If the leader is not able to carry the load, or drops out due to illness or personal problems, someone else often automatically takes over leadership responsibilities. Over time, if this is not discussed and clear agreements are not made, problems usually arise.

Dutch Deputy Prime Minister Kajsa Ollongren fell ill in 2019 and was absent from the cabinet for six months. The cabinet was reshaped a little around her illness. A week before the new ordering took effect, they started talking about it. It was her portfolio, she thought it was very important that she could be replaced in a good way. [. . .] But she was very ill and not able to do much at all. The State Secretary at the Ministry of Foreign Affairs was the logical replacement for her. But he and the

Deputy Prime Minister quickly agreed that the whole portfolio would be impossible to handle, because he already had his own portfolio.[11]

Confusion about place can only be resolved through clarity. Often a ritual is needed to free up the place for the incoming person. To do so, it is not enough to just get up from that place and give it to another. A small but important ritual is needed: together, you look at what that place has or has not brought, so that it is truly free and the past does not cling to it. And really freeing up that place also ensures that the outgoing leader does not continue ruling over her grave, even if the newcomer does things differently than before. The outgoing colleague must (be invited to) take it all, heart and soul, with her when she leaves, because it belongs to her. Otherwise, she cannot truly leave and the newcomer cannot truly arrive, as his or her place is still, to some degree, occupied.[12]

Timothy, as the new, and young, leader of the telecom giant's sales team, is not really able to take his place. Andrew, his predecessor, had led the team for more than five years and taken sales to unprecedented heights. The team exhibits resistance, which veers between teasing, and deliberately sabotaging assignments. Both Timothy and his director are at a loss for words, and the latter is also growing impatient. At an evening meeting of the Young Executives Association, Timothy brings his concerns into the group. A colleague asks Timothy "Did Andrew properly pass the baton over to you? I mean, has Andrew said, in your presence, to the team members that you are the new leader they should follow?" The answer is no. The next morning Timothy calls Andrew and asks him if he is willing to stand together in front of the group. A few weeks later, Andrew attends the end of a team meeting. He is happy to see 'his' people and the feeling is mutual. Andrew addresses the group. He acknowledges the special bond they had and how grateful he is for it. At one point, as a symbol, he hands the projector pointer to Timothy. There is silence in the room. "I'm turning over the leadership of this team to Timothy", says Andrew. "He is your leader now. And it is important that from now on you also allow him to be the leader of this team". A few months later, Timothy tells the YEA club how surprised he is that this (emotional) moment caused such a major turnaround in the team dynamic.

In a family system, the greatest confusion occurs when generational boundaries are crossed. This happens when a child receives inappropriate tasks and responsibilities from a parent, or just takes them on himself. These are tasks and responsibilities that do not belong to the child, that he takes on unnoticed, or the child is encouraged to take on by the family environment. "How good that you help your father so much", now you are the man of the house".

The child gets used to carrying a (too) heavy burden and so continues to do so, unconsciously, as an adult.

Steven Colbert was a 10-year-old when his father died. Being the eleventh and last child, he was a kind of gift to his mother, he gave her a purpose. But he also had to take care of his mother. The house became very gloomy and quiet when his father died and the ordinary things that belonged to childhood were suddenly gone. In one blow he was an adult while, developmentally, he considered himself a bit behind when his father died.[13]

Taking care of your parent(s) is called parentification. Children then become a secure base for the parents, as it were. This leads to them developing special qualities, which is why you come across them as adults in social work, health care and, often, in the leader's chair. Problems arise when the young child's learned behavior of taking on responsibilities and tasks is unconsciously carried through in the contact with colleagues. When someone, whether the circumstances demand it or not, unconsciously exhibits that 'over-caring' behavior, that person takes things out of the hands of those to whom it rightfully belongs. As a leader, you pamper your employees; you don't ask if something is needed, because you've already done it. Constantly caring, while the daring 'switch' is permanently off. Perhaps all this caring is pleasant for the other person initially but, after a while, it results in confusion, irritation and anxiety.

> She comes to her coach because time after time she gets stuck in the organizations where she works. She keeps finding herself in teams where the leader doesn't take responsibility and, seemingly automatically, all eyes turn to her. And then, 'naturally', she takes over. After some time she becomes furious inside, because she is the one who has to do the difficult stuff. Her pattern is that she then ends up in a fight with the leaders she works for. When the coach asks if she knows this from anywhere, she realizes that, as a child, she did this for her father during the conflicts between her parents.

In such a case, there is an empty place – the leader not taking his position – and an old dynamic from childhood that is unconsciously repeated, again and again. Adults who leave their right place often receive a reward for this. Yet, at the same time, they experience it as a burden. They are often critical of (their) leaders and find it difficult to work with people who do not pull their weight and do not feel appreciated for the tasks they have taken on.

They attract tasks and responsibilities to themselves, evoking gratitude but also irritation, because they don't give their colleagues a chance to grow and develop through responsibility. And sometimes they load so much on their back that burnout is inevitable. From a very young age they have a special eye for what others need. They take care of everyone but themselves and eventually become exhausted. If they gain insight into this dynamic and take their right place, the organization can make optimal use of their qualities and they do not drop out of the work process.

As a leader, it is important to become aware of the patterns of your employees and your team, and also your own patterns: to recognize what is happening, when it is happening. Ask yourself "To what was this once the solution? How did it come about? What did it bring? And what did it cost?" Next, it is important to make the inner decision to let go of this pattern. It is likely you'll need to speak out, to your colleagues and/or to your boss.

Martine visits her coach because, for quite some, time she has been at odds with her director at the healthcare institution where she has been working for four years. "And I'm drawing the short straw". She talks about her son, age nine. "When I come home, and I feel bad, I call him to me. I hug him and then notice that this calms me down. But I also feel that I am burdening him with it. He reacts nervously when I call him . . . And he keeps his body tense when I try to cuddle him". The coach takes a Miffy doll from a basket in the practice room and gives it to Martine. She resolutely puts the doll down beside her.

"Suppose you had a Miffy at home, what would you say to her, if your son wasn't there for a hug?"

"That I'm scared. Of losing him. And of being sent away". She cries. She recounts a memory where she saw her mother in panic in the hospital with her father. Her mother was shocked when she saw Martine, and sent her away.

Martine decides that, on her way home, she will buy a Miffy from the toy store she passes on the way home. "A bit strange for a grown woman, if I'm honest", she says before leaving the coach's office. She practices at home. Every time she wants to call her son for a hug, she goes to her bedroom and says what she needs to say to the Miffy doll. A few weeks later, Martine has another session with her coach. Her eyes shine in amazement. She tells how the dynamics in her family have changed. That her son moves more freely in the house, plays more. And that she is crying an incredible amount. "That hurts", she says, "but is also liberating. Although sometimes I don't know when or if it will stop, and that makes me restless". And she has come to an understanding. "I don't have to be a perfect mother, but I am doing everything I can to break with my history. My son is allowed to be free. I have to deal with my stuff, not him".

At work, she has a conversation with her supervisor; about her fear of not belonging to the team, of being sent away. This turns into a couple of open, frank conversations about tasks, meaningful work and being able to experience support. "Vulnerable" she calls these conversations, "and also tough. But they are helping to break this old pattern".

Balance of giving and receiving

In interactions between people, a balance is constantly sought between giving and receiving. Between parents and children there may be an imbalance, because parents give children life and take care of them. The older children get, the more this comes into balance. But in horizontal relationships, such as between friends, partners and colleagues, there is a constant question whether giving and receiving are in balance. In the organization, there is constant balancing; this dynamic is also necessary because otherwise there is stagnation. As a leader, you might ask your team to temporarily step it up a notch, because this is necessary for the success of a project. But afterwards, the balance must be restored.

> *During the Corona crisis, a retail chain's staff were asked to put in extra effort. They had to work more, perform new tasks such as door duty and trolley cleaning, addressing customers when they did not follow the guidelines. These were tough tasks, especially for the younger employees who were mainly part-time. But the store manager made no distinctions and involved everyone in consultations about the changes in their work and the extra effort that was required. She was frequently present on the work floor to instruct or adjust the approach and was available for questions or support. And, regularly, the employees received a present such as a big bar of chocolate as a reward for their extra effort.*

In this case study, the organization works with every aspect of the system. Everyone is included. Permanent employees, shelf stockers, on-call workers, everyone is included in the process. The leader takes her place and is also present as a secure base. Finally, she ensures that the extra efforts are recognized, rewarded and appreciated. For the customers, this approach is also extremely pleasant, even though the strict door policy means they often have to wait in line outside. There is clarity and their safety gets priority.

In an organization, employees receive income, a place to work, safety, challenge, encounters, opportunities to develop and so on. And they offer the organization their time, qualities and talents, commitment and creativity. If there is no balance in this exchange, and/or if it is of a longer duration, the chance increases that employees become ill, or that unwanted attempts to create balance take place. The latter can manifest itself as obstructive behaviors, theft, doing personal work during business hours, maintaining strict working hours or refusing to put in extra effort when asked.

Breaking through behavioral patterns

Behavioral patterns originate at an unconscious level and can only be broken through when they are seen and brought into awareness. Behavioral patterns can obstruct the flow of the organization considerably, also because they can easily become fixed and repetitive. Just as in the family system where you resolved not to try to be like your father and, one day you look in the mirror and still see your father's eyes; you can, as a leader, also unconsciously maintain old patterns within the organization.

Tijsse Klasen[14] suggests four interventions to break through unwanted patterns.

- **Becoming aware**. When you are aware of the pattern, you can choose whether to keep acting it out or not. Recognizing the pattern is the doorway to breaking through or reducing its effect.
- **Unraveling**. When you understand how the pattern is related to other patterns in the organization, you can untangle the knots, allowing for more space and freedom of action.
- **Growing beyond it**. If you are able to take the pattern – with all that belongs to it completely as it is – to acknowledge it in all the ways it is good or not, then the possibility arises to put it behind you and continue your growth.
- **Disruption**. Crisis is a mechanism that so strongly disrupts and destabilizes that it makes room for new patterns. The Corona crisis removed all the obstacles to remote and digital work, in business and education. We discovered that for meetings and consultations you do not always have to take the car, train or plane, but that video calling can be very efficient, even pleasant.

Projection and (counter)transference

As you have read, at the beginning of this chapter, time and again you unconsciously repeat the table seating of your home, of the family in which you grew up. Later, when you take new places in your life and in your work, in new systems and in new arrangements, you bring all your experiences along with you.

In all these places, you are programmed to expect rules and forms of interaction similar to your family of origin; that is what you consider normal. From that perception, you will then react to events, easily repeating old behaviors that do not fit the new situation. Reactions to a situation or a person that are based on feelings, thoughts or beliefs, that belong to situations or persons from the past, are called transference reactions. You unconsciously stick something on another person that belongs to a person or situation from your past. For the other person, it is difficult, if not impossible, to be able to understand this transference reaction. Because of hierarchical differences in the organization, employees might, for example from experiences of having too little say and not feeling heard, react to the leader as if he were the father or mother who did not listen to them. These reactions are actually about the child's past struggles with the parent(s). By learning to see through your own themes and patterns, you can prevent yourself from falling into the abyss of learned responses.

> *Karel's mother had abandoned the family when he was young. She had left with another man, with whom she had been having an extramarital affair for some time, and had built a new life and a new family elsewhere. She never contacted Karel again. His father had taken Karel into his confidence and told him everything. His anger at his wife's cheating made a particularly deep impression on Karel. Although he was not the oldest in the family – he had an older sister and a younger brother – the weight of this knowledge and the breach of trust caused by the cheating weighed heavily on him. The message his father gave him was literally that no woman could be trusted. He later had relationships, but they never lasted long. He distrusted his girlfriends and controlled them. Sooner or later they all left. That only confirmed his learned image of women. When he made a career as an IT executive, it was not so noticeable at first. Few women worked in the department and control was part of his management style. Only when a female director was appointed as his line manager did things start to go wrong. He could not take orders from her, simply could not be subordinate to her. It led to a situation where, to the surprise of everyone in the management team, a fierce battle ensued; this was not how they knew him at all. Only in the mediation that followed did Karel's underlying convictions emerge, much to his surprise.*

Projection is a specific form of transference reaction. You are looking at the other from your own perception, as if that other person had exactly your feelings or thoughts. This perspective forms your truth about the other person and hinders the possibility of open observation. The other person becomes, as it were, a screen on which you are projecting your own inner world. As a leader, it helps to be sensitive to projection and transmission mechanisms, your own and others'. When you keep open the possibility that a coworker is unconsciously confusing you with a parent – and if you can do so during actual contact, you will better understand what is happening, and can react differently. For example, you might say "The intensity of your reaction surprises me. What is really going on? Are you willing to explore that?" Knowledge of transference phenomena gives you, as a leader, more tools with which to communicate and offers the possibility of avoiding struggle and confusion.

Contact and (psychological) contract

Every contact unconsciously creates a contract: a psychological contract[15] that defines the unspoken and unwritten rules for how you and the other person will relate to each other. It also covers expectations about the degree of confidentiality, depth and vulnerability that each will allow in contact. Because the psychological contract concerns unspoken mutual expectations and is not explicitly negotiated, the contract remains implicit and susceptible to unintentional violations that can have a major (negative) impact on the relationship.

In a work situation, in addition to the explicit employment contract, there are several implicit psychological contracts: between you and the organization, between you and your immediate supervisor, and one with every colleague with whom you have any kind of interaction. All these contracts are bi-directional because the other person also expects something from you. Violations of the (expectations in the) psychological contracts subsequently come not only from the other person but, despite your good intentions, also from you.[16]

As the expectations in your psychological contract are implicit; the assumptions underneath are mostly unconscious. Yet these are precisely what guides your behavior and, because one behavior evokes other behaviors, you often get reactions that confirm – and thus reinforce – your assumptions. Think of the *set-up-to-fail syndrome*, which you read about earlier. Your assumptions and beliefs color your expectations of the other. Therefore you will, in the main, unconsciously see in the other's behavior confirmation of your assumptions, thus reinforcing your existing image of the other person and the outside world. We call these cognitive filters. If the other person changes and shows different behavior, your cognitive filter will not let that change through. You only allow yourself to see it when you notice your own assumptions and expectations and thus adjust your filter.

Psychological safety and team performance

Working in groups comes with a huge variety of dynamics, which can throw up real challenges in your life as a leader, especially in times of stress and change. In team situations, people repeat the patterns of feeling they experienced when they did or did not feel welcome in groups from earlier in their lives. And, of course, no group has more impact than one's family of origin.

Leading transition is also a group phenomenon, and a learning place par excellence. In groups we encounter two distinct opposing phenomena: on one side the *wisdom of the group*, and on the opposite side *groupthink*. The *wisdom of the group* is based on the conventional wisdom that "two know more than one". A good example is from the nineteenth century English scientist Francis Galton, who had bystanders at a market guess the weight of an ox.[17] To his surprise, the average of all the guesses was closer to the actual weight of the ox than the estimate of an expert. On the other hand, we have the phenomenon of *groupthink*, where the quality of decisions in a group actually decreases, despite the increased levels of knowledge present. This latter phenomenon occurs unconsciously when the solidarity and unanimity of the group is felt to be more important than the outcome, with members of the group making their rational considerations and critical thinking subordinate to common agreement.

Amy Edmondson examined what distinguishes excellent teams from underperforming teams. She discovered that within excellent teams there is a shared belief among members that the team is a safe place to take risks in interpersonal relationships. She came to call this *psychological safety*.[18] This belief usually takes the form of a tacit assumption; one that is not spoken aloud by individual team members or the team as a whole. Psychological safety is the confidence that the team will not ridicule, reject, or punish someone who speaks up.

Trust within teams is characterized by the expectation that actions taken by others within the team will work out well for the interests of all the team members. It is this trust that gets every team member's buy-in to those actions. Psychological safety at the team level includes, but also transcends, interpersonal trust between the individuals that make up the team. Another necessary condition for psychological safety at the team level is that team members can be completely themselves from a position of mutual respect, despite differences. This requires that team members hold the same perception of psychological safety within the team. Shared experiences in the team are helpful in arriving at such a shared picture.[19]

Amy Edmondson discovered psychological safety, she says, "by accident" during her research into the relationship between medical errors and team effectiveness. Whereas she expected that more-effective teams would result in fewer medical errors, her research indeed revealed a statistically relevant relationship between team effectiveness and the number of medical errors.

To Edmondson's dismay, however, the relationship turned out to be inversely proportional to her expectation: more-effective teams made more errors. Her eureka moment came when she posited that more-effective teams might not make more errors but, through greater openness, reported more errors. New research confirmed a relationship between team effectiveness and openness to discuss risks and mistakes, in order to learn from them. This culture of openness in teams when discussing risks and mistakes and the willingness to learn with and from each other is what Edmondson would later call psychological safety.

In a psychologically safe environment ideas are shared openly, leading to better innovation and decision-making. There is a certain level of comfort in admitting failure and the team learns from failure. This leads to an upward spiral of performance in a team experiencing psychological safety, because ideas are openly shared. The opposite occurs in an environment where there is no psychological safety: team members are less likely to share different of opposing views, leading to a 'common knowledge effect'. Fear of admitting mistakes and a tendency to blame others, leads to a downward spiral of decreasing team performance.[20]

Although the concept of psychological safety was not new, Google's Aristotle Project marked its breakthrough into the public realm. The Google project examined more than one hundred different teams within its own organization, looking for the secret behind the most successful teams. First, Google looked for it in the teams' composition: which mix of personal traits, characters, competencies and knowledge made one team more successful than another? Despite hundreds of interviews and extensive data analysis, they couldn't figure it out. Neither the personnel of a team nor mutual friendships outside of work had any impact on success.

Nor did strong management or less-hierarchical direction make any difference. Even similarly set-up teams that shared certain team members turned out to achieve very different results. Only when mutual norms and behaviors within the teams were examined – from the perspective of psychological safety – did everything fall into place.

Working on psychological safety

How can you strengthen the psychological safety of a team? Edmondson suggests a number of approaches or tactics. She suggests you begin by emphasizing the uncertainty of the environment, and that interdependence within the team is essential to achieving the desired results, especially working in a dynamic and volatile environment. By stating that everyone's input is desired and needed, you are also stating that it is necessary for everyone to speak out. You then approach the work as a learning environment, not as a problem to solve. This is a learning-oriented mindset. We'll examine this in Chapter 5. By being genuinely curious about the other person's story, you avoid the trap of thinking in terms of guilt and innocence, of judging the other person, of creating an atmosphere of blaming.

By acknowledging your own fallibility, you provide safety for everyone else to speak up. When you make explicit the limitations of your knowledge and experience, alongside your own insight, you indicate that team members are crucial to supplementing your knowledge and experience.

By asking lots of questions, you encourage your team members to speak up. In doing so, you simultaneously awaken their curiosity. Curiosity arises when you address the other as one human being to another. Just like you, the other is someone with universal basic needs, such as respect and appreciation. The other person is also, although possibly from different interests or insights, looking for their own particular desired outcome, just like you are.

By always seeing the other person as someone who is "just like me", the likelihood of a desirable shared outcome increases:

- The other person has beliefs, viewpoints and opinions, just like me.
- The other nurtures hopes, has fears and vulnerabilities, just like me.
- The other has friends, family, and perhaps children, who love him, just like me.
- The other person needs respect, recognition and appreciation, just like me.
- The other wants peace, joy and happiness, just like me.

This includes asking for feedback to gain insight into your blind spots:

- What went well and what could be improved in the way I addressed this?
- How was it for you to hear this message?
- How could I have presented this proposal better?

The benefits of psychological safety in your team, are higher levels of engagement, a greater willingness to tackle difficult problems, greater learning and development opportunities as a team and higher performance.[21] Psychological safety is a prerequisite for transition and it is up to the leader to create the conditions for psychological safety.

Psychological safety and learning

Psychological safety is necessary to promote a learning-oriented mindset among employees. Fear, as a tool to inspire desired behavior, is actually counterproductive to learning. A leadership style based on instiling fear is based on the belief that people only work hard to avoid punishment or sanctions. However, this is only true when the controlling force is present and, more importantly, only for simple routine tasks where no unexpected problems might arise or where no improvements need be made. Knowledge-intensive or innovative work, where success depends on collaboration and knowledge sharing, benefits from the open exchange of ideas, asking questions and suggesting alternatives. The human tendency is to exhibit risk-averse behavior within a group. If employees feel psychologically safe, they usually rise above this.

Yet psychological safety is not the same as a work environment where everyone is just being nice to each other, where everything you say is valued unconditionally or where dissent is not tolerated. Psychological safety is about respect and value for differences in input and vision, where feedback, just like input, can be given openly and honestly. This may not, and does not, always have to be put nicely, but the intention must be positive: to learn from it together and to become better together.

So psychological safety is about caring and daring, with a leader as a secure base, so allowing the team to also become a secure base for the team members. This enables the team to achieve higher performance.[22]

Important insights to take away

- Your oldest experiences of being or not being welcome and belonging have a strong effect on your behavior. In every encounter, especially in new or exciting encounters, these old experiences come into play.
- Unconsciously, you tend to repeat old patterns and to overlay old events onto new contact situations (projection and transference). However, with awareness you can consciously make new choices and break through these patterns.
- In systems – both family and organizational – it is important that there is an order, and that this order is respected, that each is included, and that there is a balance between giving and receiving.
- Every contact leads to a psychological contract, often unconscious, with mutual, unspoken expectations.
- Psychological safety – the confidence that your openness will not be used to ridicule or reject you, but to learn from together – is essential to performing as a team.

Questions for self-reflection

1. Take a look back at your family of origin.

   a. How were you welcomed into the world?
   b. Which child were you in the line? What was that like for you?
   c. What space was there to show emotions?
   d. What attention was there for you? What, if anything, did you have to do to get attention?
   e. What was talked about, mostly, at the kitchen table in your home? What remained unsaid?
   f. How much interest did you experience in what occupied you day-to-day? Were you given space to continue when you shared your challenges and emotions?

2. How do the previous questions affect how you function in and lead teams?
3. How do your past experiences affect how you make contact in your present life?

   a. How do you give attention to others? What, if anything, do they have to do to earn it?

  b. What does the balance between giving and receiving in your relation-ships look like to you?
  c. What or who do you tend to exclude when things are stressful or when you experience anxiety or loneliness?

4. What expectations and unwritten rules make up the psychological con-tracts you enter into with others?
5. What degree of psychological safety do you experience in your own (man-agement) team?

  a. What is the reason for this?
  b. How can you (further) increase safety?

6. What degree of psychological safety do your colleagues experience in your team?

  a. What is the reason for this?
  b. How can you (further) increase their sense of safety?

Questions for you to ask of the people around you – your person effect

1. How do I welcome you when I meet you? How does it affect you and our bond?
2. What do you see me doing to make team members feel welcome? What could I improve in that regard?
3. In what ways do you feel I contribute to the safety of this team? What detracts from it?
4. When do you get enough attention from me and when do you not?
5. What do you sometimes have to do to get it?
6. When do you experience my attention as genuine and when not?
7. How do you appreciate the openness in our contact and how might we deepen this?
8. What do you want to know about me – that I haven't told you yet – to get to know me better?
9. What may I know about you – that you haven't told me yet – so I can get to know you better?
10. May I share with you what I expect from our contact, and would you like to share with me what you expect?

5 In Your Vulnerability Lies Your Strength

Attachment and Resilience

About attachment and resilience

Martine is a leader that people hold in awe. She is energetic, always cheerful, gets a lot done, and her team members can always rely on her. But still . . . Martine contacts a coach and says "Something's not right with me. But what?" A recent radical experience in her personal life made her realize that something needs to change in the way she does things. She solves everything herself, pushes away negative emotions by working harder and pushing herself in the gym, and feels lonely and abandoned. "Who is there for you? Are you even there for yourself? Who do you let see your vulnerability? How do you look for bonding at a deeper level? Who do you allow to look inside you and accompany you on this painful journey?" Through the coaches questions she realizes how she was taught from an early age to do everything herself and never to seek help. As a child, Martine had to figure everything out on her own and to comfort herself. Through this she developed many qualities, but also the feeling of loneliness and abandonment with which she now struggles.

We see in Martine a woman who, as a child in the relationship with those who raised her, adopted the belief that she was on her own in life. She has been unable to let go of this conviction, not even when secure bases are available.

In studies of adult attachment, it is seen that most people continue their childhood attachment style into adulthood.[1] This affects both their personal and work relationships. Knowing about adult attachment helps you better understand your colleagues, and yourself. Here's a short overview of attachment styles.

Attachment and attachment styles

John Bowlby – the founder of attachment theory – together with Mary Ainsworth, in the middle of the last century, showed how, as a child, you shape

DOI: 10.4324/9781003409922-5

your attachment style based on your experiences with the safety and availability of your attachment figures and secure bases. By attachment Bowlby meant any behavior that would result in a person achieving or sustaining closeness to a very specifically defined other, who is considered better able to cope with the world. The awareness that an attachment figure is near and available gives someone a powerful and pervasive sense of security and encourages them to perceive and continue the relationship.[2]

Attachment is the *unconscious* behavior by which proximity to an available other is sought. This is necessary for survival because the child is dependent on the caregivers for its safety and care. If a child has enough experiences that a secure base is present in cases of disappointment, frustration and (temporary) separation, it develops a healthy behavior pattern that leads to resilience. It experiences that it can bring emotions into the relationship without running the risk of rejection. If, during those same experiences, that attachment figure was not available, what Bowlby calls *separation anxiety* and protest behaviors arise. That anxiety and that behavior will persist until the secure base is available again. Depending on the availability of the attachment figures we make a distinction between *secure* and *insecure attachment* styles. We discuss both attachment styles briefly here and will return to them more fully, in the context of the work environment, later in this chapter.

Secure attachment

In a secure attachment, the child has access to secure bases. It can go to them for support and comfort, and they provide a safe haven – a comfort zone – to get to know the world, to explore and to take risks. And if the world feels unsafe, the child can return to the safe haven to be reassured and soothed and resume his journey. In this way, the child is given time to explore the world and, supported by his secure bases, develops resilience and the ability to cope with setbacks and disappointments. A secure attachment is the foundation that enables the child to deal with the bumps that life throws at her.

Insecure attachment

Not all children are fortunate enough to have available secure bases, and so develop an insecure attachment style. This is not an emotional disorder, but the result of attachment problems, and will manifest in both personal and professional lives, but is rarely recognized as an attachment-style issue. Often what arises is seen as innate character, while it is, in fact, learned behavior. If you, as a leader, have insight into this, it dramatically widens the palette of responses you can draw upon.

The most common insecure attachment style is one in which there is too much demarcation. These children get cold-shouldered when they turn to their attachment figures for comfort and support. They reach out but there is no one there to accommodate them, especially emotionally. The parent doesn't ask what the child needs, and says or radiates that the child has to take care of it themself. When this happens repeatedly, children develop the belief that they are on their own in life and must solve the problems that arise themselves, without help. Even as adults, they do not ask for help, even when it is available. They are hard workers, but usually not good at cooperation; they pull work and responsibility to themselves. Like Martine in the earlier example.

A second insecure attachment style is one in which there is too little demarcation. The child seeks comfort but is confronted with the adult's emotions, overshadowing the child's needs. The adult is upset herself and is not available to calm the child. The child is not asked what he needs; the adult imagines the problem and solves it immediately, because he cannot endure the child's emotions. Thus, the child does not learn to stand on their own two feet and remains dependent.

You might, for the first time now, be looking at your parents, caregivers, and yourself as a leader, through the lens of secure or insecure attachment. You have an existential, inalienable bond with your parents. Probably, you'd prefer to emulate what was good and leave behind what has not served you well.

Inquiring into your attachment history can create an uncomfortable tension. You might say, "At my house, it was safe. My parents loved me. Stuff happened, of course, but nothing serious". Investigating your attachment history can create a conflict of loyalties between yourself and others. For example, the thought might be "After so many years, it's not for me to blame my parents; they just did what they could". Or, "I'm not going be seen as a victim of my childhood". In short, looking at the real impact of how your upbringing has affected your leadership, can give rise to the idea that you are fouling your nest.[3] Paradoxically, true freedom only arises when you acknowledge the deep bond, its sunlight and its shadow.[4]

Oscar is 48 when he is fired by the international organizational consulting firm where he's worked for seven years. His employer told him to create a PIP (Performance Improvement Plan) for himself. Not for the first time in his career, he was accused of passivity, of coasting. This passivity led, among other things, to sloppiness in projects he led. Oscar also knows that he is passive in his relationships, which leads to tension. While exploring the theme of encouragement *in his life, he tells how he was "given all the space" to take the initiative. "Nothing was put in my way. There was never criticism if I couldn't do something, or a feeling that I had to perform". When asked how results and school choices were discussed, Oscar says there were never any doubts. "My father was a kind, warm man. He was interested in what I was doing, but he didn't ask many questions. I think it was often a bit too much for him, too. He was tired a lot. My mother liked to say that 'good is good enough' and encouraged me to go to college in a nearby city instead of university, although I would have preferred the latter. So I could continue to live at home, which I liked. But I think I also did it to please her: I gave in, I suspect".*

Being able to trust another person, or not, forms beliefs in the child's brain, which develop into internal working models that children take with them into their adult lives. If you have an eye for it, you will see these working models in abundance on the shop floor or the office. Both in your employees and in yourself.

Are you the leader who is emotionally available to your employees and, from that availability, do you also encourage them to take on new challenges and increase their potential? Or are you the leader who leaves his or her employees to their own devices based on the motto "they must take their own responsibility" or "this is a business, not a social project" or "emotions do not belong in a professional environment". And, as a result, are you not available as a secure base? Or are you the leader who 'sees' all the problems before anyone else and has already solved them before the employee realizes he has them? These internal working models, anchored in your mind's eye, form the basis for your personal and professional relationships. The mind's eye is the part of your brain that determines and directs your focus.

You could compare it to a kind of flashlight that illuminates either the positive or the negative. The fundamental experiences the brain uses to focus your mind's eye come from your first attachment figures. The more secure the attachment, the more the mind's eye focuses on the positive.[5]

Yet an insecure attachment in your past does not preclude your being able to focus on the positive. On the contrary: using secure bases, it is possible to change your brain's responses by creating new neural pathways. If you (can) walk the path of trust repeatedly, using your secure base, you make a kind of 'elephant path' – a short, broad path between two points. It may not be complete yet, but it forms as it is used. The paths leading to negative focus then become less used, overgrown. This is known as *rewiring the brain*. In this way it is possible to develop a form of 'acquired' secure attachment later in life.[6] This is primarily a matter of doing the hard miles, of not giving up. Although talent is not acquired, nor leadership, a secure attachment **can** be acquired by focusing on learning, practicing vulnerability, having the courage to ask for help and being willing to receive full and frequent feedback.[7] It is becoming increasingly clear how (the practice of) mindfulness also can contribute to rewiring the brain.[8] In this way you ensure that you can assess employees more fairly, and offer more and better alternatives for moving forward. Because you are no longer assessing them based on your 'old' patterns.[9]

Writer Bart Chabot grew up with a father who reprimanded him physically and, when not beating him, would crush him to dust with words. His mother would just sit there doing nothing to protect him, staring down at her plate. Also at school he received no recognition or confirmation from his teachers. All this changed when he met Herman Brood and Jules Deelder who saw something in him and encouraged him to go on the stage and to write. His wife also became a stable factor in his life and he succeeded, unlike his father, in developing into a loving father of a family with four sons where it was possible to say anything. "In a way, I am indestructibly optimistic. Despite how things were at home, I discovered how wonderful life can be. That it is worthwhile, even if you are unhappy or have no money. Even then you can just go to the beach: the waves are free, the clouds float by for free. The children, too, have this confident and joyful outlook".[10]

As an adult, it remains important to have secure bases to whom you can turn for (emotional) discharge, dialogue, advice and counsel, especially in stressful situations. Having and using secure bases – in the form of asking for help – is perhaps the most critical factor in preventing leadership from being derailed. We will return to what attachment means, in the context of life and work, in more detail later in this chapter.

Peter Ottens, founder of the YETS Foundation, grew up on the edge of one of Rotterdam's disadvantaged neighborhoods. Already at a young age he is fascinated by the great differences he encounters on the streets. On the local basketball court he is certainly not the best, but he has a dream. A dream that he makes come true: to become a professional basketball player in the United States.

Once in the U.S., he wonders how he managed to get there while more-talented boys from his neighborhood did not. He realizes that he owes this to the strong home base he had. Whatever happened on the streets, at home there was love, structure and attention. Something that many of his peers never knew.

Back in the Netherlands, Peter wanted to give something back, to help young people who were not as lucky as he was; the possibility to develop their talents from a safe and supportive home. He started a mentoring program for vulnerable young people, based around sports. This program grew into what is now the YETS Foundation. A place for young people who, for whatever reason, do not have the secure base at home that they need to become the best they can be.

The YETS Foundation is a place where young people not only find a safe haven for guidance with their problems, but are also challenged by playing sports together. Above all, YETS is a place where sport, fun and development come together. The approach is unique and impact-ful. Being welcomed, playing and having fun and then having conver-sations about what young people are faced with, their struggles. This is a reversal of what many young people actually experience: often their parents impose rules and conditions they must meet if they are to receive the love and attention they need. Surprisingly, Peter and his coaches also work with clear, nonnegotiable rules. Notorious is his *ten push-ups* if you are late for an activity. The rules provide not only clarity, but also safety. In the right order: first the welcome, then the rule. Both are unconditional, and neither is without consequences.

Many of the young people who work at YETS or participate in the programs lack the presence of an available parent and so lack structure and a role model. This is precisely what they find at the YETS Foundation. As one young person says, "At YETS, I got to meet new 'fathers'.

The YETS Foundation is an (inter)national example of young people being guided out of situations of insecurity through the use of sport and play. The YETS Foundation has already received many awards and Peter Ottens is often invited globally – among others by the United Nations – to share the power of the YETS approach.

Attachment and secure base

Bart is driven. An HR department head who is always at the office because of his tendency to work too hard. His manager Remco talks to him about this. Bart says he doesn't have much confidence in his abilities and is afraid of being exposed. He thinks he doesn't have the caliber for the role. When Remco asks Bart why didn't he raise the alarm sooner, he doesn't answer. Remco asks, "Did you ever learn to ask for help?" Bart tells how his father was always working and was never there for him. He set the bar very high and Bart was only 'seen' if he performed well at school or in sports. Remco again "Do you know the feeling of having your father standing behind you?" Bart remains silent. "Can you remember a time when you felt like your dad was totally there for you?" Suddenly Bart's eyes light up. "Yes, when skiing. I skied endlessly down the baby slope, safe between his legs until I dared to do it alone. I had completely forgotten about that". Remco suggests he use this image as an anchor. Not the times when his father was not there, but precisely these moments when he was totally there and was incredibly patient. "Your father was there for you then, and I'm here for you now, at work, when you need help. Asking for support is a quality. And know that you are more than capable of doing this job. I'm asking you to knock on the door if you're feeling a bit out of your depth, not when you're already in over your head".

Remco's intervention is effective. He elicits a forgotten resource in Bart – his father as a secure base – and offers himself as a secure base at work. This kind of bonding conversation can ensure that someone does not give up at work, even when things get difficult, and learns that he doesn't have to go it alone.

As you already read, our first secure bases in life are usually our parents. But children also discover very early on that there are other secure bases, such as cuddly toys or pets. They serve, even later in life, as powerful *transitional objects*.[11]

A *transitional object* could be described as something that 'objectively' seems to be only a thing, only what it looks like. For the person in question, however, it is just as much a part of himself and of his inner world. With children, these are, for example, cuddly toys, pets, songs, games. They give children a sense of belonging, security, being seen, support and warmth. With adults this works similarly and can apply to things like jewelry, particular books, clothing (a hat for example), the framed picture of the founder of the company, the team mascot and so on. Transitional objects can thus serve as powerful secure bases during change. They provide a sense of stability, and inspiration for the next step. Transitional objects are powerful anchors that help facilitate the transition from one situation to another. Often they become part of rituals.

> *It is exciting for Luciano to present his project for the first time to a larger group of colleagues. Holding the microphone in his hands, he looks around. He feels as if everyone can see right through him. He feels fear squeezing his throat and is afraid he might panic. Then he catches the eye of his supervisor, with whom he always feels comfortable. Under his warm gaze, Luciano can breathe again and feels himself becoming calm. After all, he is not on the stage to be torn apart. Then he is able to see that his colleagues are also waiting, interested, open to what he is going to say.*

As an adult in situations of stress and change, you need contact with a secure base to help you regulate your emotions. You 'know' you are not in danger yet still you can panic. Throughout your life, you tend to keep an eye on those to whom you are most attached. This applies to both their physical and emotional presence and availability. Attachment is not a childish dependency, but an abiding human need for a secure base. Through secure bases you constantly improve your ability to distinguish between *being safe* and *feeling secure*. The fact is that the world – including organizations – is rarely a safe place. Changes and risks, sometimes physical but mostly emotional, are always lurking in the shadows. In the 'small' – the exciting conversations, the presentation to the team – and in the 'big' – the (imminent) resignation, the transfer, becoming a partner, the death of a colleague – change is the constant; an unpredictable insecurity. You *are not safe*. Learning from and with your secure bases allows you to access your internalized secure bases whenever necessary. You can think of those internalized secure bases as powerful memories based on previous positive experiences of handling tension, stress, fear, disappointment, danger and risk. Those memories teach you something about how you acted then and give you the confidence to act well now. Your resilience is always at hand. You feel *secure*.

The leadership quality that employees worldwide say is most important is respect. On the one hand, the respect that everyone deserves, that the leader owes to his employees out of decency and basic human kindness (*owed respect*). On the other hand, the respect that employees earn based on their performance or merit (*earned respect*).

When this is adhered to and evident in behavior, it creates a sense of security and trust. Respect is the key to trust, and trust underlies the relationship between the leader and his employees and colleagues.[12] Trust is at the root of teamwork. Absence of trust creates fear of conflict, which always stems from a fear of rejection, which in turn is linked to the separation anxiety you read about earlier. It further leads to less bonding, and group members who no longer take responsibility, which also erodes the focus on results.[13] In situations of stress – as you'll see later in Chapter 8 – the leader's skill at building trust is put to the test. It can just disappear: "Trust comes on foot and goes on horseback".[14] This means that the leader must be able to see and name reality, especially painful reality. George Kohlrieser introduced the metaphor of *putting the fish on the table*.[15] By this he means discussing difficult and painful themes that can get in the way of bonding.

After all, a fish kept under the table is still going to stink. Putting hard issues on the table substantially reduces failure. But, more positively, and unsuspectedly, it also contributes to profit, and the growth of both employees and the organization.[16]

In short, the essence of the secure base is to establish and sustain trust. Feeling the trust of secure bases, you build self-confidence and become able to 'create' it in others. In this way, trust inspires action and movement, especially where stagnation is a threat. Leaders who have the impression that they cannot trust their own bosses will adjust their behavior so that they still feel secure. They try to protect themselves from the behavior of their bosses. They think they have to take care of themselves because they don't expect to get help when it is needed. They are, in fact, insecurely attached to their organization and will exhibit behaviors that reflect insecure attachment. All types of behaviors are possible here, but in particular insecure attachment will often result in the leader rigidly adhering to rules, procedures and processes. This gives the illusion of safety, because the environment appears predictable through control and mastery, while in fact it is not.

The leader experiences no secure base in the organization and feels forced to construct one himself. He wants to feel safe but creates a false sense of security for himself. The leader's behavior in this regard is not without consequences. The effect of his lack of felt trust in the layer above him transfers down and across in his own environment. The consequence is that his team members lapse into what Eric Berne calls game behavior.[17] Team members (consciously or unconsciously) deploy behaviors that avoid showing real emotions.[18] Through this game behavior they get stuck in undesirable roles, undesirable for everyone involved. Initiative and ownership are the first to die, given the heightened risk of emotional rejection. The insecurely attached behavior of the leader actually minimizes the chances of deepening the relationships. His team members will also start to feel less safe.

Thus, there is a strong snowball effect directly related to the presence or absence of a secure base leader at the top of an organization.[19] Even in profound loss situations, a secure base at work can make the difference between work as a resource or as hardship. When it becomes the latter, calling in sick is an easy option.

> *25-year-old Bas's sister dies, suddenly, in dramatic circumstances. He graduated only a month earlier and is starting his first job at a high-tech institute. To the surprise of many, he manages to do his job well despite his grave personal loss. Bas's manager, Mart, is in his early thirties and lost his father as an adolescent. They often take a lunch walk together. Not that they talk much about the losses, but the quiet presence of Mart is a secure base for Bas. Without words he feels that he is allowed to be there with everything that is going on at the moment. But, alongside Mart, work itself is also a secure base, a safe place where everything simply continues and where Bas doesn't have to hold his breath. Outside of work, when he next meets his parents, the loss is fully present again. In the months that follow Bas continues to function well at work, so that promotion became a real possibility.*

In times of transition, times when employees are expected to let go of their bond with the old situation, they need a leader who offers the security of a secure base from which they are challenged to take the leap into the unknown. For them, a situation of certainty and knowing where you stand, changes into an uncertain situation. This results in discomfort, which is registered by the brain as pain and can therefore evoke fight-or-flight reactions. This is a natural human response to uncertain, and therefore unsafe, situations. It is worthwhile for you as a leader to investigate how your employees bond with other secure bases, to stimulate these bonds or to make them possible, if necessary. What anchors, what sources of strength are present in your employees' networks? Everything that inspires (emotional) movement and growth can serve as a secure base. Like Beethoven in the following example.

> *Jan Kortie, vocal coach and 'voice liberator' is inspired by the way Beethoven overcame his suffering. Beethoven has known a lot of suffering, Kortie states, but after a great struggle and despite his misery Beethoven had the feeling he had a lot to give to the world. Kortie feels Beethoven's music in his heart. When Kortie broke up with his last girlfriend, he tells, he listened for hours to Beethoven's fourth piano concerto. He could hear in the music exactly what he was feeling: the frustration, feeling*

flattened like a pancake. In the slow part of the piece, Kortie explains, the piano is small and modest and the orchestra, which for him represents the world, is very big and bright; that's exactly how he felt.[20]

As a leader, if you can look through the lens of safety/insecurity, rather than the lens of resistance, the view is very different. You respond mildly and are able to explore how you might make things safer. When employees lose a familiar and safe situation, if you recognize and acknowledge their loss, and realize that this also involves a form of grieving, people can bond again easier and sooner. This is something we will explore in more detail in the following chapters.

The relationship between you the leader and your employees has characteristics similar to the relationship between parents and children. As a result, unconsciously, similar and old patterns are quickly evoked. If you do not learn to recognize these old patterns, you run the risk of holding the other person responsible for your unfulfilled desires and unspoken expectations. This is an unspoken dialogue: the other is responding in a similar way. The hierarchical relationships within organizations carry the risk that employees who as children internalized that their parents always knew better, adopt a dependent attitude. Or that they evoke the struggle they always had at home with their parents.

> *During the first meeting of the newly formed project team, one of the older employees displays a very critical, almost hostile, attitude. Willem, the (external) project leader, feels criticized and the atmosphere slowly but surely deteriorates. When Willem raises this issue with his client, they look together at what this critical employee's attitude brings up in Willem. He would prefer to run away, to leave the room and give up the assignment. But he knows he can't, so he becomes increasingly rigid and consequently no longer able to hear what is being said or to respond appropriately. The client asks if he has experienced this feeling before. This brings them to Willem's demanding and critical father who made his son really scared if something did not work out as expected. It seemed that this old feeling was evoked by the critical employee. The client advises Willem to share with the employee what his behavior brings up in him. Willem bites the bullet and tells the employee that he grew up in a family where there was always conflict; you had to be ready to attack first, otherwise you could lose.*

Here again you run up against the phenomenon of transference: someone's reaction to a current situation is based on feelings, beliefs and expectations that are connected to situations and persons from the past, often from the system of origin.[21] Originally, this reaction was correct – as a child you could not do otherwise – but now it is no longer appropriate. As a result, it evokes confusion, incomprehension or irritation, as in the case described.

In this way, employees project their unspoken expectations, unconsciously from a child's perspective, onto you. The inequality that employees can experience, around the distribution of influence and power, further
encourages this. When the communication continues to take place at the
content level, it becomes difficult to discern these patterns of parent-child
transactions and to bring them out into the open. Based on your specific
attachment style, when things get tense and feel unsafe, you tend to either
seek closeness or distance. When two different attachment styles use different strategies in this way, it increases the level of problem complexity
and diminishes the possibility of coordination and cooperation. A situation
that is far too close and therefore threatening for one person pushes them
to increase distance. A distance that the other person's attachment style
experiences as unsafe and threatening. When you, as a leader, learn to see
through your patterns and their effect on others, you can maintain bonds
and address mutual needs.

*Janneke is creative director at an innovative company. She tells how irri-
tated she used to get by employees who came to her for every little thing
and constantly asked for her attention. When you thought you'd sorted
out one problem, they would come up with another. It had helped her
enormously during a management training to get insight into attachment styles and especially into her own style: avoidance. She is someone who can work very independently, is not inclined to ask for help
and doesn't like colleagues near her. She thrives on distance. She has
discovered how this came about in her family of origin and now knows
both the pitfalls and the qualities of this attachment style. She has built
up an allergy to colleagues who are not independent, constantly ask for
closeness and come into her personal space. But now she can handle it
gently, seeing her own part in it. She knows better how to work with this,
not by avoiding contact, but by setting clear boundaries and indicating
when she can be available.*

Attachment and the brain

Your brain is innately social; it was already online before you were born and
is continually exchanging with its environment. Your parents are in the *brain-
building business.*[22] In the beginning, mother is the one up on the scaffolding
and father makes sure that the scaffolding provides enough support. Because
your brain and nervous system, unlike in most other species, are still im-
mature at birth, you come into the world as a kind of fetus psychologically.
The rate of brain development in the first year of life is enormously high as
the brain catches up with the infant's physical development. That is why this
first year is so important to the rest of your life. During this period, you are
completely dependent on your secure bases. You can't manage in the world
on your own yet.

The attachment system is activated when children experience stressors such as hunger or pain. When an adult (usually one of the parents) is sensitive and offers an attuned and predictable response to this stress, children return to a state of calm and peace. It is precisely in the degree of predictability of the response that you as a child unconsciously learn that you can endure the stress and thus develop resilience.

An attuned response between parent and child triggers the release of hormones (such as endorphins and oxytocin), which play an important role in brain building. Oxytocin creates feelings of well-being and pleasure in both parent and child. It also contributes to feeling safe and calm.[23] During this hormonal release, neurons are active in those areas of the brain associated with social recognition and bonding, and so reinforcement of existing neural connections and growth in the number of neural connections takes place; think back to the elephant pathways. At the beginning of life, in the safety of the presence of emotionally available and attuned parents (caring), the way is cleared to start exploring your inner and outer world (daring). Secure attachment is an internal resource that can absorb the shock of stressful events, allowing you to land a little softer.

These internal working models are recorded in your brain's neural infrastructure and have an enduring lasting influence on your attachment orientations. According to Manfred Kets de Vries, Professor of Leadership at INSEAD, they set the tone for future relationships, and that means you have to deal with your (and your colleagues') internal working models in the workplace too.[24]

The human brain is distinguished into three main parts. At birth, it is mainly the primitive part of the brain, the reptilian brain, that is online. Here the basic bodily functions that ensure that you can live, such as breathing, heartbeat, blood pressure, body temperature and your survival mechanisms are regulated. The second part, the limbic or emotional brain, is still largely in development. This is where, among other things, emotional development and attachment are located. Together, these two parts of the brain are also called the 'lower' brain.[25] The third part is the 'higher' brain, the cognitive brain or neocortex, which is not yet mature and still a work-in-progress at birth.[26] It is involved in important cognitive abilities such as making informed decisions, planning, organizing, reflecting, inhibiting undesirable behavior, the sense of social norms and values, and emotion regulation. But because the upper floor is still wrapped in scaffolding, as a young child you need your parent's higher brain as a kind of external emotional hard drive.

The brain grows from bottom to top, but also from right to left. At birth, the right hemisphere is already developed and active. The left hemisphere, which is more linguistic and factual, only develops from the age of about eighteen months. The contact between parent and child during this first period is right brain – right brain communication. The words do not matter so much (that is left brain), but the way in which the words are pronounced, i.e., tone, rhythm and sound, does matter. As do things like eye contact, smell and touch. How your parents communicated with you during that period – smell, sound, touch, eye contact – is stored in the body as unconscious memories. Situations at work can awaken these old memories and lead to reactions that are not immediately understandable.

> *Evelien is a young, enthusiastic teacher. Her principal is very satisfied with her and with the way she deals with her students. He does notice, however, that during team meetings she falls silent if things become a bit heated. She no longer contributes to the conversation and seems to be frozen in her chair. When, after a lively meeting during which emotions ran high, she indicates during the break that she is not feeling well and wants to go home, her director decides to talk to her the next day. He keeps returning to the issue of what happens to her when people disagree with each other and the tone of a conversation becomes angry. "Is this familiar to you in your life? When did you experience it before?" At first, Evelien can't answer. Eventually, it turns out that Evelien's parents got into a nasty divorce the year after she was born. She has no conscious memories of this. She does recognize her impulse to flee when voices get a little louder. Then she just wants to leave. If she can't, she sits, as if frozen, and cannot hear anything of substance. The director discusses with her how she can work with this theme, so that she can stay fully present and contribute meaningfully during team meetings.*

Emotional regulation

Babies and young children cannot regulate their emotions and quickly become upset with stressors such as hunger and cold. Because they cannot endure their emotions, it is the job of the parents or caregivers to help them do so. They pick up the emotion from the chaotic, emotional mush of the child, give it words and acknowledge it to the child in a bearable form. "Ah, that's not very nice, a wet diaper. Daddy will give you a clean one right away". The baby experiences the reassuring and comforting sound of the voice and the calmness with which the parent talks and acts. "Has that tower you just built fallen over? That's not nice. Come, Mommy will help you. We'll rebuild it together". The parent describes the confusing and unfamiliar world to the young child, lowering the stress level. Through this 'co–regulation' by your parents, you gradually and accurately learn the meaning of what you feel and what an appropriate response to it might be.

Bessel van der Kolk, Professor of Psychiatry at Boston University School of Medicine, is a specialist in the field of (traumatic) stress. His work shows that you should take the identical approach with adults who are under great stress. You might already have experienced this yourself in many areas. Just take an echocardiogram in the hospital or an MRI scan. You receive constant explanation and reassurance, and the 'strange' world is pointed out to you.

"The next scan will take four minutes and you will hear a loud sound that some people find unpleasant". The way you are spoken to is also important, as we saw earlier in right brain to right brain communication: the words are less important than the sound, tone and rhythm. This has a calming effect on the child's brain, and on adults too. Then there is *containment*: a warm and calm framework that radiates safety.

> *Lianne is a spirited young woman who has had a lot to deal with in her life and tends to isolate herself in her workplace. She works for a quite unstructured company where everyone is left to do their work however they wish. Therefore, it is not clear where one person's work ends and another's begins. As a result, Lianne has regular conflicts with colleagues and is repeatedly discussing this with her line manager. Her struggles with colleagues are, in fact, a repetition of the struggles she had with her parents. She finds a position with another employer and immediately notices that things are different there. The work has structure; each person having clearly defined responsibilities. Overlaps and role uncertainties are discussed with each other. Her manager keeps her on her toes, but also gives her confidence and praise. Only now does Lianne notice how much peace this structured approach gives her. She realizes how much energy her previous job cost her.*

In her childhood, Lianne was in an unsafe environment with little structure. Her parents were unable to acknowledge or reassure her. As a full-grown adult, she is unable to reassure herself; she only knows the way of struggle. As a child, you need your parents to calm your brain. Most often, most adults can do this themselves, but in cases of great stress you need extra support – from a secure base – to manage this. Babies and young children have a chaotic inner world and cannot yet find their own way in it. If you grow up in a context in which your parents are sensitive to your emotions, are responsive and take you by the hand emotionally and make connections for you between feelings, words and actions, then you learn, increasingly, how to distinguish these feelings yourself and how to communicate about them. This gives you an anchor as a child and your inner confidence grows. Self-regulation is an important quality that significantly influences your ability to work, and feeds and stabilizes your working relationships. It is something that every person uses every day. It is the human ability to understand and control your thoughts, emotions and behavior. You use this skill to navigate through everyday situations and to work with other people.

> *When you practice self-regulation,*
> *you bond with the secure base within yourself.*

Self-regulation means that you develop the ability to take a bit of distance from yourself, see yourself objectively, and coach yourself through different, and difficult situations. For example, by talking to yourself, by giving yourself instructions and encouragement.[27] As we described above, you learn this as a child via co-regulation. "I am sad, so I want to sit on mummy's lap" becomes "I had a nasty contact with a client, I want to see a colleague to talk about it and get support". As a child, in the attunement with your parents you experience whether or not you can count on them when you need something or want to be comforted. When you have grown up receiving this confirmation, as an adult you know that although you have to do it yourself, you do not have to do it alone, that there are always others who are prepared to support you when you face setbacks.

As a child, you are a budding researcher who collects data about the possible outcomes of seeking contact.[28] You figure out how different ways of seeking attention work and adapt your behavior to the most successful way. If protest turns out to work, this becomes your primary strategy. If this doesn't work and you don't get attention, perhaps because your parents become impatient or dismissive, you fall back on follow–up strategies. A primary strategy is to increase activation; amplifying the behavior that initially seemed to help in order to get attention. However, this also increases stress and causes escalation. The child becomes upset and exhibits externalizing behavior: the emotions are expressed through (undesirable) behavior in the hope of getting attention and care this way. The second strategy is less visible and therefore less disruptive for the environment, but much more distressing for the child. He suppresses his feelings of stress, withdraws and might even go completely out of touch. The need-for-attachment switch is unconsciously turned down or off to prevent frustration and unbearable stress.

Geoffrey is a valued employee who always delivers good results. He is seen as a quiet force who never bothers anyone and gets on with his work. During his performance review, his leader expresses her appreciation for his work. Geoffrey is clearly pleased with this. When it comes to discussing the next step he would like to take and how he would like to develop, Geoffrey falls silent. When the leader makes suggestions and then a generous offer, Geoffrey stammers. "I don't know, I really don't." The question is too complex for him. He doesn't even manage to say, that as far as he is concerned, things are fine the way they are, as he's unsure if it's allowed to say this. Over the course of the conversation, his discomfort grows and his confusion increases.

Often, people like Geoffrey look absolutely fine on the outside, but on the inside they are anxious, insecure and sometimes very confused. Then words and explanations no longer help because the first thing that goes off-line when stress increases is the cognitive brain. The switch goes off and the connection between upper and lower brain is severed. Logical thinking, reflecting, organizing is then no longer possible. As a leader, you can speak to the employee, but your information does not reach the cognitive brain. You first have to calm the other person down by offering safety and reestablishing the connection. Only then can someone return to the here and now and be approachable again. It is important to realize that the other person is not unwilling, but for those moments he is being held hostage by the primitive parts of his brain.

As a leader, if you can look at people from this perspective and act appropriately, it can save you a lot of energy. You've probably experienced talking to someone, but nothing seems to be happening on the other side, as if that person is no longer present. And that's true, because 'inside' the other has left. When someone is held hostage by their lower brain, the upper brain is hermetically sealed away. This can happen in a way that bothers you, but doesn't really scare you: there is no contact and the other sits with glassy eyes, staring into the distance. But it can also be violent.

There is a huge racket coming from the staff room: shouting and crashing noises. When the principal goes to check, he sees one of the teachers freaking out and throwing dishes against the wall. Coffee is dripping down the paint; colleagues are looking on in bewilderment. One of the students has apparently gotten so far under the skin of this teacher that she is completely out of control.

According to American trauma expert Bruce Perry, the most effective strategy in the event of this kind of disconnection is as follows:[29]

- The first step is **Regulate**. That means making sure there is enough safety so that the other person's brain can calm down and come out of the fight, flight or freeze response. How you provide safety will be different for each person. Taking the person out of the stressful environment, going for a walk, getting a coffee, making careful physical contact, talking in a calming way (just like a parent talks to a child to reassure her). You need to make sure that the person returns to the here and now. (Because you should assume that she has retreated inside to somewhere else: a *there and then* place.)
- The second step is **Relate**. You restore the connection by making contact in an attuned way. This enables the other person to make the journey from within back to the here and now. This is most visible in the eyes. Are they really looking at you again?
- The third step is **Reason**. If the first two steps are successful, you can start appealing to their cognitive abilities, their capacity to think and reflect. If someone had totally disconnected, you'll sometimes notice that they have forgotten parts of the event, as if they had taken place completely outside them.

Only after these three steps is the connection between upper and lower brain back again.

Attachment: the basis for life and work

During the attachment period, children learn to use their bond to others to soothe their own inner pain.[30] This basis of secure attachment provides a good foundation for life. These children grow up trusting others, are able to learn, manage stress and deal with the challenges and crises that life brings. They learn that attachment can be broken and this break can be repaired: attachment – break – repair.[31] Securely attached leaders are able to provide such a foundation to their team.

Insecure attachment

There are, unfortunately, many people who were not fortunate enough to grow up with parents who were sufficiently sensitive and attuned. Perhaps you, personally, had to learn how to get along with a parent who was not sufficiently available emotionally (because they were reserved, inconsistent, physically absent, unpredictable or clinging). Perhaps because your parents had to work hard, or had not been taught by their own parents to deal with emotions, or had a parent who had to live with loss, trauma, or mental illness. If you are a child of such parents, it affects the development of your self-confidence, self-efficacy (belief in your ability to complete tasks successfully), and your self-esteem. It also affects the formation of your identity and you are somewhat more likely to enter into less-stable personal relationships. But you will have also developed many qualities simply by dealing with this: qualities such as perseverance, the ability to work hard, imagination, humor. Many leaders recognize this, both in themselves and in their employees. At the same time, it is important to keep an eye on its pitfalls, which can include collaboration problems, an overabundance/lack of purpose, and dropping out through burnout.

Dealing with divorce, death, mistreatment or abuse in your childhood intensifies these attachment challenges.[32] But these experiences of loss can also become powerful sources of energy, if and when you dare to face them and work through them.[33] Kets de Vries shows that the nature and quality of repeated interactions with your attachment figures determines how attachment patterns develop. The degree of responsiveness and attunement of the attachment figures forms the blueprint for the child's internal working models for all relationships. By this we mean that your expectations for how others will respond to your needs, are based on your earliest experiences with your caregivers. These can be positive (people stand by me when needed, they can be trusted) or negative (people are untrustworthy, they hurt or use me, I am alone in the world).

The Hedgehog Effect

The great German philosopher, Arthur Schopenhauer, drew an analogy between the discomfort humans and hedgehogs experience with social proximity. When it is cold, hedgehogs huddle together for warmth, but soon they begin to hurt each other with their spines. If they then move apart a little, they soon get cold again. Finally, after much shuffling back and forth, they find the optimal distance for warmth and comfort. For human 'hedgehogs', that paradox – our simultaneous need for closeness and distance – is a fundamental reason why people often find it so difficult to function successfully in groups, teams, organizations and civil society.[34]

Too few boundaries

There is also an insecure attachment style which involves too little delineation. Here people develop a great deal of dependence: inside they are continually afraid that the other person will not be sufficiently available.[35] Their self-regulation is insufficiently developed. They are little hedgehogs for whom the closeness is never enough, even if it hurts enormously. They are often not very good at problem solving. When one problem is solved with the help of a colleague or supervisor, the next problem is already in sight, so to speak. This is because they are uncertain whether they will get their mentor's full attention next time. You come across them in the workplace as colleagues who demand a lot of attention and often act dependent, clingy, insecure and sometimes panicky. They need a lot of approval and are afraid of rejection.

As a leader, you may be tempted to pamper them and give them everything, or, depending on your own attachment style, become very irritated because of their attention-seeking behavior. They constantly ask for caring and avoid daring. Their need for closeness can have a suffocating effect, so that colleagues become reticent and take more distance. It is precisely this vicious cycle that feeds their fear of rejection even more. Sometimes they 'test' the other person to see if they will remain available in spite of everything. In this way they achieve the very thing they fear most: more distance. Because they take up so much energy, they are often passed from one team to another, which only fuels their fear.

Too many boundaries

There are, however, many people who find intimacy or proximity difficult and erect a wall to maintain distance. This can take a mild form, but these 'walls' can also be sky-high, as in the Midas Dekkers example (see page 70).

You could say that people with this attachment style were, as children, pushed out of the nest to fly on their own, while their wings were not yet fully developed. To survive emotionally, they more or less had to disconnect from their feelings. They had little caring but, consequently, lots of daring. In fact, their self-regulation is overly developed and their distance button is set on 'far'. They don't feel comfortable being close to others. They are the hedge-hogs who prefer some space and don't mind getting a little chilly. They don't like being pricked, are afraid of being hurt.

Biologist and writer Midas Dekkers writes, in his book *Full License* how, as the son of a pub owner, he was an orphan with parents. He did have a father and a mother, but they weren't there. At any rate, not for him. The customers came first. And if there were no customers to serve, then his parents would serve themselves. His father, in a drunken stupor, beat up his mother, and his mother, in a drunken stupor, wasn't any nicer and eventually ran off with someone else. Dekkers experienced that a café is populated by transmitters (people who talk), not receivers (people who listen), and says that because of this childhood he grew up to be a rather independent person, a loner. And there was no place here for vulnerability. He thinks making yourself vulnerable is the stupidest thing you can do. Why should you make yourself vulnerable? Then you get hurt. Imagine that you are a knight and think: this armor's heavy, I'll throw it away; I'm going to make myself vulnerable during the next jousting tournament. Little is heard of such knights anymore. So you shouldn't do that. As far as Dekkers is concerned, this also applies to personal relationships. If you allow yourself to be vulnerable, and love appears to be finite, you spend the next two years recovering from the blow, he feels. He was very vulnerable once, before he thought that Freud was a fraud. She left, with someone else of course. That really knocked the stuffing out of him. Being hurt is very unpleasant. So he is not going to get caught out again. He'll be a bit sharper in future.[36]

Midas Dekkers is clearly most comfortable with distance and invulnerability. Bonding and intimacy are avoided: he will be a bit sharper. You can see from his life story why he had to develop this attitude.

For people with too many boundaries, intimacy and closeness are a major, sometimes impossible, task. They become masters at unobtrusively avoiding intimacy, both in personal and work relationships. For example, doing a lot of overtime, hiding behind their laptops or taking frequent business trips. They are often good at being tough and taking action. Asking for help has not been learned; they are convinced they must do everything on their own. The distinction between doing things themselves and doing them alone is unknown to them. People with this attachment style can be very successful in their working lives and can be found in the highest echelons of politics and business. They pay for this success with a sense of isolation and inner emptiness.

Generally, they are highly valued employees who do a good job and cause few problems. To keep a lid on negative emotions such as fear, anger and sadness, people with this demarcation style often use 'anesthetics' such as working too hard, always looking busy, clownish behavior, withdrawal, pleasing behavior, constantly being there for others. Some are actually addicted: to alcohol, drugs, gaming or working out. Henri Nouwen calls this "entertainment" – from the French word *entretenir*, based on the Latin words for between and holding: there is literally something in between.[37] It's about anything that engages you and keeps you away from the things you'd rather not face.

Some of these ways are socially very accepted, such as hard work, rescuing behavior, or being the nicest one on the team. It's a good masquerade that usually goes unnoticed, by the people that display the behavior as well as for the ones experiencing it. But eventually it can lead to depression, burnout or relationship breakdown.

> *In a responsible position, you have your tasks, that you do yourself.*
> *But this is not synonymous with doing it on your own.*
> *Being able to ask for help really is a quality.*

The emotional language of transition and the power of words

> **What your mother sings when you are in the cradle**
> **you carry with you to your grave.**
> African proverb

Your brain is a bit like a computer. It is programmed more or less the same way. What is not important is erased. The rest goes onto the 'hard drive', your autobiographical memory. Virtually nothing leaves your autobiographical brain once it is in there.[38] The same is true of words. The power that words give leaders is enormous. They can provide security, momentum and growth but just as easily create fear, oppression and sickness.[39]

As you read earlier, the human brain naturally focuses on the negative. It is always looking for threats, for error messages, to avoid pain. You can turn that around in your life by seeking out secure bases who will help you keep your mind's eye focused on the positive.

The vast majority of your thoughts are – without your being aware of it – negative. They do not help you; on the contrary, they often encourage the opposite of what you are striving for. Precisely because you are dependent on your parents in your first stage of life, your brain stores the words and phrases they say. Father says, "You should be ashamed", and you later say to yourself, "I am ashamed". Very little has more impact than the words spoken in attachment by your secure bases or those you longed would take that role. Negative messages enter more easily, go deeper and attach themselves more firmly in memory.[40] The impact of words isn't really dependent on whether they are said often or only once. What makes the difference is the person effect of the one who utters them. Words spoken during a profound loss experience, at a time of intense stress or with great emotion, make the deepest grooves on the hard drive. This applies to both negative and positive messages.

Words (also in the form of thoughts and beliefs, voices in your head – no need to go to the psychiatrist for this) that others speak and that you speak yourself can hold you hostage. Words spoken by a parent or leader (someone in a position of authority) have extra impact because of the place they are spoken from. For example, leaders evoke, in your unconscious, previous events where certain words were used (or omitted!) by people in positions of authority. Without your being aware of it, those words can easily hold you hostage and lead to an *amygdala hijack*.

The amygdala is that part of your brain that largely regulates your emotional housekeeping. It links both current perceptions and memories to stored emotions in your brain and determines your actions, such as your fight-or-flight response and the words you speak during that process. The challenge here is that the amygdala does not distinguish between 'there and then' and 'here and now'. It conflates situations. As a result, the amygdala's response is not always adequate, and often based on 'there and then'. So the amygdala becomes hostage to fear. This is at the expense of the other parts of your brain that deal with memory and processing new information. Digging up knowledge and applying it in a new situation, acquiring new knowledge and experimenting with new behavior is all much more difficult when, according to our amygdala, your life's in danger.

Anita Kentie describes the lead-up to an amygdala hijack. "There is a moment, just before you go into resistance, when you might be able to feel that something is catching hold of you. [. . .] If you don't pay attention, these signals can pass you by. And, before you know it, you have been pulled back into your old pattern of behavior."[41]

Carola is an outstanding leader who has risen quickly to the top. She and her team achieve results that the organization – a soft-drink manufacturer – have been proud of for years. She is always very tense prior to management team sessions where she has to speak or give a presentation. During one of these sessions, she lashes out at a colleague who is looking at his cell phone while she is speaking. She uses words that, she later says, she is "not proud of". Talking to a coworker, she realizes that colleagues who are "doing something else" remind her of her brother in the family home. Whenever she said something at the table,

he invariably "with those rolling eyes" shrugged and dived into his com-
puter games. Her parents did not intervene. That particular moment had
been especially painful for her, as she had just returned from school after
a presentation that had gone badly. Carola's brother had said something
like, "Yes, you should prepare better, then you'd have said something
sensible".

The amygdala hijack occurs in infinite variations and intensities. It is one of
the most consequential barriers for leaders on the road to greater success,
because it significantly negates your person effect (which you read about in
Chapter 3). The principal path out of being taken hostage is awareness. *What*
is happening to me and what is triggering me? Are you aware of the words
you choose, what your body language says? The effect of the specific words
you choose?

The feeling of being held hostage occurs when you consciously or unconsciously feel that you are being forced to do something and, during this
process, experience that you have little to no choice to do anything else. It is
the trigger for further negative actions and reactions. If you could turn on a
time-lapse in your brain, you would hear sentences like these:

- This is never going to work for me.
- I will never get over this pain.
- My boss will never agree to this.
- The team is simply not interested in what I have to say.
- I could never do without this work.
- I'm stuck.
- Without my family, I cannot be happy. I have nowhere left to go.
- I am not suited to this kind of job.

From a negative state of mind – which is, essentially, a hostage state of mind –
you cannot be an inspiring leader. So it comes down to learning to find positive ways to describe experiences. As a leader, how do you talk about your
own experiences, both with others and – as Kets de Vries would call it – in
your inner theater?

Brendan is an operations supervisor at the water company. He and his
team have now done quite a few sessions focusing on bonding and trust.
It has led to people speaking up more and more. Pain from decades ago
coming to the surface. In an emotional session, someone speaks out for
the first time about the effect of years of bullying by two former team
members. During one of the sessions, Brendan is unable to be there
in the morning. In his absence they seem to be letting everything out,
sharing their concerns. Bart, a somewhat anxious man, tells how he has
presented a plan to the team three times and, each time, Brendan con-
signed it to the wastebasket. He is at his wit's end. In the afternoon, it is

noticeable how Brendan mumbles a string of conciliatory words when Bart tells again of his frustration. "You really don't need to worry. It's all going to be okay". Bart has had enough: "You keep telling me what I should and shouldn't feel, but you don't ask me anything and I end up spending days, alone, sweating and toiling. I sleep badly. You offer these beautiful words of support, but when it comes down to it, you never deliver. You just say, 'I'm sure you can do it', and I'm back to square one".

Neuroplasticity

Neuroplasticity is the ability of your brain to reorganize itself throughout your life by forming new neural connections. This allows your brain to adapt to the environment and compensate when damaged. It also involves significant *pruning* to make room for new and stronger connections.[42] Neurogenesis is the ability to continually create new neurons, not only in childhood but also in adulthood. The idea that as an adult you only *lose* brain cells is false. You are continually able to adapt and improve yourself, since neurons that fire together, wire together, according to Donald Hebb.[43]

The brain's neural networks form when neurons fire and connect with other neurons. The more often these pathways are followed, the more solid the networks become. This is also how attachment memories are recorded. "When I can't do something, Daddy gets angry" or "When I'm sad, Daddy comforts me". When these experiences are repeated, they lead to implicit expectations that are stored in implicit memory, which is still largely un-conscious. "If I don't do my assignment perfectly, my leader will get angry", or "If something doesn't work out, I can ask my supervisor for support". You notice that the presence of your close colleague does you good, that you get very restless at the smell that a certain colleague has or you feel tension during a meeting but you don't know exactly why. This usually has to do with sensory memories linked to previous experiences in life. Only when you are eighteen months old does your hippocampus, which links time and place to experience, start developing, and autobiographical memory emerge.[44]

Use it or lose it.

The statement *use it or lose it* also applies to your neural connections. When neural pathways are no longer used, they disappear; this phenomenon, men-tioned earlier, is called pruning. This tells us something about the brain's neuroplasticity.

Changing the processing in your brain is easiest in the part that developed last, the cognitive brain. But changes are also possible in the lower brain through new, repetitive experiences. This means that you don't have to strug-gle throughout your life with the burden of an attachment that wasn't quite optimal.

Changing attachment patterns is not an easy task. Yet positive changes can occur through transformative relationships.[45] This is called *acquired attachment*. It involves encounters with trustworthy, responsive others, preferably over an extended period of time and repetitively, which creates new neural pathways in the brain (think of those elephant paths again). This can happen in a therapeutic setting, but also in contact with a teacher at school, the father of a friend, a grandparent, partner or parent-in-law, a colleague or manager. This person can be a secure base and provide the support and/or challenge that was not there at the beginning of life. The supportive presence of another, a secure base, makes all the difference.

Most therapeutic interactions take place outside of the therapy practice, according to Bruce Perry. He refers to – possibly brief – encounters in which a person feels safe and respected. It is not so much about what you say but about the way you are present.

This view by Bruce Perry can be applied seamlessly to adulthood, partner relationships and the workplace. Research shows, for example, that someone can grow towards a safer attachment pattern within five years in a relationship with a securely attached partner.[46] One can imagine that the influence of a securely attached leader can also make a difference in that sense. You could say that good leaders are in the brain-(re)building business.

Amir did not have a happy childhood. He was barely two when his father left and contact with him soon stopped. Amir's trust in humanity and especially in men was gone. At school he had constant authority problems. Now, after many jobs haven't worked out, he has an apprenticeship in an auto-assembly plant. His boss Arie is a quiet, amiable man, who uses clear rules and gives Amir confidence in his ability. Mistakes are followed by questioning but, contrary to what he is used to, Amir is not fired. Slowly but surely he begins to believe that there are men in the world who stay and who can be trusted. Over time, he goes through hell for his boss and becomes one of the most motivated employees. Arie becomes one of Amir's secure bases, for life.

The calm brain and resilience

When someone gets upset, bursts into tears, or erupts into anger, the first thing you need to do as a leader is to stay calm yourself. A deep breath is an important first step and can also stop you from taking what's happening personally. If you, as their leader, can't stay calm, you immediately make things worse. Daniel Siegel, Professor of Clinical Psychiatry and Director of the Mindsight Institute, combines his neuroscience work with, among other things, mindfulness. His work is congruent with that of Bruce Perry. We'll go into this in a little more detail here. Siegel advises that in difficult situations, when the other person is upset, you should first identify which part of the person's brain you need to address. He describes the following steps (remember that being or becoming calm yourself precedes this):[47]

Restoring the broken contact

Before you bring someone back to the issue at hand, you first need to restore the broken contact. This can only be done with right brain to right brain communication, because this calms and stabilizes. You can't do anything with your left brain to calm down the other person; that's wasted energy. That sounds to the other person like "Blah blah blah", no matter how wise and sensible your words are. Only when the other person is calm again can you start guiding him.

> Nathan is a strapping Antillean man who is loved by everyone. But one day, when a colleague makes a remark about his father, everyone is shocked when Nathan freaks out and leaves the room. He is totally upset and stands facing the wall in the hallway. His department head, Mariska, goes to him and tries to make contact. Only when she takes the lead and politely asks him to look at her, to grab her hands and squeeze them hard, does she get a response. She keeps inviting him to look and squeeze until she notices that he is back in the here and now and making eye contact.

Become calmer by giving it words

If the first step is successful, you can also engage the left brain. Then both parts are active. This is the time to calmly explain what happened and give a name to the feeling.

> Mariska suggests to Nathan that they go and have a cup of coffee together and discuss what to do next. "I think you were very shocked by the comment about your father. Am I right Nathan?" He nods. "You don't have to tell me what happened, but let's see how we can both get back to the office. I was wondering if you are embarrassed and if that is making it difficult to face your colleagues again. Shall I ask Robert to come here for a moment? Then you two can return together, when you're ready". This conversation makes Nathan calmer and when the coffee is finished, he feels able to go back with Robert to his desk. Mariska had sensed into it well on two counts. Returning was easier with a trusted other, and that Nathan needed the help of a male colleague.

A trouble shared is a trouble halved

When people can talk about their experiences, with both hemispheres of the brain online and the upper brain also switched on, a coherent story emerges. They can look not only back to the past, but also forward to the future. In Nathan's case this might mean that, for example in the absence of a father figure in his life, he would see that he has a secure base at work, in the form of a male mentor who would support, but also challenge him in his work.

Calming the brain while at work can be done in many ways. Going for a walk with someone safe, holding someone for a moment (with permission and in an accepted way), having a cup of tea together, a short mindfulness or breathing exercise, stamping your feet together for a moment or other ways of getting into the here and now, such as throwing a wad of paper and shouting "catch". The important thing is not to exclude or marginalize people, no matter how 'strange' or unexpected their behavior might have been, but to find ways to include them and keep them in the team. If you don't manage to do this, the unwanted behavior will repeat, ad infinitum.

> *Sue Johnson, globally successful author of books about Emotionally Focused Therapy, tells how she could sometimes be upset after a session with a couple, because what she had envisioned had not worked out or because things had escalated between the spouses rather than improved. Then she would walk over to her 'real English' colleague who would speak to her in a soft voice, inviting her to sit down and have a nice cup of tea. Then she would feel the stress subside and, slowly but surely, she'd calm down.*[48]

Even people who are very successful, like Sue, need a secure base to be able to return to a *baseline* of calm and quiet. Having such a supportive presence allows a leader to get herself back into balance.

When you have good emotional regulation, you are better able to calm your brain on your own. There is integration between the upper and lower brains and between left and right brains. This ensures you do not lose the connection, so that you can keep your wits about you, even when you are under pressure, without violently suppressing your feelings. You realize that there are ups and downs in life and if you get upset about something, like everyone does, you are able to bounce back. A secure attachment forms the basis for the development of this mental resilience, enabling a stable basis for emotional and cognitive functioning in life and work.[49]

Developing resilience, or not, is closely related to the secure bases that were present in a child's life. If there was no secure base at home, yet the children still developed resilience, there was often a secure base outside the family, such as a grandparent, a teacher, a sibling, or a sports coach.

> *Resilience* can be described as the capacity to recover or rebound. It is the ability to adapt successfully despite difficult or threatening circumstances and the ability to maintain a stable balance.

A second characteristic, after having a secure base present, is that these children did not identify with the family, but followed their own path and did not take responsibility for the things that adults should do. As a result, they grow up to be mentally resilient individuals able to take the rough with the smooth. They develop a mindset in which they dare to take on challenges and want to develop themselves.[50]

Mindset

When you follow your calling, you choose to embrace new challenges. You step outside your comfort zone because that's where you will develop and learn from new experiences. And, essential to doing all this, is a growth mindset.[51] Leaders with this mindset have a positive attitude towards challenges. They are not content with repeating what they have proved they already can do. They like to take on new things, even and especially if they are more difficult than anything they've done before. They also understand that they must do this, as much as possible, in bonding, collaborating with others. They see this as an opportunity to develop and learn. Experience has shown them that failure does not lie in a task or assignment not being achieved, but rather in giving up before you've tried every avenue. The power of the growth mindset cannot be overstated. The belief that you **will** succeed at something is **the most important prerequisite** for success.[52]

It appears that, as a child, you are sensitive to the *type* of compliments you receive when you are successful at something. When the compliment is focused on how clever or smart you are, you seem less inclined to take on a more difficult task afterwards. However, when you receive a compliment about the amount of effort you put in, you seem to be more motivated to attempt tougher tasks. You are in charge of how much effort you put in and you run less risk of losing the compliment when trying a more difficult task.

It is precisely the combination of security and challenge offered by secure bases, that leads to resilience and helps develop this growth mindset. With a secure base, you do not experience setbacks or disappointments as major threats. When you see not achieving a goal as failure and – historically – failure led to rejection, you begin avoiding risk and start developing a fixed mindset.[53]

When you are able to integrate setbacks and disappointments into your life story in a positive way and can see how these events have also contributed to your personal growth, you will experience more wellbeing than people who are unable to move past the disappointments and see the possible benefits.[54] What is needed for this, at least, is the ability to share one's story with others. It is precisely in the vulnerability and intimacy of this openness that the opportunity for learning arises.[55]

In developing a more growth-oriented mindset, you will recognize a number of intermediate steps. You are able to accept a little more challenge, a little more feedback and put a little more effort into difficult tasks. During this development you become increasingly aware of your potential and your ability to look, from a growth perspective, inward at yourself and outward at your environment. With a severe and prolonged focus on results you miss the opportunity to learn through the journey. Just think of how highly talented musicians, athletes, neurosurgeons endlessly practice, reflect with a coach or mentor, look back and improve. Anders Ericsson became famous for the "10,000 hours guideline", which says that in order to develop a talent, that's the minimum number of hours needed. It is more nuanced. The hours themselves are not the most important thing. It's about three things: practicing, practicing correctly – that is, being able to make adjustments – and having a secure base.[56]

So you are able to take these steps because secure bases offer support and challenge by inspiring, mirroring and giving feedback. You further develop your resilience, via your attachment dynamic, by focusing your mindset more and more on growth. In doing so, you also open a door that leads to developing your qualities in the areas of Bonding and Intimacy, which we will discuss in more detail in the next chapter. We return to resilience in Chapter 8.

Important insights to take away

- Your attachment is the basis of your ability to feel safe with others and to grow, learn and develop.
- Your childhood attachment-experiences accompany you on every step of your adult relationships. Even if there is an unsafe, original basic attachment, you can still develop a secure attachment style when you have the help of new secure bases.
- Your resilience to cope with adversity develops based on your attachment history and your ability to reach out to secure bases.
- Your own emotional regulation, your ability to keep a calm brain and not be held emotionally hostage – hijacked by your amygdala – allows you to better sense into another person's emotions.
- The words you speak as a leader have a major impact on the safety your employees feel. Your person effect can amplify this impact positively and negatively.
- Your mindset determines how you look at your environment and at challenges, and whether you see them as opportunities or as threats. You can steer the direction of your mindset from your mind's eye.

Questions for self-reflection

1. In general, do you prefer distance or closeness in your contact with others?

2. When you were growing up, what were the elements of secure and insecure attachment? How have these affected you in how you view (emotional) risk-taking?
3. How safe do (did) you feel with your father? How has that shaped you?
4. How safe do (did) you feel with your mother? How has that shaped you?
5. What are the pros and cons of the way you attach?
6. How safe do people – your family members, friends, colleagues and team members – feel with you? How do you know?
7. Who are or were your secure bases? Who believed in you even in moments when you might have doubted yourself? How do you approach them for support and challenge? Do you express your gratitude to them?
8. What other secure bases did or do you have? What secure bases are needed for you to continue to grow as a leader?
9. For whom, in turn, are you a secure base? In what ways do you support and challenge?
10. What words/messages do you remember from painful, potentially shameful, disappointing, or otherwise emotionally negatively charged moments? How did these words shape your leadership and the words you speak to others?
11. What words/messages do you remember from joyful, successful, or otherwise emotionally positive moments? How did these words shape you in your leadership and the words you speak to others?
12. Do you tend to see challenges as opportunities or threats? How does this mindset manifest itself in your behavior, the words you speak, the questions you ask?

**Questions for you to ask of the people around you –
your person effect**

1. Who are or were secure bases for you who also believed in you at times when you doubted yourself?
2. In what ways can I be a secure base for you?
3. How do you experience being in my company, my presence or absence?
4. Do you experience me as near or distant? What do you see me doing in that?
5. How safe do you feel with me? What contributes to that?
6. When do you feel like I'm rescuing you from something you can take care of yourself? What is the effect of that on you?
7. What do I do in this team that makes you feel safe? What do I do that makes you feel unsafe? What is the effect on our shared achievements/performance?
8. What risks can I take, for you as a team, so that together we can grow more?

9. What could I do or not do that would make you feel safer with me? How would that affect your development?
10. What setbacks and challenges have you seen me face in recent times? And how have you seen me respond to them?
11. What setbacks and challenges have you been faced with recently? In what ways did you respond? What do you need from me in this?
12. What negative message(s) have I ever given you that still bother(s) you?
13. What positive words have I ever said to you that you still hold on to?

6   First Bond, Then Lead

Bonding and Intimacy

About bonding and intimacy

Attachment, as you saw earlier, is about the *unconscious* side of emotional relationships, the basic pattern which is initially fixed by the relationship between parent and child. Bonding is about one's *conscious* approach to others in order to deepen a relationship. Thus, bonding is always the result of a choice, even when feeling vulnerable, to get closer to someone else. Here there is both an (albeit unconscious) desire to relate to the other on an emotional level, and a functional need to relate to others – for example at work. In collaboration, bonding is not without obligation; it is a necessary condition for jointly achieving results. As a leader, you have a strong influence, from the example you give, on the degree of bonding that employees perceive as appropriate to the organization's culture. People automatically judge others, and certainly their leaders, on two main aspects: how loving the other person comes across (how empathetic, warm, affectionate, reliable) and how decisive the other person comes across (how strong, capable).[1]

> *As the only girl among all her brothers, Rebecca had developed a natural ability to fight for her place. She was able to hold her own among the boys and was quite proud of her ability to take the rough stuff and to dish it out when necessary. Not only did she stand her ground verbally, but she could also physically push back when it mattered. Like her brothers, she played rugby, and she was captain of her team. She enjoyed the speed of the game, the agility and the tough but honest character of the sport. The fact that soon after graduating Rebecca found herself in a managerial position did not surprise her or those who knew her well. However, she did not find management easy initially. Giving clear instructions and defining what results were expected seemed not enough to get things done. To her surprise, her initial performance assessment was not very positive. She was so driven and direct that her example and the standards she set discouraged rather than motivated her staff.*

DOI: 10.4324/9781003409922-6

In order to bond with employees and within teams and at the same time give the kind of direction that achieves results, a balance between these two aspects (loving/decisive) is needed. Leaders who are perceived as both powerful **and** compassionless are likely to evoke fear. Awe can accompany fear, but at the expense of the psychological security that is precisely what is needed to innovate and perform, as you saw in Chapter 4. Fear can be unquestionably effective in the short term, but must keep growing in intensity to maintain its effect. In the polarity of power versus powerlessness, a leader whose style is to dominate – see also the section on leadership styles later in this chapter – runs a great risk of creating powerlessness in his followers. A powerlessness that often hides in the undercurrent, waiting for the right moment to bite back.

However, merely coming across as loving is not enough either. Leaders who are perceived as loving **but** not decisive often bring up a kind of sympathy or even pity in their employees. This results in employees who are inclined to help at first, but eventually lose respect for the leader and, usually indirectly, begin to ignore him. Due to the absence of a felt and lived vision or the ability to execute it, the organization with a nice-but-weak leader – *Mr. Nice Guy* or *Ms. Nice Woman* – will not achieve its goals. Strength that stems from love for the organization and its employees creates the confidence to take decisive action at times when it is needed. Then there is enough invested in the bonding to accept hard and necessary decisions.

Maggie is HR manager of a large law firm. An extremely friendly and charming woman who, we find out as soon as we get acquainted, is rather subservient. "As long as my employees are getting what they want, so am I". Gradually, as our program unfolds, that turns out to be the case, but only in part. Employees really like her. Her door is literally always open. She makes time for everyone, listens, and mediates when necessary. But the firm's partners give her pretty stern feedback. They feel that objectives are not being met sufficiently and they see that staff turnover is above average, with employees moving to other firms that are reputed to be more academic.

Maggie talks about her family. A special combination of enormous love and warmth but also a bit suffocating. "When I hear about secure and insecure attachment, I actually don't know if I really did feel all that secure. My mother was always on my case. It wasn't hard to see that she loved me, but her daily meddling with homework and sports, basically with everything, was more smothering than mothering. I mostly kept my mouth shut; only after I'd left home did I speak up a little more. After high school I had to make a choice: should I choose the academic route or the vocational? My father said, 'It's fine whatever you choose'. He pointed out the disappointments that would ensue if I chose university and it didn't work out. I also wonder why my father and mother did not question me. Ask me what I would like to do myself. They saw danger everywhere. It did feel easy somehow, because I knew I didn't have to climb 'higher' to earn love from them. Yet, I also see how much they projected their own fears of failure onto me. I always imagined I would do that differently. I have to laugh now, because the feedback I get from many colleagues during this journey, is that they get irritated by my 'What would you do?' sentences and yet miss a deeper dialogue to go with my empathy. That's quite a critical mirror".

In the previous chapter you read that a deeper exploration of the roots of your leadership can bring discomfort, perhaps also feelings of shame or guilt about how things went or a sense of restrictive loyalty. As long as those experiences are played out in your private domain, your inner theater, you probably feel 'safe'.

However, your leadership gets its meaning from its context, in its connection with your environment. That context can become an important source of power for your leadership, if vulnerability is granted the space in that context, that it needs.

Vulnerability

The way you are attached establishes the foundation of your ability to bond with others, the ease or discomfort with which you do this. From a secure attachment it is easier to bond with others as equals. From an insecure attachment you might take a distant attitude and avoid bonding. Or you might become dependent. This automatically and enduringly binds the theme of bonding to the openness, vulnerability and dialogue that are essential to searching for and allowing intimacy.[2] This is the vulnerability that goes back to your experiences with early, real bonds and rejections, experiences that are stored in the deeper layers of your brain. At the level of your attachment style, these unconscious memories impact every conscious act of reaching out to another. Every attempt to bond also touches on the mostly unconscious but fundamental fear of rejection.

Connecting is also about taking responsibility for your own emotions.[3] Your emotions arise within you as signals that your needs are or are not being met. Emotions like *afraid, angry, sad* are signals that your needs are not being satisfied; *happy* tells us that they are. So there are not so many positive and negative emotions; emotions are mainly signals telling you whether or not your needs are being satisfied. By becoming aware of your emotions, you can also become aware of your underlying needs at that moment.

However, as long as you make the other person responsible for fulfilling your needs, you remain in a state of dependence and are an emotional hostage. This makes you less effective in your actions. It is highly likely that you will keep repeating old patterns (as you saw in Chapter 4). By becoming aware that your needs are yours and yours alone, you acknowledge ownership of them. By doing so, you accept responsibility for your feelings when it comes to whether or not your needs are met. This ownership provides you with autonomy in respect to your feelings. You no longer hold the other person responsible for how you feel or where you end up, beyond the question of whose fault it is that you feel this way, given that you are in a space where you are free to grow and enjoy yourself. In that free space you can make choices about how you want to react or relate to the other person. You start to experience that the behavior of the other person can contribute to how you feel, but that the real cause – the fulfillment or unfulfillment of your needs – lies within you.[4]

Erik de Haan and Anthony Kasozi – both associates of Ashridge Business School – show how leadership is easily derailed if the leader does not examine and acknowledge his own needs. Learning in leadership goes hand in hand with getting to know your shadow side. The side of yourself that thinks or says that it already knows and can do it all. The side in yourself that believes you have nothing to do with power and influence. The side in yourself that is convinced that *wanting to belong* has no role. Or the side of you that believes that you would never hurt others. Learning requires surrender to others, to your teachers. But this surrender invites conflict, for instance between your pride and your remorse, but also between your very best intentions and your deepest shame, and between your optimism and your sense of reality. De Haan and Kasozi marvel at the remarkably limited willingness of leaders (especially at the top) to look at themselves and address their deeper needs.[5]

After Rebecca received a negative review, her first reaction was to try even harder. That's what always helped her overcome setbacks. However, her supervisor took her aside and asked her to compare the situation at work with her favorite sport. (Which as we learned earlier, is rugby.) What was her own role, and how was the team doing in the match? She realized that she naturally and unconsciously saw herself as the captain and not the coach. She was running the hardest herself. When her supervisor asked her if the team was playing the same game she was, it hurt. It felt like failure. However, when he then asked what the team needed and what she herself needed to enjoy the game, the penny dropped. In the next team meeting she told them honestly about her disappointing evaluation and that she realized she was not making enough use of the qualities in the team by trying to do so much herself. She started asking more questions, even when she thought she already knew the answers. She let employees come up with proposals about possible approaches, and gave them room to investigate them. In addition to the feedback she was used to giving, she also consciously started to obtain feedback. She took the time to spar about the collaboration and to listen. This enabled her to pay attention to what was important for the other. Team members who, it turned out, had been on the verge of leaving the team, became enthusiastic again. Within a short time, the team was functioning really well.

Needs

From birth on, you respond in whatever way gets your needs met. And the way is by showing your emotions. Before language is available to you, expressing your emotions is the only tool you have to communicate with the person who is critical to your survival. This is also how you learn to manipulate your parent, educator or other secure base on some level that gets your needs met. You cry, when you are still a baby, when mom or dad leave the room and you don't want to be left alone. You scream when a need must be met, whether it's hunger or pain. You screech when someone else is playing with your toys and your boundaries have been crossed.

Throughout your life, social and cultural codes (etiquette) grow in frequency and complexity. You could call these codes a 'group conscience'. You learn, consciously and unconsciously, what works and what doesn't, what is and what isn't 'allowed' within this system. These commandments and prohibitions can take the form of "boys don't cry", or "girls don't get angry". This is how you learn to bottle up your emotions. However, the emotions and the underlying needs that trigger them haven't gone anywhere. Thus there are no good or bad emotions. However, there is a fixed link between our (basic) needs and our (basic) emotions:

- Scared   – need for security
- Angry   – need for boundaries
- Disappointed – need for support
- Happy   – need for joy in life

In every social and cultural context, there are rules, overt or covert, about what behaviors and emotions are desirable or acceptable. This can be very confusing. Within the common management and leadership jargon, time and again *need* turns out to be a loaded concept. It appeals to a notion of vulnerability, and the first movement you usually observe in those present, is one of *away from vulnerability*.

> *On the management side, they paid attention to handling stress, so that employees would be as active as possible and would be able to work to their full potential. Not looking back at the causes, but forwards to how to do things differently and better? This appeared to work until the moment there came a deluge of personal losses: a divorce, the serious illness of a child, a terminally ill parent, a seriously unwell director, and the death of another director's best friend. The usual – and so far, apparently adequate approach – no longer worked; the needs had changed. But in this deeply vulnerable space, as leaders, they felt very uncomfortable. They had to stop and work with their vulnerability. There was a lot of discomfort, and at the same time they noticed that developmental opportunities arose for them when they were able to endure the discomfort.*

Linked to the rules you learn, is an incredibly strong – albeit unconscious – sense of loyalty to your system of origin. The place where your first needs were fulfilled or not, the place where your first secure bases were there for you, or not. It is this loyalty that makes it possible, for example, for you to have an opinion about where you come from, but does not allow others to express a similar opinion.

If expressions of emotion were (implicitly) not allowed to be there as you grew up, then these emotions get suppressed or hidden away under other socially or culturally accepted expressions of emotion. For example, you become the leader who always smiles, even when he feels pain, anger and disappointment. A leader like Marc. At home, he mainly heard that "emotions can be diabolical; you'd be better off using your common sense and just getting on with whatever you were doing". Marc learned early on to laugh difficult things away. Now, at fifty-five and after a session of painful feedback, he finds that strategy no longer works. By laughing a lot, Marc was still getting some of his needs met.

So he became convinced that, with his friendly smile, he was always welcome. However, he was also focused on not just seeing kindness in his environment, but demanding it too. Marc discovered that he was no longer authentic; he manipulated not only himself but also, in a suffocating way, those around him. Exactly as he had been 'suffocated' at home.

Becoming aware of one's emotions, and expressing them while in contact with another, is a strategy that helps you take a step forwards in responsibility, a step towards maturity and towards an equal relationship with the other. So it is also a step up in leadership. Communicating in a bonding way can also help you to stay out of the 'drama'.[6]

Communication is a process between 'I' and the 'other'. And there is no context without implicit or explicit manners, conventions, norms. Over two millennia ago, Aristotle called for *directing the right emotion to the right person, in the right place, at the right time and to the right degree*.[7] For Aristotle, dealing with emotions was inextricably linked to the pursuit of virtue. For him, virtue consisted of finding the right middle ground between two extremes, just as bravery is the middle ground between cowardice and recklessness. That precise middle, however, can rarely be determined in advance by using fixed rules and standards. So the 'right' elements in Aristotle's quotation are not only to be found in the field of tension between 'I' and the 'other', but first and foremost in the tension within yourself: becoming aware of your emotions and the needs which activate them.

In determining how much emotion to express, and when and where, context is vital. In business, for example, most people experience that there is less room to express emotions.

This creates a tension between speaking out your emotion and the constraints of the context in which the relationship with the other is happening. Your responsibility extends beyond your own inner world. It also applies to expressing your emotion in relation to the other person in the most bonding way possible. The other person is then responsible for how he or she interprets your message. At the least, you have taken responsibility for personal virtuous action.

Delay judgment – express compassion

Actually, it is impossible for humans not to judge. You depend for your survival – from an evolutionary perspective – on being able to assess, in a split second, whether or not something carries a threat. The lives of your hunter-gatherer ancestors actually depended on being able to correctly interpret signals in an environment that contained many threats. Although threats in your current work environment don't come from wild animals waiting to pounce, your brain is still assessing your environment in that way. It has an emotional counterpart, in the form of social rejection and isolation, that is equally perceptible at the neurological level. In other words, physical pain (e.g. the bite of a dog) lights up the same parts of our brain as the parts that are triggered and activated by social pain or discomfort.[8] In fact, psychological factors such as uncertainty, conflict, lack of information and lack of control are considered the most stressful stimuli, which the brain interprets as highly threatening.[9] And also, with this emotional pain, your brain activates survival behaviors in order to keep you safe, when it recognizes situations similar to previous moments of emotional pain in which your needs were not adequately met. In this way, your brain tries to keep that feeling of discomfort from arising again. An undesirable consequence is that the memory of the old pain severs the connection in the here and now.

Becoming aware of your emotions, and the needs that trigger them, is often difficult, especially in a business context. A mnemonic device could be *every judgment is an unmet need, and unmet needs evoke emotions*. By becoming aware of your judgments, and moving beyond your instinct to want to be right or get even, you can come to understand that you are often being 'played' by your unmet needs and emotions. For example, you might become angry if you get the impression that the other person does not respect you, when this impression might be totally false. Your judgments about others act as a mirror: they can teach you a great deal about yourself and your own needs. By always wanting to and choosing to take responsibility for your own emotions and needs, you are able to postpone judgment, remain curious about the other person's intentions and, vitally, stay bonded.

Negative judgments go together with severity. Gentleness about another's behavior or in your communication helps to delay judgment. Gentleness and compassion carry the ability to be touched, and to experience a desire to relieve suffering: yours or the other's. For in addition to your judgment of others, you often judge yourself just as mercilessly. Your internal critic cruelly judges your mistakes, your failures. To bypass that inner critic, you must look kindly at yourself. Being compassionate to others often proves easier than being compassionate to yourself.

Compassion has a number of synonyms besides mildness, such as sympathy, tolerance, gentleness, all of which have a slightly different sound and color and can evoke different feelings. Perhaps one word resonates more in you than another.[10]

You can quite easily recognize when you are judging by the language you use: "I find . . .", "It is the case that . . .", "How it is should be, is . . .", "Everyone does . . .". Judgments and standards are closely related and block your natural ability to have compassion for another. They divide the world into *good* and *bad* and separate you from your own needs. Yet you are so used to looking at the world from your standards and through your particular lenses that you have no idea that you are doing this. You determine your own position partly by judging. In doing so, you are not aware that your judgment is based on an unmet need of yours. Nor that your emotions, which prompt you to act, are triggered by that unmet need.

A well-known fallacy is to think that your emotions are always right; after all whatever you are feeling cannot be denied by another person. Certainly, you feel what you feel. However, the question is: Are you aware of the trigger and are your feelings an appropriate interpretation of that trigger? Often emotions are misattributed. Your subconscious brain is usually much too quick for you and compares situations in the present with similar situations in the past with lightning speed. That process became fully automated as you grew up. Your slower conscious brain doesn't get the time to consider if the situation is, in reality, comparable to the old memory, and whether you are still the same person you were in the old situation. The realization that you no longer need to react in the old way, because in the meantime you have developed new skills that equip you to react differently, usually surfaces later.

In retrospect – especially when there were emotions involved and they have subsided a bit – you can tell the other how you would have preferred to react. But beware . . . the harm has already been done.

By realizing that these are your own unmet needs, you can take responsibility for your own emotions. No more of: "I feel . . ., because *you* . . .", but: "I feel . . ., because *I* need . . .". By becoming aware of your own needs, you also come to realize that the other is not responsible for your needs being met. In this way you can distance yourself from looking for blame in the other person, or in yourself, and learn to look beyond your judgments. This requires you to look, listen and perceive with compassion. Noticing your own needs, you can then respond compassionately to the other. That other who is human, just like you, with human needs just like you (see also the paragraph about psychological safety and team performance in Chapter 4).

Compassionately responding to the other person can be done by naming the emotion you perceive or suspect in yourself or the other. Through this form of feedback you support the other to get in contact with what's happening. By acknowledging that emotions are at play and checking that the other agrees or recognizes the emotion, the possibility arises to compassionately ask the other if the emotion concerned is an appropriate reaction. It is possible that the other person has not interpreted something you did as you intended. By making the intention behind your words or behavior explicit, a connection is created at the level of intention and need: "You look angry, is that right?" "Yes, because you don't take me seriously". "It's not my intention not to take you seriously. Do you feel this way because I interrupted you?" "Exactly! You're not letting me finish and I find that very annoying". "I'm sorry I interrupted you. I really want to hear what you have to say. Would you be kind enough to tell me again?"

Dialogue and the four keystones of bonding

> *Dialogue is the search of two or more people for*
> *a greater truth than they previously knew.*
> *Dialogue is characterized by mutual curiosity,*
> *acceptance and empathy.*

Elisabeth Kübler-Ross described her approach to people as having four aspects. Through these she expresses in dialogue the completeness of the human being:

- The emotional aspect – feeling.
- The cognitive aspect – thinking.
- The physical aspect – the body and bodily sensations.
- The spiritual aspect – the philosophical, the religious, sense and meaning.

These aspects, which influence each other, emerge in the exchange that characterizes real dialogue.

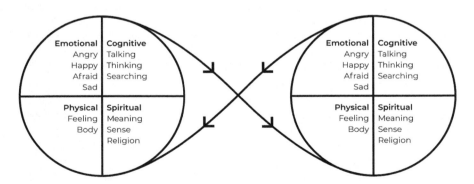

Figure 6.1 Dialogue model – Transactions and Signals – by George Kohlrieser, based on Elisabeth Kübler-Ross. From Care to Dare – Unleashing Astonishing Potential Through Secure Base Leadership (2012, John Wiley & Sons Inc), reproduced with permission of the Licensor through PLSclear.

These quadrants are not separate parts inside you, but do help to make the different aspects visible. When faced with dramatic events you might be inclined to react from the quadrant where you feel safest. From a survival point of view this quadrant has 'taken over'. From the **emotional** quadrant you can overreact, overcome by feelings.

From the **cognitive** quadrant, you might resort to rationalizing. From the **physical** quadrant you might seek refuge in sports, exercise, hard physical work, or drink and drugs. From the **spiritual** quadrant you might seek refuge in religion or the search for meaning. The art is to address all quadrants equally in the dialogue and to explore together what needs attention. Using words to convey inner experiences in such a way, that the other person can also understand them, is extremely difficult. Either because you do not know exactly what is going on within you, or because you experience discomfort in admitting and acknowledging what is going on. Or because the other is not yet able to receive the message. Attunement is needed, together with practice in asking questions that help with reflection and dialogue, such as those found at the end of each chapter of this book.

> *In the biographical film* Chasing Mavericks, *surfer Frosty Hesson saves his eight-year-old neighbor Jay from drowning.*[11] *Jay lives alone with his mother; his father abandoned them. Jay looks up to his surfing neighbor immensely. Frosty decides to take Jay under his wing and train him. His approach is to build in Jay the four pillars of a strong human foundation: physical, cognitive, emotional and spiritual. Jay will need to become physically stronger, learn to perceive better in order to make decisions and life-defining choices, face his biggest fears in order to control his moods, and find his deepest calling; because this is about more than surfing. It's about finding that one thing in life that will set you free.*
>
> *When Frosty's wife dies suddenly, Jay confronts him with his own surfing and life lesson that there's always a way through the waves. When Frosty doubts his own strength to deal with his loss, Jay offers himself as the fifth pillar Frosty can lean on.*

Dialogue and the voice of the (whole) team

In the section on psychological safety in Chapter 4, you learned about the processes of "groupthink" and "wisdom of the group". The wisdom of the group can ensure that the group's answer to a question comes closer to the truth. But most of the time, the questions facing an organization have no simple answer. There is no absolute truth to which even the collective's knowledge can bring you closer. The problems always require collective agreement in the sense of support for a particular approach to solving a problem. This collectivity needs a dialogue with the entire team, if you are to draw out every point of view, opinion, position, feeling, belief and perspective.[12]

> *As a director, Lorenzo had no time for 'coaching'. He disliked, in his words, "people who just stand to one side giving advice but never want*

to get their hands dirty". He had built a successful business, and he ran it with a firm hand. He knew everything and had an opinion about everything. He had no doubt this was necessary, because what was your value as a boss if you did not know more about everything than your employees. He worked hard to maintain this position and worked very long hours. When his finally wife told him that she wanted a divorce, because his work was clearly more important than her or the family, his knee-jerk reflex was to work longer hours to avoid the tension at home.

However, he couldn't just give up on the relationship. So, for the first time ever, he went with his daughters to watch their field hockey team. To his surprise, they were coached very differently than he had been as a young athlete. In his time, coaches were tough. Usually, men who had been better at their sports than the boys they trained, and they weren't shy about showing it. Also, the boys were constantly compared to each other and no one was ever told that they had done well. How different things were with his daughters! The coach complimented their effort and what they did well, regardless of the result. Lorenzo saw the fun they got from working as a team, how all the team cheered when a goal was scored and how the players raised each other's spirits when their opponents scored.

At first he thought it was because the field hockey coach was a woman and the players were girls. But he noticed that other girls' teams had male coaches who had a similar style of coaching. Afterwards he spoke to his daughters' coach and let her know how surprised he was. She told him that she deliberately created an environment where making mistakes was accepted, so players could learn from them. He learned, in turn, that when feedback was based on effort rather than results, it contributed positively to the development of the players and the team. It had been shown to improve results too. Back in the office, the following Monday, he looked at the faces of his Board as they arrived for the regular start-the-week meeting, and decided to do things differently. A week later, Lorenzo had engaged a coach, who joined the meeting and, for the first time, Lorenzo explicitly asked for feedback from his team.

That first feedback had been tough: his managers felt that they always failed him and that he did not appreciate their input. With the help of his coach, he adapted his leadership style, started asking more questions and giving more space. He also told his management team about his relationship crisis and that his work was not worth losing his wife and family. He delegated more, relinquished authority and started giving compliments in his environment when he saw people taking the initiative and making their own decisions. He noticed that, for the first time in ages, he could relax, make time for his family and be more attentive at home. His management team not only turned out to be perfectly capable of managing the organization but, within a few weeks, and again as a first, product innovations were suggested and implemented.

Dialogue and conflict

A dialogue is characterized by the fact that the outcome of the conversation is not fixed, the outcome is still open, neither side has a monopoly on the truth. A conflict is characterized by the fact that the conversation begins by establishing that neither of the parties intends to reach an agreement while their interests are at stake. The goal of a conversation **about** a conflict is usually to reach a shared outcome. During a conflict there is often a lot of tension, because there are opposing views and emotions such as anger, disappointment and fear: all are symptoms of underlying unmet needs. This tension often makes it more difficult to communicate well, to interpret the content, the relationship and intention aspects of the other person's message, and to shape one's own part well, as the context is difficult. One often feels threatened because one's own needs are unfulfilled, leading to a certain degree of hostage-taking of the brain by one part: the amygdala hijack.

At first glance it appears logical that conflicts might seem unsolvable because of conflicting interests. This is certainly the case if both sides claim that they are right or if they are trying to settle old feuds. Here too, gentleness and real interest in the other person can help to unwrap the conflict and find out what it is really about. You make an effort to clarify the other person's intentions and needs and you speak out your own, quietly and clearly. Conflict transformation does not mean that you have to agree, but it does mean that you both know exactly what you disagree about and what that means to both sides.[13] It means that you can accept what the other is saying without having to agree. Listening is the core skill here. Listening with the intention of wanting to understand, not to judge. The golden rule is: want to understand first; want to be understood second.

Thus, the most important skills in conflict fall within the competence of 'active' listening. Although listening might seem to be a passive activity, as someone else is speaking, as an active listener you are consciously engaged in receiving the message. You are aware of environmental factors that can cause noise and, likewise, of factors within yourself that can cause 'noise': filters that prevent the other person's message from getting through accurately and entirely.

In the context of listening

Think of a leader that you felt trusted you. A leader who saw something in you and motivated you. Someone to whom you could turn, with whom you felt seen, valued and encouraged. A leader who had a lasting impact on your own leadership. And then think about how this person handled the ratio between speaking and listening. We are willing to bet that this person had excellent listening skills.

No matter who we work with, no matter where in the world, no matter how much leadership experience is present, one thing is common: the way leaders struggle to listen and paraphrase. Paraphrasing is an art and skill, a particular tool a leader uses to ensure not only that he is listening, but that his person-effect is inviting his 'audience' to listen too. Paraphrasing is giving back to the other person what you heard and observed and making a bridge between it and what the other person shared with you. This can be done in literal terms – sometimes called *Paraphrasing 1.0*. But it can also be in explaining your experience of the essence of what you heard and saw – we call this *Paraphrasing 2.0*. However, there are two factors that can have a significant negative impact on the leader's listening skills: stress and hierarchy. The more stress and/or the deeper the hierarchy, the more difficult it often appears for the leader to receive the message cleanly and to have the tranquility or courage to check the message by paraphrasing. You can overcome this – to some degree – by not only paraphrasing yourself, but regularly asking for the other person to paraphrase what you have said: "Will you give me back, in your own words, what you think you just heard me say". This increases the likelihood that the dialogue will be a success for all involved.

In practicing this – what is also known as *active* listening – you might experience that you are developing some kind of 'trick'. As if by doing it that way, you are no longer authentic, and could come across as false. Do you recognize this in yourself?

Then think back to what we saw at the end of the previous chapter, about how practice enables mastery. Ask your partner, your children, your colleagues, your team members and your own supervisor: How do you experience my listening?

Leadership and active listening coexist in a special way. Active listening is the ability to see and hear what is being said, and what is not being said. It means not just collecting data, like an analyst, but wanting to know why someone is saying something, with what kind of energy and from and in what context. This only becomes possible when you can postpone your need to react. It might help if you can say to yourself, "I already know my story, so let me invest in hearing the other person's story". That way, instead of reacting from a primal impulse, real responses and useful answers are given time to emerge.

When you actively listen, you also focus on body language. In a team meeting, you are alert to whether everyone is really present and, crucially, willing to (gently) call out anyone who seems to be elsewhere, describe what you see, and ask why. You have probably experienced countless meetings, gatherings and presentations in your life where you struggled to not fall asleep, because hardly anyone was listening and you were distracted by other thoughts. Your body was present, but your mind was somewhere else: the lights were on but there was nobody home. The leader who actively listens and thus leads by example – without disappearing behind his phone, tablet or folded arms – supports team members to mirror his behavior.

So active listening requires your involvement, attention and focus with your whole being. Many leaders lose bonds because, while listening, they get sidetracked by their brain investigating whether they agree with something or not. Remember what you read earlier about the important difference between accepting or agreeing to something?

"I disagree" often presages the beginning of the end of the dialogue, and the point at which the leader takes charge in order to explain why he disagrees. Remember that the purpose of listening is to establish and maintain bonds. You want to foster creativity, hear other voices, identify pain points, discover what gets in the way of growth and fun, and all that other good stuff.

Try it. The moment you feel that the other person is wrong, that his appeals to you are unreasonable, or he's clearly ill-informed, hasn't done his homework, ask, "What is it that makes you experience it that way?", "Will you share with me why you think that?" This allows you to build on what the other person has shared with you and it prevents the other person from feeling blocked, ignored, patronized or belittled.

Paraphrasing means always looking for phrases and words that promote bonding and dialogue. Some examples:

- From: *I understand you're disappointed.* To: *Will you tell me what you're so disappointed about?*
- From: *You have nothing to be ashamed of.* To: *Can you tell me why you feel so ashamed.*
- From: *I really don't understand how you can be so intimidated by your colleague.* To: *What actually happens for you when your colleague responds like that?*
- From: *We agreed that you would lead this project. Right?* To: *How do you recall the agreement we made about this project?*
- From: *You're complaining, but do you know who's really struggling?* To: *What issues are you bumping into then?*
- From: *I know exactly what you're feeling. How I solved it is . . .* To: *How does it feel for you? Can you tell me a little more about that?*
- From: *You tell me you're very tired lately. Have you been to the doctor?* To: *Will you share with me what is costing you so much energy?*

To be sure of listening well, paraphrasing is essential. It is one of the most important tools to avoid taking the easy route and solving it for the other person before anything has been asked. Paraphrasing is your ability to restate what you heard in a way that promotes bonding. Leaders who listen well are able to reiterate the other person's words in their own words, so that both parties are sure the leader has understood those words, feelings and experiences.

- "Is it true that you heard me say that . . .?"
- "I get the impression you want to say . . . Am I correct?"
- "I think I'm talking too much now and that you don't really feel that you have the space to say what's bothering you".
- "When I start talking about this project, I see that, all of a sudden, you start to fidget and look away from me. Does this sound right to you?"
- "I am shocked that you raise your voice to me like that. You are, I think, very angry?"
- "Have I understood you correctly when I say that the way my predecessor habitually reviewed progress with you, left you so disillusioned that you now expect the same to happen with me?"

Paraphrasing *does not* mean listening endlessly in silence or 'parroting' without some shift taking place. On the contrary. By paraphrasing you give direction to the dialogue – after all, as leader you are leading it – and you offer space for new choices. When you start paraphrasing you might hear yourself thinking, "I don't have time for a long conversation". Or, "If I start a dialogue here, I'll get lost in endless sessions about feelings and stuff". Yet, if you practice, you will discover that it actually allows you to stay in control and helps the other person to focus their mind's eye.

- "If I understood you correctly, the source of your anger lies in how HR handled the problem. What is more important for you? To discuss this further now, or to look at how you might approach HR again and what I can do to help you in that?"
- "You say you have symptoms of chronic fatigue. Do you want to tell me about this, or would you prefer that I put you in touch with a colleague or, perhaps, someone else?"
- "In our previous conversations, you indicated that you would address an issue with one of your team members. You just told me that you have yet to do so. This isn't what I expected from you. Shall we talk privately about what seems not to be said or heard in our conversations or would you prefer that we discuss this with the entire team?"
- "You asked me to look at your project plan with you this afternoon. I won't be able to do that. I can ask Marieke to take my place or I can sit with you tomorrow morning. Which would suit you best?"

- "You say that you are finding it difficult to organize Bart's farewell. That we need to give him a good send-off is a given, but the question is should the whole team be involved or should we do it differently. What do you think?"

  The better you learn to paraphrase, the more positive your person effect will become. People will find it more pleasant to be around you, feel safer and feel seen in how they take responsibility. Paraphrasing and offering choice calms the brain and the heartbeat, promotes learning and development, enables people to experience autonomy and, from there, to tap into and improve resilience. The leader who paraphrases builds psychological safety and a secure-base team. In this way it becomes possible, for example, to deal with conflict constructively.

Cognitive filters such as judgments cloud the message. You do not hear exactly what the other person says; you mostly hear what you are expecting to hear, and you are already preparing your response. Listening without judgment, or at least postponing judgment, remaining curious about the intention behind the content of the other person's message, and remaining tranquil about the form in which the message might come, helps you to understand and bond with the other person at a deeper level. From that deeper level it becomes easier to ask the other person to listen to you. Conflict requires an open attitude: an open heart to continue to be touched in the relationship and an open mind to explore the possibility of the other person being right.

Conflict versus fight

If the willingness on both sides to actively listen disappears, a conflict will arise, escalate and become a fight. Where a disagreement can still be a bonding difference of insight, opinion or need, conflict is a hardening of stance. A conflict is never about the here and now. In conflict, earlier, unresolved quarrels are fought out. Conflict touches on old pain, where old patterns are repeated and positions taken solidify. Conflict takes place with a closed heart – you will not let yourself be touched – and a closed mind, where there is no room for the possibility of the other person being right.

This old dispute, which you couldn't win before, is being repeated without you realizing it. Your fast-paced lower brain hits out, triggered by events in the present that activate behavioral patterns from the past. The slower-responding cognitive upper brain simply looks on. The lower brain memory interprets the current situation as threatening, and activates a stress reaction in the here and now. Stress hormones are then released which give you physical feelings of being attacked, confirming that there is clear and present danger. Then the circle is complete: you feel the threat, so it must be real. You mistakenly think you are reacting appropriately to the current situation because you are confusing *then and there* with *here and now*. Behavior evokes behavior. The other person knows nothing of your old memory and reacts from his own old defense mechanisms.

Then it quickly turns into a drama in which both people are trapped in old patterns, engaging in and continuing the fight and no longer excelling. The first and only way to break through the drama of conflict is to become aware that you are in it. But that is fiendishly difficult. Because once you're in it, your capacity to act rationally diminishes; instinctively, being right becomes more important than bonding with the other. The trick is to look at yourself and the situation from a distance. Is the situation really threatening? Your cognitive upper brain is slower than your unconscious lower brain. Stress hormones are flowing through your blood, preparing your muscles for fight or flight, your heart rate is accelerating in this state of readiness, all making de-escalation very difficult. Counting to ten before reacting is always good advice. It can give you just enough time to switch on your cognitive brain, bring your awareness to your breath, relax a little and take stock of what is happening inside you. Then you also have to switch between the different levels of communication to try to find out what trigger you are reacting to. Is it the content, the packaging and form of the message, a disconnect between message, intonation and body language? What unmet need of yours is making you respond in this way? By responding with careful questions, rather than being led by your assumptions, you avoid pressuring the other person. Counting to ten not only delays your response, but gives you a moment to suggest taking a short break which both parties might use to engage with a secure base. You might find that taking a walk, or actually consulting someone, brings about a change in your mood and thinking.

A colleague had asked Tristan to take over a client and he had agreed. During the first customer contact, it turned out that Tristan's colleague had delivered an overly committing proposal to the customer. Tristan became confused and the conversation came to a standstill. Afterwards he immediately wrote an angry email to the colleague with words like "unfriendly", "behind my back", "unprofessional". Fortunately he didn't press Send, but took a short walk around the block and then called a colleague he knew well and asked if, together, they could look through the email he had composed. The ensuing conversation revealed to Tristan that he had felt, very strongly, that he had been misused. On the advice of the colleague-friend he wrote a new email that was based on asking questions to get clarity. "I just spoke to that client you handed over to me. I learned that your project proposal to him is, given my experience, overly generous. Would it be okay for you to let me know your thinking around this? That will help me in my negotiations with the client". Freed from the 'control' of his old pain, he could feel how this was a much better solution.

From a position of gently deferring judgment, you are able to be curious about the intent of the other(s). By not only naming aspects of the content, but also aspects of the process and the relationship, the chance of bonding increases. To show our vulnerability when emotionally triggered is rarely our first impulse. However, by being curious about the other person's intentions, we often learn that it was not their intention to hurt us. The other person is also primarily concerned with getting their own needs met. From the shared experience of this human need, a path appears from conflict to dispute, dispute to disagreement, and disagreement to mutually acceptable solution.

Four leadership approaches

When making decisions, especially when there are many actors offering many 'insights' and a host of potentially conflicting interests, when you're trying to overcome long-standing blockages, the good and bad of your leadership style falls under a harsh spotlight.

The Gordian Knot

The expression "cut the Gordian knot" is used for someone who is not shy about making difficult decisions. It had its origins in Greek history: Alexander the Great, during his conquests, came to the city of Gordium. There, in the temple of Zeus, stood an ancient chariot whose yoke and drawbar were connected by what was known as the Gordian knot. An oracle had said that whoever untangled the knot would become ruler of all Asia. After wrestling with it for some time and without success, he stepped back from the mass of gnarled ropes and proclaimed, "It makes no difference how they are loosed". He then drew his sword and sliced the knot in half with a single stroke . . . or so the story goes.

Since the oracle had said nothing about how the knot should be untied, the sword brought the solution and Alexander the Great cut the knot.

Another Greek story shows the threat that power carries: the sword of Damocles represents continual danger; unavoidable and uncontrollable. This idiom refers to the sword which the ruler Dionysius hung on a horse's hair above the head of Damocles – a courtier who aspired to power and wealth – in order to make it clear that the position of a ruler was not always to be envied.

The two stories together symbolize the situation of a leader, where decisions must be made constantly. The question is whether taking it upon yourself to slice 'knots' apart is the best solution.

The road to any leader's failure – and his or her eventual fall – is paved with good intentions. Wanting to, but not being able to. To desire, but not to act. To feel, but not to speak. To be able, but not to dare. To dream, but not to do. Failing – and falling – leadership is exemplified in the famous 'Man in the Arena' speech by Roosevelt, where the credits do not belong to the critic, or know-it-all, but to the man actually in the arena.

As a leader, you can't escape wielding the axe and accepting that your 'guilt' will be visible, your culpability. You cause damage and pain along the way, sometimes leading others and making decisions and sometimes avoiding both. This applies at work and, of course, at home in your relationship with your family. So you always have choices to make and, if you are aware of the consequences of your choices, you grow. For many leaders, it is very difficult to admit they are guilty. To see past 'Yes, but I really did it for the best' to the real effects of their actions. Most prefer to wash their hands of it. Only if you admit your guilt, are you able to mend what you have broken. Which, as we'll see, is an essential leadership quality.

Mending

Let's imagine the leader as a fisherman. He sails out with his ship and casts his nets. The catch is brought in and, as always, there is a bycatch. Other fish and garbage also get caught up in the net. Is this bycatch just *collateral damage* or does it perhaps have value that he might overlook in his focus on the goal: catching as many fish as possible? And then there's the net. Every trip it gets damaged, gets new holes. When the fisherman comes ashore, he will have to repair his nets; buying new nets for every trip is not an option. The craft of repairing nets is called *mending*. We see *mending* as an essential leadership quality. It is recognizing that damage has occurred and doing whatever is necessary to be able to continue 'fishing'. To *mend* is thus – beyond the rationale of right or wrong, guilt or innocence – literally to mend the bonds that have been broken.

Being able to deal with shame and fear, with uncomfortable emotions, in all their manifestations and at all their levels – right up to existential fear – requires a combination of daring, decisiveness and caring. We consciously write "combination of" and not "balance between" to avoid the misunderstanding that caring and daring are two extremes on the same line. Each, however, has its own axis.

The quadrants depict four styles of life and leadership:

1. **Excelling**: the combination of the willingness and capacity to combine caring with daring, leads to a mindset of investing in the relationship and the bond, seeking the optimal result for both, and to learning and developing. Here you are willing when necessary to embrace conflict, with an open heart, from your strength. This is the quadrant of psychological safety; even though it can be frightening to feel vulnerable, there is clarity and openness.

2. **Avoiding**: is when you show affection and emotion, but do so in a weak, inadequate way, as if you do not own those emotions. At best you try not to lose: you try to maintain a good relationship, but you do not dare to go for the optimal result. Here there is the chance that your caring not only comes across as vulnerability, but that it is weakness: you procrastinate, saying and doing nothing useful. You offend nobody but, on the other hand you please nobody, not even yourself. You avoid conflict, even when you must step into the fire to achieve your goal, your desired result.

3. **Withdrawing**: when you don't want to show your caring, yet don't show any daring, the effect will be that you are withdrawing. You stay away from any conflicts. Maybe you physically don't show up. But, for sure, you don't speak out. You just let things roll where they will, you don't make any choices other than to avoid, you don't take a stand anywhere. Living from this quadrant is not living. Leading from this quadrant is not leading.

4. **Dominating**: when you are unwilling or unable to allow or show caring, and you do muster the daring to go all out for the result, you get into a situation where you are dominating. Perhaps without it being your intention, you have this effect on the other; this is your person effect. The other will react to this and, pretty quickly, the conflict will become hostile. After all, your heart is closed, your shield is up, you've got your armor on: you will not be touched.

The approaches in the 'weaker' quadrants can come in handy at the appropriate time, but they always come with a price. Living and leading from these quadrants means that you try to avoid specific pain or fears. When you are *avoiding,* you are trying to escape the pain of not belonging, being left out, being left behind because you're a loser. When you're *withdrawing,* you try to bypass both the fear of winning and getting attention, and the pain of failing and being rejected. When you are *dominating,* you try to avoid the fear of being a follower, being led, and the pain of losing control. You can say to yourself that there is always a moment when, in leadership-survival mode, you decide to choose one of the three styles where you are not *excelling.* However, you can also, moment-by-moment, look in the mirror and ask yourself whether your assessment of each moment is correct. Have you not chosen a style because even to consider it evokes fear and pain. And, although this choice reduces the chance of conflict, it also reduces the chance of winning. Being constantly reflective gives you the opportunity to learn and to make a better choice next time.

The strategies around vulnerability are based on beliefs about scarcity. The brain has evolved from ancient times as our key survival tool, in such a way that the unconscious focus is on (avoiding) loss and pain. An expected loss carries twice the impact of an expected gain of the same magnitude.[15] And when millionaires and billionaires are asked when they think they will have amassed 'enough' capital to feel secure, they all mention at least double their current net worth. Even the rich who already are worth double what others

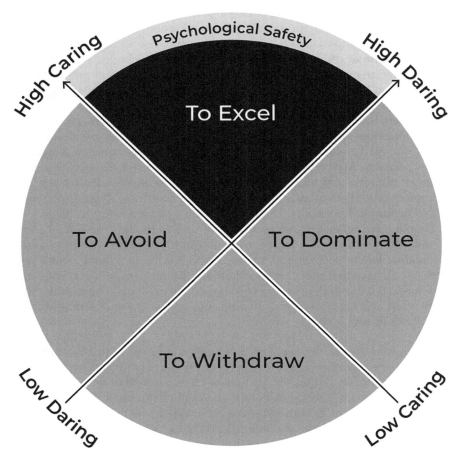

Figure 6.2 Window of Excellence. Klaartje van Gasteren, Marnix Reijmerink and Jakob van Wielink. [14]

are worth.[16] This unconscious focus on avoiding pain and loss has positively affected human survival since ancient times. However, in the absence of secure bases and lack of the trust they give you, it can lead to a mindset of "never having enough". However, this neurological blueprint of avoiding loss and pain does not mean that you are genetically predestined to go through life as the character in Eric Carle's children's book *The Very Hungry Caterpillar*, always busy trying to get more food.[17] Humans also possess the ability to empathize, to understand and share the feelings of others. Parents can respond appropriately to the needs of their children through this empathic ability, and every person can be touched by the emotions of others as a result.

This mechanism is also crucial to the survival of humanity. Your capacity for compassion and empathy, although a stark contrast to your possible tendency to be A *Very Hungry Caterpillar*, is equally at the foundation of your humanity.

> *As CEO of a large company, Lance sends out an invitation to his executives, to let them know about some impending changes. However, the invitation contains an extensive appendix which everyone has to read before the meeting. It also says that if anyone has questions they must submit them by email at least three days in advance, and that no more questions will be permitted during the meeting. The 'official' reason given is to allow the CEO to properly prepare for the meeting. The real reason is that Lance is trying to avoid the misery of having to deal with embarrassing questions. The meeting will be mundane with a low energy level and little excitement. But, since receiving the invitation, the frustration of the executives is growing more tangible day by day.*

When you get caught up trying to avoid or ignore your uncomfortable emotions, you also lose your ability to excel. You lose your ability to bond with the other.

You can no longer understand the language of the other properly, truly hear what is being spoken or to intuit the intention of the other by 'reading' between the words and lines. This inability hinders you from determining what nourishes the relationship with the other, with the risk that you retreat into the hypocrisy of your isolation, adding more armor to prevent further hurt.

> *Rowan's office partner, Head of Purchasing, dies suddenly. When Rowan returns to work, he cloaks himself in silence, drinks coffee alone and goes out alone on his lunch breaks. His supervisor chooses to believe that Rowan wants it this way and leaves him to it. Both Rowan and his supervisor retreat, each into his own small fortress, afraid of discomfort and hurt.*

Lonely at the top?

That it is, or should be, lonely at the top, is a leadership myth. Yes, the leader is at the helm and determines the direction and he will have to make (sometimes tough) decisions himself, solve wicked problems, cut Gordian knots.

> *Dick Bouman is the principal of an elementary school in a well-to-do neighborhood in Apeldoorn. One morning, just after 8.30 a.m. the father of a student is shot dead outside the school gates. As soon as Dick arrives at the scene, he becomes very focused and immediately knows he can't do this alone. He gathers the parents who witnessed the killing and asks another father, whom he knows is a doctor, to take these*

parents into the school building and care for them. Dick asks three peo-
ple, including a member of the school management team, to form a cri-
sis team with him. With them present, he makes arrangements with the
press and agrees a short-term plan with the team and a police spokes-
person. In this way, he delegates tasks, allowing him to do what he sees
as his clear responsibility: take care of his people. In person, he visits
each classroom and informs each teacher of what has occurred. He is
***caring** in a **daring** situation. His school management-team colleague is*
his secure base, with whom he can spar. This keeps him on track. And
at home, his experience finds a sympathetic ear so that, in spite of this
stressful situation Dick can remain calm and peaceful. He excels as a
leader, as evidenced by the purely positive reactions afterwards from the
highly educated, usually critical parents.[18]

Leadership is also about the willingness to "get your hands dirty". Sometimes
you have to do things for which there isn't a beauty prize. We call that culpable leadership. You can't avoid it. Trying to avoid it leads some people to
procrastinate too much or to not act at all. As you ambitiously made your
way to the top, it is highly unlikely that everyone you met on the climb has
become a friend. The higher up you are in the hierarchy, the less space there
is. As you climb the corporate ladder, some people are inevitably squeezed
off as the number of roles reduces. Competition for these roles can be fierce.
In order to survive in an environment of power and prestige, to experience
your culpability at every level of the organizational pyramid, you cannot
avoid straining existing relationships. When reaching the top you might, perhaps, find that you have also paid a price for it in a relational sense. This often
(unconsciously) leads to feelings of loneliness.

Being able to ask for help, having a sounding board, not only prevents feelings of loneliness but, in particular, reduces the likelihood that you'll make
serious errors of judgment. And, in the collaboration with your team and colleagues you will experience bonding and encouragement. Because, basically,
the team should also be a secure base for the leader. The bigger the change
you want to implement, the more important it is to feel this bond. Seeking
bonds with his secure bases is one of the ways in which leadership is distinguished from management.

Geert van den Enden had to adjust his leadership during the corona cri-
sis, when his hospital at the epicenter of the Dutch outbreak was tested
to the limit by the huge influx of Covid-19 patients. Van den Enden is
CEO of the mid-sized Bernhoven hospital, where the ICU was stretched
to triple its normal capacity. He and his management team pushed each
other to find solutions to the tidal wave of Covid-19 patients arriving at
the hospital.

He is stable and calm by nature, van den Enden explains. But he dis-
covered that some people took him to be a bit distant, and they needed

to be explicitly given space to say how they felt and to hear how he felt too. In one particularly heated meeting, a team member told van den Enden that she did not believe he was really affected by the crisis. Van den Enden, who was shocked by the reaction, interrupted the meeting. He expressed his fears and doubts to his staff and told them how the spread of Covid-19 was making it difficult for him to sleep. He then invited his staff to share their worries and fears.

The trust issues were resolved immediately. Van den Enden remembers. They all wanted the same things and offered different perspectives. It united them and he was able to let go of control. He gave them the freedom to do whatever they felt they should do. Van den Enden later contacted one of his senior managers and asked him to be his right-hand man for as long as the country was in the crisis. He told him he would not be able to do this without him. The senior manager became emotional and asked if van den Enden really needed him? They realized – both emotionally – what that meant to the both of them to say that.[19]

Important insights to take away

1. Bonding with others at work is necessary to achieve results through collaboration. Your attachment history forms the blueprint for how you seek and allow bonding.
2. Your emotions signal to you whether your needs are being met or not. The courage to be transparently vulnerable in acknowledging your emotions and thus your needs, forms the bridge of bonding.
3. Dialogue is the search together powered by curiosity, acceptance and empathy, for a greater truth than you knew before. The skill of paraphrasing is essential to bonding and to achieving optimal (team) performance.
4. Excelling is the leadership style that combines your willingness to care and dare in making decisions. As soon as you compromise on caring or daring, you find yourself in less effective leadership styles such as avoiding, withdrawing or dominating.
5. The will to engage in conflict is indispensable to your development and growth. However, if you end up in hostility, you end up repeating old patterns that no longer serve you.
6. It doesn't have to be lonely at the top, if you are able to bond authentically, speaking out on what matters to you.

Questions for self-reflection

1. How close do you let others get? And what is your favorite way to keep others at a distance?
2. Do you feel that you focus predominantly to excel? How would the people you live with and spend your time with answer that question?

3. When do you choose to take a different approach than excelling? What message or warning do you hear within yourself at that moment? What need must be met in order to return to excelling?
4. How much fun do you have at home? How much fun do you have at work?
5. What conflict is going on right now? What conflicts are you going to deal with and bring to an end?
6. What is the most difficult conversation you have ever had? Why? What did you learn from it? Looking back to that conversation, is there anything that you would do differently?
7. How emotionally bonded were you to your parents when you were growing up? How has that affected the way you think about vulnerability?
8. What struggles are present in your life right now? What pattern from the past are you repeating in these struggles?
9. What past difficulties are still getting in your way?
10. How good are you at listening? How would your partner, children, colleagues, your team members and your boss answer that question?
11. Do others experience you as having a genuine interest in them? How do you know that?
12. How do you use and hear the words "I love you" and "I'm sorry"?
13. When was the last time you said sorry – unconditionally – at work? At home? What makes it easy for you to say sorry? What complicates it?
14. Do you experience love for the people you lead and with whom you work? How does that manifest itself?
15. Do you experience love for what you do?
16. How much intimacy do you experience in your intimate relationship right now? How does this affect you in your personal life and at work?
17. How much intimacy do you experience with your children? And they with you?

Questions for you to ask of the people around you – your person effect

1. How approachable do you perceive me to be?
2. What is the hardest conversation you ever had to have? What did you learn you from that?
3. How do you think I listen? What could I improve? How would that affect you?
4. When do I talk too much? How does that affect you?
5. Are the conversations we are having in this team/organization ones that really matter? How do you notice that? What is the effect of noticing it? What, in this context, could I do more and/or better?
6. What bond do you experience with me and how would you like it to be?
7. Do you enjoy working with me? What is instrumental in that? What detracts from it? How does this affect your (and our) growth and development?

8. Do you experience enough depth in our contact?
9. What do you miss in our dialogues?
10. When do you see me avoid risk-taking in my leadership?
11. When do you see me putting results before relationships in my leadership?
12. What conflicts, if any, do we still need to resolve together?
13. Where might we still end up in a fight about something? And what, in that, do you still need from me?

7 To Welcome is to Learn to Let Go

Loss and Separation

About loss and separation

It is perhaps the only certainty in life, that all things change and pass away. Loss, and with it the separation that lurks within it, is always real.[1] Separation is an interruption of the attachment and bonds that existed. It presents itself in the form of change, loss, disappointment or frustration. It evokes – especially when it comes to your bonds with secure bases – powerful emotions that can act as both engines for growth and for decline. An impending divorce, an upcoming change in the organization[2], the imminent massive redundancies[2], the impending resignation[3] and even a self-chosen career move[4] can affect you in such a way that you have the tendency to avoid saying goodbye or to say it with a closed heart. Though, no matter how difficult it is, do not burn your bridges. Even if that seems at first – out of shame or anger – to be the best solution.[5]

Looking back, you might discover that something positive remains after the loss. Life is enriched, a new perspective emerges that would not have been there without the loss.[6] Thus, growth is possible after loss.[7] Growth can manifest, for example, in an increased ability to cope with adversity.[8]

Sheryl Sandberg – the COO (chief operating officer) of Facebook – put the topic of adversity and grief at work on the global map after the sudden death of her husband Dave. Together with Professor of Organizational Psychology, Adam Grant, she wrote the bestseller *Option B*, in which she tells how she found her way back after Dave's death. The authors introduced the idea of "springing forward". That growth is possible after loss, by building on the resilience that was already there. For Sandberg, her greatest wish is that something good will come out of the terrible loss of Dave. She sees comfort or strength that people have drawn from what she has shared as a tribute to Dave's life, who did so much for others during his life. Sandberg hopes that her book will speak to people and become a part of his legacy. She would like to see it as their common calling.[9]

DOI: 10.4324/9781003409922-7

Loss touches on the fragility of life. Sharing (or learning to share) your losses can lead to greater self-confidence and, at the same time, a greater focus on the other.[10] (A process that you will encounter, in the last chapter, as a journey through the valley from the 'first' to the 'second mountain'). In spite of the reality that control over life is an illusion, growth can arise from experiencing greater appreciation or gratitude for that same life or for having experienced that which has been lost. This is also sometimes accompanied by experiences of spiritual or existential growth.[11] Life is more 'values-full'. Things that were previously experienced as important might come to be seen in a different, broader perspective. Growth after loss can also be expressed as an increased bond with others. This growth will always be based on having the will to respond to the loss. To let that loss become a source of inspiration.[12]

Changes and other forms of loss:

- Loss of attachment (With whom, what or where do I feel safe?)
- Loss of intimacy (Who or what am I bonded to?)
- Loss of ground (Where do I belong?)
- Loss of structure (What is my role?)
- Loss of identity (Who am I?)
- Loss of the familiar world (What can I hold on to?)
- Loss of future (Where am I going?)
- Loss of meaning (What's the point of all this?)
- Loss of control (I feel overwhelmed)[13]

Embracing by letting go

Saying goodbye at work. This little phrase evokes a diversity of experience. There are the everyday goodbyes, ranging from "good evening and see you tomorrow" to the teasing "half day?" on a rare day when you leave the office early. You probably also know the inevitable goodbye of a colleague who is retiring or another colleague whose career aspirations mean a move to another company, a 'better' job. So far, so good, it seems. Perhaps you once resigned with an exciting and challenging new job on the horizon. All are forms of saying goodbye within a known and expected framework, the safety of the predictable within work. But when a colleague or a manager dies, through illness, a car crash, an industrial accident or even suicide, the insecurity that reflects the unpredictable nature of loss can permeate the organization.[14] Reorganizations, mergers, acquisitions, relocations, redundancies and layoffs are forms of loss that can evoke a range of feelings and a range of intensities.[15] Emotions that, if not addressed, can affect the functioning and performance of employees and, by extension, organizations.[16]

Philippe Bailleur talks about the combination of letting go (detaching) and embracing (attaching). In his classification you can see the four aspects of Kübler-Ross's model, which we described in Chapter 6 in the context of dialogue.[17] The table below is largely based on Bailleur's classification.

Table 7.1 Bailleur's classification: Detaching and Attaching

	Detaching	Attaching
Emotional	Saying goodbye to colleagues, leaders, management, customers.	Bonding with new colleagues, leaders, executives, customers.
Cognitive	Letting go of beliefs about quality, service, accuracy, commitment, customer friendliness.	Embracing new perceptions of quality, service, precision, etc.
Physical	Letting go of familiar work processes, machines, applications, workstations, buildings, company names, logos, coffee and lunch places, websites, work times, achievements, etc.	Learning how to work with new equipment, new applications, integrating new ways of working, moving workstations or buildings, using a new name, following new guidelines and agreements.
Spiritual	Letting go of the original mission, contribution of the organization to society, etc.	Embracing a new mission and values, following a new calling.

In Chapter 5, you were introduced to the impact of attachment on your leadership. This forms an important basis for understanding the impact of loss on leaders and their organizations.[18] From your first experiences with *separation* and *separation anxiety*, you develop your ability to really say goodbye, or to totally avoid saying it.

> *Arthur is a young father of three children. He's a manager in the music industry, for Benelux and Scandinavia, and he travels a lot. They are all relatively short trips. Saying goodbye to his children, especially the eldest two, invariably results in much upset and fuss in the form of anger and sadness. He always leaves the house with an unpleasant feeling. "It usually takes me half a day to come back to myself. It also makes traveling to anywhere tough". Arthur tells how, as a young child, he regularly went to stay with uncles and aunts. "On the one hand that was a relief, because at home the relationship with my mother was suffocating. She was a well-meaning micromanager. With most of my uncles and aunts there was freedom. But there was also another side. My mother always said, 'If there's any problems, you can always call me. I'll come and get you'. I came to realize, much later, that there was an implied threat in that message. Apparently I had to be alert to danger; maybe it wasn't safe. To this day I have trouble with transitions. I come and go. In a way, traveling really suits me".*
>
> *The coach asks Arthur if he has a set ritual with his children around saying goodbye. This question surprises him. "No, I don't think I have even a fixed pattern, let alone rituals". Arthur is given a suggestion. Suppose you give each of your children a small wooden chain they can put in their trouser pocket. And one for you too. Every time you go away,*

you agree with your children that when any one of you holds their neck-
lace, it makes the others think of you and be with you in your heart, just
as you think of the one who is holding the necklace. Arthur responds,
"I've got to say it sounds a bit wishy-washy to me, but I will try it".

Two months later, Arthur is back with his coach. "I had a strong resist-
ance to doing it, but I committed to doing it every time. I've been away
five times, since our last session, and perhaps most importantly, the way
we say goodbye is now much more bonded. I really make contact, we
look at each other, and that gives a kind of peace to us all. The necklace
works really well. I notice that I'm often holding it, sometimes uncon-
sciously, and that brings a smile to my face. I feel calmer when I travel
and the children are much less stressed. We now also joke around at
night when we are FaceTiming. 'And, do you remember, this afternoon,
when I held the necklace?' This whole idea is so beautifully innocent".

If you never had the experience of being supported when faced with the fear
that separation brings up, you cannot build the inner confidence needed
to handle loss and 'stand tall' when painful goodbyes must be said. When
you have experienced having such support, you develop trust. And so you
learn that within the loss lies the possibility to make new contacts and new
bonds.

Saying goodbye is often accompanied by a certain degree of embarrassment and not precisely knowing how to act, which you have to learn how
to work with. The whole human system is naturally geared towards avoiding
situations of saying goodbye that involve pain and discomfort.

Bram is in charge of the part of the ambulance service that works to-
gether with the police and the fire department. There is a lot of resist-
ance to this collaboration among the employees. This mainly concerns
matters such as the way in which people work together (or not) while
on shift, the way in which time waiting to be called out is spent and
other (apparently) trivial issues. Each department has its own habits,
and once one thing has been brought into the open and resolved, the
next one needs attention.

Mariska works within the staff of a service organization and felt frus-
trated: "We were not going to reorganize, the organization was going
to change direction. Seriously, that's what we were told. It transpired,
however, that people would have to leave. But it seemed the manage-
ment wanted to avoid talking about a reorganization, as if ignoring that
changed anything. Someone from outside was hired to make it clear
to us what our roles would be after the change. Everyone was asking
themselves what it was that was wrong with the company, but nobody
offered any answers. When we asked what we would have to do differ-
ently, we were told not to be so critical, and to be loyal and cooperative.
The consultant was highly experienced and was a nice woman. She also

saw that the real conversation was not taking place. But she wasn't hired for that. She finished her story and we went back to business as usual. Such a waste of money. And it didn't change anything either".

The hesitation to act around saying goodbye contrasts with the idea of social engineering, a common concept within the still-dominant leadership thinking in terms of being a 'man' of action and taking control, of blueprint thinking and command. In this chapter we want to stay in the 'place of difficulty' and reflect on what is involved in loss and in leaving, how it affects your leadership and what you and your organization can learn from it.

Leaving in the context of organizations

Organizations, like people, have a life cycle of creation and emergence, via growth to maturity, leading inexorably to old age, decline, bankruptcy perhaps or a merger/takeover as a symbolic death. This means that organizations also have a lifeline with a cyclical pattern in time. Bailleur calls this the history line. He compares organizational renewal to plowing a field: what's under the ground comes to the surface and the deeper you plow, the more surprises you turn up.[19]

Within organizations, departments and teams have an even greater dynamism in their life cycles. In organizations, their larger cycles of rise and fall contain several shorter cycles of change that have their own dynamics of saying goodbye and starting over. With every reorganization or change in strategy, departments and teams are regularly broken up because no place has been made for them in the new organization or the new strategy.

Organizations are constantly adapting to changing conditions in their environment: among consumers, in technology, the market, the economy. As you saw in Chapter 3, every change in an organization begins with an end, the end of the previous situation.[20] Being able to say goodbye properly is necessary in order to develop the capability to commit to a new situation, again and again.[21]

As managing director of the company his father had founded, Mats was unable to steer the company safely through the financial crisis. A takeover was the only chance of saving the jobs of the employees. Fortunately, he found a good buyer for his company. His staff kept their jobs. As a result, he was able to live with the fact that his own position changed from that of manager to that of adviser to the new management. But the fact that they had to move to the new organization's building, away from the building where his father had once started, hurt him. When the new managing director asked him, on the day of the move, to unveil a painting in the lobby of the building that celebrated his father as co-founder of the new organization, it touched him deeply.

Saying goodbye professionally

Within work, your professional roles will inevitably involve forms of leaving, of having to say goodbye to someone or something. Here, too, reorganizations or mergers can lead to loss, when, for example, there are more people than roles. But self-chosen career moves and job changes can also carry the experience of loss. As the saying goes, *you don't know what you've got until it's gone*. This is like the employee who transitions from subject-matter-expert to manager and no longer has any content involvement. No matter how challenging the new function or role might be, such steps often bring with them melancholy and regret. Like Rachel Naomi Rhenen states, the way we deal with loss shapes our ability to stand fully in life. Expecting to be able to face loss without being affected by it, she says, is as unrealistic as to think that we could wade through water without getting wet.[22]

> Things had been a bit messy at the top of the organization for some time. Directors were at each other's throats, although outward appearances were always maintained. It was only a matter of time before the chief executive officer (CEO) would have to intervene. When he did, the official story was that the directors had been asked to voluntarily resign from their positions and that their resignations had been accepted. However, when the news hit the papers that evening, the story was that the directors had been fired. Given the uncomfortable and contradictory atmosphere, it was not possible to organize an official farewell.
>
> Christiaan came in to succeed a supervisor who had left under a cloud. The atmosphere in the department felt like that of a small village, where the gossip was shared in the local pub. The only real difference here was that people gossiped about their colleagues in their offices behind closed doors, and were nice and polite to each other 'in public'. The team were curious to know what had possessed him to accept this job, but the question already contained the answer: healthy curiosity. He came with an open attitude. He listened, asked questions, created space by taking a step back and thus inviting the employees to take the initiative. He challenged people in a positive way and literally asked to them to challenge him. In no time at all the atmosphere in the department had flipped into positive. Later he told his new colleagues about the burnout he'd recovered from, and his conscious decision, thereafter, to live and work in a different way; that he had chosen to stay bonded when feeling vulnerable and that he considered he could be 'invulnerable' as a leader only by being fully transparent. His example inspired others to step out on their own leadership journeys.

The team as a secure base plays a crucial role in shaping change. The way support is offered within the team and the way you as a leader facilitate this support, is immediately a good measure of the degree of psychological security within the team.

Boris runs a chain of luxury goods stores in Bulgaria. Over the last seven years the business has been growing at an incredible rate. Boris believes the growth is down to "unbridled commitment, sharp focus and good market conditions. And in that order". A couple of years ago, two board members (also co-founders) abruptly left the organization. "They no longer felt motivated or able to continue shaping our growth", says Boris. "They left on the same day, sending a shockwave through the management team. Although I am convinced that their departure was a good thing, growth has flattened out since then. We are not back to the growth level of the first five years".

As part of a group of five entrepreneurs from different countries, he is following an intensive leadership program. In preparation, the program leader has sent a 360 degree feedback questionnaire to all Boris's management team. During the program Boris hears the feedback for the first time. It is critical and painfully surprising to Boris.

The course leader asks him if he's up for an experiment. "Bring it on!" he laughs, a little hollowly. A circle is formed with a chair in the middle, and Boris is asked to take turns at sitting on the chair. Each turn, the chair represents the place of one of his fellow board members. He steps into their shoes, as it were. The course leader, who is sitting in Boris's chair, has, as if he now is Boris, a short conversation with each of 'them'. Each tells something about how they experienced the abrupt departure of their two colleagues. How intense it was and how little room there was to talk about emotions. One of them says how it hurts him that feelings of friendship, which were there before, have been pushed totally into the background and that there is a constant feeling of stress, which makes the team much less productive and effective.

"Of course, I knew all this," Boris sighs afterwards. "That pressure to perform made me think I had to keep on top of everyone. I see now that I've had no space for anybody's feelings. And to learn that this might cost me Dragan's (one of the board members) friendship . . . it's just not worth it to me".

Back in Bulgaria, Boris brings the team together for a day of relaxation and bonding. They spend part of the day drawing up a 'profit and loss account' for the last two years of work together. This involves many courageous and honest talks in which much is shared. They also say goodbye to the two board members. A few months later, Boris emails his contacts from the leadership course and tells them how the atmosphere has radically changed. "What my management team appreciates most is my willingness to come back to their issues. I have the feeling that the 'business' just followed suit, as it were".

The effect of hidden grief on leadership

You might not be aware that you are, perhaps, carrying hidden grief within you.[23] By hidden grief, we mean losses for which no ownership has been taken. They are there, but they are not recognized or acknowledged.[24] Sometimes this is because you don't want to acknowledge the loss. Just continuing as before, a common survival strategy, seems to be the best or only thing you can do. Sometimes, however, it can be that the meaning of what was lost is not yet clear to you. Or events are not allowed to become public. The grief lies, as it were, wrapped-up in your unconscious. Not recognizing or acknowledging loss is a common phenomenon. But even if you can see all the losses along your lifeline (at the beginning of the book, in Chapter 2, the Route Planner invited you to create your lifeline) you still might not understand how these losses are affecting how you carry yourself now, your person effect in the world.

The way in which how you live your life has been affected by that loss.[25]

Jaap is in his late fifties and the leader of a company in the renewable energy sector. He wants coaching because the unexpected death of his best friend from corona has hit him really hard. He is sleeping badly and feeling a lot of anxiety. Together with the coach he explores where he gets this fear from and begins to tell how, as a twelve-year-old, he 'lost' his mother to depression and to psychiatric hospital.

There was no one emotionally available at that time to reassure him, and he was left to deal with his questions and his deep sadness and anxiety alone. In many ways, he managed to keep the fear and the grief of losing his mother at bay. The mother who could no longer be there for him emotionally. By working hard, making a career and taking care of his family, he didn't have to feel the pain of his deep loss. But now the anxiety seems to be demanding attention. The sleeplessness, worry and restlessness in his body are debilitating. He responds emotionally to the coach's suggestion that he write a letter to the frightened twelve-year-old boy. It feels right to him. As an adult man, he's going to take care of that twelve-year-old boy and walk with him. A second step is giving recognition to the frightened little boy, so he resolves to confide in a friend and tell him about twelve-year-old Jaap. Making these decisions, which bring up a lot of vulnerability, he suddenly feels his strength again and his confidence increases.

Research in cognitive neuroscience has provided much insight into what is called 'implicit memory'.[26] Past experiences can affect your behavior without you being actively aware of them, or wanting to be reminded of them. The effect of that neurobiological process is to bury unpleasant experiences. That's how the architecture of your brain tries to protect you from pain. The flip side is that even though you don't know this hidden grief is there, it continues to affect your behavior and your leadership.[27] Your attitude, your worldview and the people around you thus become part of your identity in a negative way, and frustrate your efforts to live your calling. So it needs some tough work to put the pieces of the puzzle in place.

First, there has to be a real desire to make or repair the bonds, to investigate where your current unconscious blocking behavior is connected to previous losses. Through not wanting to feel pain, you quickly end up in a fairy-tale land where you are busy "doing what needs to be done" and expect that "time will heal all wounds". But time cannot heal any wounds if you, as a leader, do not take action yourself. Denial of loss is like decaying concrete: it can take a long time, but eventually the structure collapses.

Brenda is participating in a secure-base management development program for senior executives. She talks about how she no longer dares to go out at night when the sky is clear. This has gotten worse in recent years. At the beginning of her marriage it was okay. But since she has had children, the thought of being outside in the dark has become unbearable. Except in winter, when it's cloudy.

Her work has many evening commitments, their number is increasing and logistically it's all becoming very difficult. She has to do them, and she wants to: many are presentations about her work as head of a large research department in Dubai. She has a crystal-clear story that she feels needs to be told, and in which she feels her calling.

The coach asks her when she first remembers having this fear. "From when I was nine", she says. He asks her what happened then, and she says her mother died, suddenly, of a heart attack. "There one moment, then gone. I stood there, at the funeral, screaming. I stamped my way into the church, making a lot of noise. My father didn't know what to do. He loved me but didn't dare to hold me. But my grandmother did. When we got home, she told me that my mother had become a star in heaven. I remember sitting on her lap. "Then I'll go find her", I said.

For months I walked outside at night. Looking for the star in the sky that was my mother. I became desperate: the longer I looked, the further from her I seemed to be. I was scared to tell my father how I would stand in the street or the garden searching the sky. After a while I stopped looking. And with that, I slowly I became increasingly afraid to go outside at night".

It is evening and outside it's dark. The coach asks Brenda if she would like to go outside with him. He walks on her left, holding her hand, and a woman from the course walks on her right. Brenda looks down, hesitant. She squeezes the coach's hand, harder and harder. He asks her to look to her right, at the woman walking beside her. "I miss my mother", she says to the woman, "she was my light when things were dark for me. She reassured me when I was scared in bed, or when things weren't going so well at school". The two women hug each other while Brenda cries. "Just hold her for a while", says the coach. After a while, the two women separate. Gently, Brenda raises her head. Her body shakes a little. She takes a breath, "I believe it's time for a new piece of heaven", she says with a smile. "I believe it too", says the coach.

Denial takes many forms. The simplest is "It's no big deal, I'm resilient. I can handle it". And the most persistent is denying that it ever happened. Sometimes this 'helps' you see reality as you want to see it, but not as it really is. For a while it can be very helpful, to avoid experiencing the painful reality in its fullness (as you will also see in the next chapter). But if it continues, there can be no healing.

The next step, and a critical one, is to recognize the negative impact denial has on your leadership. To face the reality of loss and, ultimately, to be able to really say goodbye, a personal vision is needed. That vision might include, for example, experiencing more joy, relaxation or success. Working with emotions of loss is no casual, superficial exploration. It means moving towards and into the pain, establishing a relationship with it in a way that allows something else to take its place.

The most common outcome, for leaders with hidden grief, is they become emotionally unavailable. As a result, they never achieve their full potential. They have difficulty bonding with colleagues and, probably, the same problem at home with their partners, children and friends. They have a preference for avoidance, so they don't take the risks necessary to the learning, growth and development of themselves and the teams they lead. Hidden grief often manifests itself in (subtle) cynicism, being unfairly demanding, bullying, lack of trust, fear of conflict or, on the contrary, an exaggerated tendency towards confrontation, or passivity or withdrawal. They are not team players and cannot face reality healthily. Violence and aggression are often lurking in the shadows. The leader loses his own inspiration and with it his ability to inspire others.

Some get stuck and this lack of impetus, of energy, of desire can easily lead to addictive behaviors. It could be alcohol, or the work itself, porn, social media, binge-watching, excessive gym time (often alone), or a preoccupation with others (we'll look at this in more detail in the next chapter). These leaders' negative emotional state of mind keeps them from truly bonding with their team members. They no longer feel inspired, they feel anxious, their focus becomes negative. The leader is, albeit in 'innocence', facilitating a culture of *blaming* and *shaming*.

Luis, in his 40s, works in a Portuguese bank. He is head of the risk management team. He has contributed to the success of the bank, but he wants to get more out of the job. For a number of years, however, he has been hitting a ceiling and he doesn't know why, or how to change things. Many of his team members speak about a culture of fear and micromanagement. Team turnover is unusually high. The CFO has made it clear to Luis that something has to change. Luis agrees, but is at a loss about what to do.

With a coach present, he shares his lifeline with the group. He tells how he and his wife almost lost their child in the days following her birth. "Our daughter had a lung infection and she and they fought for her life for ten days. She made it and is now a picture of health. But something changed in me. It was the most frightening period of my life. I felt totally powerless. I had no choice but to surrender to others."

A few days later, Luis is in a group coaching session, doing a role-playing exercise to explore how he can improve dialogue with his team. He gets stuck while practicing and asks for feedback from his fellow coachees. "You just charge at everything like a bull at a red rag. You don't give the other person any space at all. You fire off five or six questions at a stretch!" one of them says. There is an uncomfortable silence in the room; Luis seems to be staring out the window. A moment later he turns, wide-eyed, to the trainer. "Now I see what I've been doing. Instead of creating an atmosphere of trust within my team, I'm making them feel insecure. My fear is spreading through the team like a plague".

Acknowledging loss is an important step. A step towards accepting the loss, which opens the door to saying goodbye. Accepting does not mean saying you agree that something or someone was lost. It means saying, "I lost this. And, someday, I will be okay again".

A large healthcare facility was faced with the illness of a beloved colleague, Cindy. The void in her team was palpable. When it became clear that Cindy would die, the manager called a meeting with the entire team. It was an intimate affair, held in the evening, during which a large candle was lit for Cindy. Each colleague then placed his or her own candle around the large one and said what Cindy meant to them. There were small cards on which they wrote down their feelings. These went into an envelope, together with a photo of the candles. The envelope was to be given to Cindy by a colleague, a close friend. In the closing round everyone got the opportunity to say something if they wished, and several colleagues said that they had not been looking forward to this evening, but that it had helped them a lot.

Support from the people around you is always important in cases of loss. Colleagues and supervisors are part of an employee's social network. In the event of a loss, it is important that an employee can bond emotionally with what they have lost and is given time and opportunity to deal with this. When such psychological safety exists in the workplace, it accelerates the return to productive behavior. This is one of the ways that work can be an important link in the chain of life, a source of meaning that can act as a pillar of support during loss and separation.

The unexpected effects of loss

Broadly speaking, you can distinguish between expected losses and unexpected losses. Expected losses are part of the normal course of life, although they are often not immediately apparent. That your parents die before you do is such an expectation. That older colleagues leave because they are retiring is usually foreseeable, often to the precise date. Yet the effect of a foreseeable loss can turn out to be unforeseeable. The meaning of a bond sometimes only becomes clear when it is broken and the effect can be overwhelming. Unexpected losses take you completely by surprise, because they occur at moments when they actually shouldn't happen. When a loved one dies prematurely or a colleague or manager unexpectedly quits his job and leaves, you are confronted by how little control you really have and can find that you have time-travelled back into the (separation) fear of your primary attachment-dynamic.

> *A care institution in the Antilles was staffed by enthusiastic people who were passionate about their work and especially about the clients. They shared a strong bond. Nobody could understand the recent, and totally unexpected, departure of a colleague to the Netherlands. She had gone without saying goodbye and that had damaging consequences; for her ex-colleagues, but even more for the clients. They were all looking at each other, wondering "Who else here is planning to leave?" Their trust in each other had been severely damaged.*

Even an announced, expected loss often has an unexpected effect, despite people knowing, in some way, that it was inevitable. *People do crazy shit when they get fired.*[28] When a reorganization – with job losses – is announced, it often creates a kind of anticipated loss. Often, usually in fact, certain functions/departments are more, or less, affected by a reorganization and have to be reduced in number. And often who will have to leave can be decided in advance. It makes no difference whether the selection is based on seniority, years of service, capabilities or any other factor. But it is made clear in advance who will be affected. But often the effect of the loss, despite being known, does not fully sink in until the decision is finalized and the redundancy letters are handed out. Only then can you feel the whole of how this will affect your life.

> *In preparing for the reorganization, Zahid knew that his position would become redundant and that 'his' duties would be divided among three new positions. He would have to reapply for one of those new positions, or do something else entirely in the organization. It wasn't a surprise. Zahid had been tasked with writing job descriptions for these new positions and setting up the new department. Because he simply took great pleasure in the range of responsibilities he'd had, he had no interest in any of the three new positions. Early in the process, Zahid had decided to continue applying within the organization. To his own surprise, however, he was very upset when the letter announcing his redundancy fell through his letterbox. It was only when he saw it in black and white, in*

the formal language that it always seems to be written in, that it really sank in. Zahid was overwhelmed: shocked and angry. The organization didn't need him anymore. That was how he felt it. That it was not about him personally, that the function would no longer exist, was a nuance he could not grasp at the time. It affected him so much that he found himself unable to apply for any job. He had lost his self-confidence, his self-esteem.

Saying goodbye: shaping a continuing bond

The best way to avoid the pain, discomfort or disappointment of change is to not commit. But for those who really want to live fully, and lead fully, this is not an option. Not bonding leads irrevocably – and earlier – to death, both metaphorically and literally.[29] So saying goodbye is necessary to be able to continue, to bond again, even – and often crucially – with that which was lost. You cannot provide a welcome if you haven't said goodbye.

"How do you say goodbye?" is a question we are often asked. The answer is as sobering as it is challenging: by doing it. By moving – in the presence of secure bases – towards the loss. Embracing it you open up a new emotional reality in your brain; you start the formation of new neural pathways. By choosing to believe that, in reality, things couldn't have gone any differently, it became impossible for you to end the grieving process. Saying goodbye is precisely the crucial first step on the path to making grieving and meaning possible. As you will also see in the next chapter, grieving is not a luxury, but a necessity: it makes a more-real future possible. Loss never arrives alone. It is usually the (hidden, secondary) losses linked to the original loss that make grieving difficult. Future expectations are seen from a radically different perspective. In addition, losses in that perceived future often recur and change form in the process: new events can no longer be shared, leading to new secondary losses. The paradox of saying goodbye is that one must first bond with that which has been lost. With awareness of the full magnitude of what that bond has brought you, but also what it didn't bring. This opens the space to grieve, not only what was lost, but also what never was and never will be.

Annelies was young when she lost her mother, long before she became a mother herself. So her mother never had the chance to be a grandmother. When Annelies was about to be a grandmother herself, she found that she couldn't just be happy for her daughter and really look forward to the expected new life. She felt sad but couldn't understand why. Then it came to her: she was grieving for her own mother and the experience she had never had.

The choice to face a new reality is also a conscious choice not to stay stuck in a dream world of "what if" or – the opposite – to have a romanticized image of what could have been. This choice is a step on the road to liberation.

Your brain is not a static thing. In Chapter 5 we talked about neuroplasticity, the brain's ability to form new bonds that ensure you can keep on learning. Your memories are not fixed either. Although you can't erase actual events, your brain does have the ability to erase the painful emotions associated with a memory and so help you disconnect from that memory. Then you are able to talk about the painful memory, and connect to it, without it holding you hostage. *Memory reconsolidation* is an act of transformational leadership in more ways than one.[30] However, you cannot do it alone. The process can only take place bonded with others. It takes a certain amount of surrender, to a person or group, to allow yourself to be questioned about personal experiences. The result of memory reconsolidation is that an often radically different perspective arises about events that have taken place. As a leader, you now own the experience; it no longer owns you. In the words of David Kessler, who worked with Elisabeth Kübler-Ross, pain after loss is inevitable, but victimization is a choice.[31]

The change of perspective about previous experiences is the main outcome of memory reconsolidation. However, before we go deeper into the process of memory reconsolidation, it's important to understand that the approach described in the following story about Thomas doesn't directly belong in the leader's toolbox. You will not be able to simply apply this method yourself. It is intensive, and radical, and belongs in the context of professional guidance. Yet we want to share a case from our practice for several reasons. First, to show the powerful and transforming effect it has. So that you can explore, if your lifeline reveals hidden grief, what memory reconsolidation could mean for your leadership. Second, the case study will portray what we call the *chair-switch*. The chair-switch can also be used separately – and easily – as a powerful instrument in support of a desired change in perspective.

So how does the process of memory reconsolidation work?[32] First, by actively looking at the loss and the story you have built around it, space is created for the emotions that it carries.

Then the negative memory is challenged, as it were, by an experience that is diametrically opposed to it, creating a 'mismatch'. It is a special step which intentionally confuses the brain. It disconnects the loss from 'its' painful emotions and the story you created about those emotions. Your identity is no longer defined by the loss. The brain learns to rearrange the existing memory so that the old pain is no longer triggered in the present in such a way that it blocks your bond with yourself and with your environment. This allows you to focus on a new reality.

Thomas, a wealthy banker, is in his mid-forties. He lives and works in both Slovenia, and Argentina where he met his wife. They have been married for ten years and have two children together. Following an open conversation, his sister-in-law, fresh from completing a leadership program, puts him in touch with a coach. In their first (Zoom) meeting, Thomas tells how he experiences aimlessness in his life and so much procrastination that he, his business and his marriage are beginning to suffer. The coach asks him what is his calling. Thomas just laughs. "Calling? I haven't a clue what mine might be. And if I ever had one at all, it lost it a long time ago".

Thomas recounts some impactful life events. "I think I'll just be totally open" he says. "When I was twenty-seven, my father was killed in a car accident in circumstances that have never been clarified. There is a strong suspicion that he caused the accident himself, since it was a single vehicle accident. It was totally unexpected for all of us".

Thomas says the bond with his father was okay but not more than that. "He was strict but fair. I trusted him, but I wouldn't describe the bond as particularly warm. He kept his emotions under wraps". Thomas's father sold his company, under pressure from foreign investors, just before he was forty. It provided him and his family with a large amount of capital. "From that moment on I saw my father withdraw. It seemed as if he could no longer find any purpose in life".

In preparation for the second session, Thomas draws out his lifeline. He sees all the events in his life one after the other. One of the things that stands out is his love of sport fishing. "That's the most intimate thing I did with my father. The week before he died, I was fishing with him". A little further along the line is his marriage. He met his wife one year after his father's death. Just a year later they were married.

"This is the first time in eighteen years that I have spoken to anyone, except my mother, about my father's death. Even my wife doesn't know the mystery around it. When I first met her, I did tell her how he died, but never about the circumstances and our suspicions. Time flew by and my sense of shame about how he died made talking about it impossible. I thought I'd let go of it, but I feel that it is coming back. My son is increasingly curious about his grandfather. And I'm also tired of avoiding the subject".

"What would it be like to say goodbye to your father after all these years?" his coach asks him. "The more I talk about it with you now", says Thomas, " the more I notice that I can't seem to stop talking. Something is forcing me to continue!" On the advice of his coach, later, at home, Thomas will write a letter to his father. "Write directly from your heart", his coach encourages him.

At the beginning of the third meeting, the coach asks Thomas to set two chairs facing each other. "How was it to write the letter?" the coach asks. Thomas says that when he started writing it, what came out was anger, loss and guilt. "I thought the anger was gone, but it's not. I'm angry that he went without saying anything. As if we weren't worth staying

*alive for. And I miss, terribly, that I was never able to introduce my chil-
dren to him. I also find it difficult that I feel guilty. Shouldn't I have asked
him stuff more often while fishing, invited him to talk?*

*Thomas sits down in one chair, facing the other empty chair and
reads the letter aloud. His feelings go up and down in intensity. Sometimes, for a moment or two, they seem gone.* "I feel guilty towards you,
and angry too. I'm forty-four now, and I notice how little I talk about my
feelings, just as you didn't. I am only now really becoming aware of that.
I don't feel like I'm going in the same direction you went, but I don't
want it to get to whatever point you came to either".

*After Thomas finishes reading the letter, he falls silent. The coach
invites him to sit on the other chair.* "Take a deep breath, and imagine
that, as if by some miracle, you can now feel what your father felt and
think what he thought. Give me a sign when you're ready". *Thomas
nods.* "What would you like to say to your son?" *the coach asks Thomas's father.* "I'm really sorry, sorry that I left so suddenly!" *he says. And
then the emotions come.* "I see now how it is for you. And I also see
what I missed by never knowing your wife and children". *"What else
would you like to say to Thomas?" asks the coach. The response is hard
to make out, but sounds like,* "Can you forgive me?"

*Thomas sits back down in his own chair and talks about how it feels
when his father asks for forgiveness.* "I think, for the most part, I've already done that, but somewhere it's liberating to hear him ask for it. *Can
you say the words to your father?"* "Yes, I can". "I forgive you Daddy,
I forgive you. I miss you and I forgive you."

Thomas returns to his father's chair. "Thomas told you that he feels
guilty. That he should have done more to engage with you. How is that
to hear?" *Thomas's father looks at the coach and says,* "That's total
nonsense".

The coach gives him a specific sentence to say to his son, "It's not
your fault," *he says, half holding his breath.* "Say it again". "It's really
not your fault". "And again." "It's not your fault". *Tears flood down his
father's cheeks.*

"Thomas is struggling with the question of his purpose in life, and
with his procrastination, so what do you think he should be doing?" *the
coach asks.* "What he's doing now. Talking. Not doing it the way I did it,
but talking to friends about it, and to his wife," *Thomas's father replies.*
"That sounds like it would help him break the chain", *says the coach.*
"Yes, yes", *says the father.*

"Is there one last thing you would like to say to your son?" *the coach
asks.* "Yes. Definitely. I love you. And go out there and live your life!"

*Once back in his own seat, Thomas shares what it is like to hear his
father speak these words.* "It's so crazy, but I feel relieved. And I never

heard my dad say that he loves me. I think I knew, but hearing those words has really touched me: I feel encouraged. I'm also not going to put off talking about it with my wife any longer. She has a right to know this story and what has just happened, and I long to be close to her again. And I know she feels the same."

Thomas's case offers a concise representation of the process of memory reconsolidation. His brain has made the painful emotions – stored deep in the unconscious – visible and palpable. By hearing messages that are opposite to those stored (including those about guilt), the emotions of the experience have become more detached from the experience itself. This creates a new perspective in the brain and also in Thomas's story. His grief process will now have space to flow. Also, the story about his father will change, creating a process which will result in Thomas experiencing him as a secure base again.[33]

A few months later, Thomas tells how, after the intensive session, familiar conversations became very different. First, with his wife. Initially she was angry that this had been kept from her for so many years. After the initial anger, however, she delighted in the increased intimacy. With his mother, and some friends, Thomas talked about the experience and about his father. "It seems like it has given others more space and relaxation too. There have been a lot of tears, of course, but my relationships seem to have more freedom and flow in them".

Thomas's coach returns over time to help him search for his calling. Who is he really, as he gets to know himself again without the heavy burden of guilt and suppressed emotional pain? The sessions in which they looked at his life-line, mapped out his secure bases[34] and, of course, said goodbye to his father, also put him in touch with old dreams, from his younger days. Activities he loved to do, places that inspired him. He also learned, step by step, to give meaning to events by sharing them with people around him.

The seat switch used in the story can also be part of a regular conversation. Sometimes you notice in a dialogue – when one or the other is paraphrasing – that your conversation partner does not succeed in putting himself in your position or in putting himself in the position of another person. At that point you can invite him or her to switch positions by actually switching chairs. If the other person can take a moment to empathize, a different experience can arise, that allows a different perspective.

While discussing the progress of Jan's project, Ayana, his supervisor, notices that he's grumbling about his client. According to Jan, the client, whom he spoke to earlier in the day, wants to quickly implement just a part of the new IT application in order to solve a pressing business problem. Jan, however, insists that a fully integrated solution is best even though it will take longer. Ayana feels Jan's frustration mounting over what he perceives as obstinacy on the part of the client. At some point, Ayana places an empty chair across from Jan and suggests that he switch and sit in the client's seat, "I feel like the two of you are not on the same wavelength. You seem to have little concern about his problems, and I can imagine that he thinks you don't care about his issues. Would you like to take a seat in his chair? I suggest you take a moment to settle into his position . . . and then talk further from there. What's that like for you?" Ayana later recounts, "From that moment on, we had a completely different conversation. Jan immediately felt what was at stake for the business, even though it was more work for IT to split the implementation. Because he stood in the client's shoes, as it were, he was able to experience the importance very clearly. In the end, we soon agreed that it was right for the business. Then I communicated this, in person, to the IT team, and asked for their understanding and commitment to the new plan and the extra effort it would involve".

Not only hidden loss but also transient loss requires attention and recognition. Temporary farewells, for example due to illness, should be 'marked' both when leaving the work environment, albeit temporarily, during handing over the work and when returning. And, during the period of absence, relationships and bonds need appropriate care, to make the return as seamless as possible. In the following example you see the necessary balance between giving and receiving. Receiving cards and presents when you are absent and giving a book with a personal dedication when you return.

Kajsa Ollongren – whom we already met in Chapter 4 – was absent as deputy prime minister for six months due to illness; during that time she experienced that Dutch politics does have a human face. She received many messages of support, cards, flowers and gifts. The chauffeur of the Dutch Minister of Justice and Security would deliver something, or the Secretary of State for Economic Affairs and Climate Policy would suddenly arrive with Easter eggs. The different political Parties, and all her colleagues have shown their care in various ways. When it was over, she ensured there was recognition, by speaking to all of them and offering a personal thank you. She emphasizes that they really do function as a team, but that this does not solely depend upon the person, but on what they agree between each other. She bought a book for each person, chosen for each individual, and wrote a personal message in every book.[35]

In the past century another important development has taken place in how psychology looks at saying goodbye and dealing with loss. Earlier insights focused on cutting the ties with what was lost, on detaching and letting go. Only then would the loss be 'processed'. New insights indicate that there are ongoing, albeit changed and evolving, bonds which we call *continuing bonds*.[36] In addition to being open to new bonds with others, reshaping the bond with who or what was lost is also one of the tasks of what we know as grief.[37] If there is no goodbye, then someone has not really left.

A secondary school was faced with the sudden death of Kerem, a young and popular teacher in the Health and Welfare Department. Two months after his death, the director called the department head. He had realized that the team was in a state of grief and that he had left something unfinished. He asked for a meeting with the team, to remember Kerem together and brought in a loss and grief specialist to facilitate the process. She asked the team members to bring something personal that bonded them with Kerem. On the afternoon itself, during the opening round, one person said the fact that the director had thought of them was actually enough; so, for him, the afternoon had already succeeded. But others thought it was 'mustard after the meal' or believed that they were 'over' it, that it was no longer an issue for them. The team members were asked to take turns to say something about Kerem and their memento. One colleague carried a jar of licorice. He had always picked Kerem up from the train station, and the jar of licorice sat between them in the car. Everyone had their own story. Those who in the beginning had felt this to be unnecessary, told their stories at the end. For everyone, it had been an intense, moving and bonding afternoon.

The necessity and power of rituals

Following a death, in particular, important moments from that life offer opportunities to commemorate personal and professional milestones: these could be, for example, the birthday, or anniversary of the death, of a deceased employee. This can be marked in the work environment and there can be attention for the next of kin.[38] A card, a flower, a phone call lets them know that their loved one has not been forgotten, even by his colleagues. Holidays also are ritual moments in human (work) life: a time when the bereaved can use extra attention and support. It is good practice to mention deceased employees by name if your company has the tradition of a Christmas or New Year's speech. Professional milestones, such as anniversaries of long-serving employees, and of the organization itself, deserve similar attention.

At a convention center, Alejandro, a chef from South America in his early twenties, died suddenly. A memorial table was set up with his photo, his chef's hat, some items from the kitchen, flowers and a candle. Colleagues were given the opportunity to write something in a memorial book. The management organized a farewell service, as Alejandro was to be flown to his home country for the funeral. Some family members who lived in the Netherlands were invited as special guests. The service began with four of Alejandro's colleagues walking slowly up the central aisle pushing a serving trolley containing his picture and the mementos from the memorial table. It was as if they were carrying the coffin containing their colleague. There were speeches, music and a colleague from the kitchen, himself a Spanish speaker, gave a short address in Spanish. A video recording of the service was made for the family in South America.

Every end, and with it every new beginning, requires a ritual, whether tangible or not: a farewell to a method of working, a department, an organizational name or logo, a workplace, a certain atmosphere or culture of cooperation. Only when people are supported to take their leave by a ritual, will they have room to bond with the new. The fact that changes in organizations often have such a hard time, as you've seen in Chapter 3, is partly because organizations do not enable their people to say goodbye.

The effect of a well-organized farewell is that colleagues who are not let go, but remain in uncertainty after a round of layoffs, wondering when it will be their turn, can see that redundancies are handled with care. All too often the organization ignores the emotional and psychological effects this uncertainty foments among those left behind. The prevailing idea seems to be that those left behind should be 'grateful' because they still have jobs. That the uncertainty can have a paralyzing effect, while often fewer people need to do more work, is conveniently ignored. It is rarely recognized that people can remain emotionally bonded to the people who are laid-off, and experience a form of "survivor syndrome" and "survivor guilt".[39] It is a question of whether you are a good employer or not, whether you see the need for a proper goodbye offered out of compassion. It is also, simply, good business sense as it can avoid a consequential loss of productivity.[40]

After several rounds of the reorganization, the cutbacks had hit the organization hard. There were severe job losses everywhere and even the management board was cut in number. The directors had to reapply for their own positions, knowing there were no longer roles for them all. One of the directors, who really did not agree with how things had been done, did, in his mind, the honorable thing. Within the organization the story was that he had voluntarily decided to make room for the younger guard. In a closed circle he poured his heart out, saying that he could no longer recognize the organization. That after so many years he no longer felt at home. And then he was gone; from one day to the next he just disappeared. No one had a chance to say goodbye. The people who remained, and knew him well, were like orphans, stranded in an organization where his spirit still roamed, but his name was no longer mentioned.

When you are unsure of how to say goodbye, especially in a work situation, it can be helpful to design a ritual for such occasions. Rituals are symbolic actions that help in those moments when everything has changed for you but the world doesn't seem to have noticed. A ritual evokes emotions and, at the same time, provides a container for these emotions. It gives people something to hold on to, brings order, gives comfort and marks an important moment. Experience shows that rituals appear to be effective when one is dealing with profound loss. It also seems not to matter whether participants *believe* in the ritual.[41] In performing a ritual, the sense of control over a situation, often disrupted by the loss, begins to return. Reestablishing your grip on the situation is an essential precursor to assigning new meaning.[42] Rituals, therefore, create a safe vehicle, supporting you as you navigate round the Transition Cycle, repairing old bonds and making new ones.

According to the famous German monk and leadership trainer Anselm Grün, you can see rituals as doors that open and close. From day to day they help you to mark the beginning and the end of what you do. Through rituals, a leader can create and maintain peace and security in a team, helping employees to experience that they belong, that they matter. From that secure base, goals can be realized together.[43]

Daniëlle Braun and Jitske Kramer looked, globally, at how groups of people (*tribes*) create order out of chaos, the ways in which they discover, together, that what they have in common is greater than what they do not. One of the most powerful rituals, that take place everywhere, are campfires: places where people come together to share stories. Where people truly engage in dialogue with each other.[44]

The executive team of an insurance company had been working intensively for about two years on relationships and feeling bonded. One of the outcomes was that every team meeting started with a check-in[45] where people talked about what they were busy with.[46]Over time, this had helped establish an atmosphere of interest and fun.

Then the CEO implemented a reorganization which led to two members of the management team leaving. Suddenly, the organization is filled with uncertainty and turmoil.

The management team feels this too, although the board members keep it hidden from each other. At the beginning of the year following the reorganization, the team went into the mountains, together with two coaches. There were long walks, intense conversations. One evening, the group is sitting around a campfire near their mountain hut. After a while Dave, the COO, begins to speak, he is very emotional. He speaks of how, six months ago, he began to miss the feeling of being bonded with the team. It seemed that everyone withdrew "to their own island" and that he felt much less safe and quite alone. "For the first time I started to think about leaving the organization". Dave's revelation leads to silence, to shock and also to stories from other members about their pain and worries over the past six months. It turns out that six months ago the check-ins had become a kind of 'formality' and more a ritual of checking out *than* checking in. *Under "the day-to-day pressure", the very thing that had made the team high-performing*[47] *– the check-in and the pleasure of meeting together – had faded into the background. Everyone took a piece of paper, wrote on it what they wanted to leave behind, read it to the group and threw it into the fire.*

Rituals come in all shapes and sizes. Every day, each of us participates in a number of rituals. From a handshake as a symbol of greeting and contact, the words you speak when saying hello or goodbye, the flowers, the cards, the bottles of wine and the speech at a farewell reception. The power of the ritual lies in its familiarity, its predictability, its repetition, a form that we know, that offers a sense of safety. The ritual forms a metaphorical bed in which someone can feel carried. During the corona crisis you probably noticed how uncomfortable people (you) feel when shaking hands or hugs are no longer 'allowed'.

Shaping a farewell ritual in an organization requires the right combination of form and involvement. A form that suits the organization and, just as important, the person leaving. And commitment that goes further than simply recounting business milestones from a personnel file. It needs the personal: a farewell designed just for that individual, with anecdotes from colleagues, explicitly or implicitly touching on what the leaver meant to them and the organization. What they know the work actually meant to the one who is gone. In the ritual, highs and lows are remembered without the need to gloss over anything, where not only the beautiful moments but also the difficult times get attention. Difficult moments, which for some will include the farewell ritual. With, perhaps, appropriate music, chosen by the departing colleague and by the colleagues who remain. Besides a last handshake, perhaps someone appropriate walks him or her to their car, waves them through the doors that symbolically close for a last time.

In addition to an individual farewell, it is also possible to organize a collective farewell for a group of employees, a kind of informal get-together with those who are leaving the organization and those who are staying. This gives the opportunity to share the loss with each other and for both 'sides' to feel less alone. From a ritual point of view, the end is marked, while a signal is given to those left behind that they are saying goodbye properly.

The reorg came like a bolt from the blue and left the place looking like a battlefield. Out of a total of 200 employees, eighty had to leave. A transition team was put together that took suggestions during the process. One was to organize a farewell 'party'. It took some effort to get the remaining management to go along with the idea. Many employees and board members were reluctant to do so. Everyone had as much time and space as needed to choose whether to come or not. Right up to the last moment. There was quiet music, a delicious buffet and no speeches: togetherness was the goal. At the beginning of the evening,

*the atmosphere was a bit oppressive. People were hesitant about mak-
ing contact. But that changed quickly: soon there was much laughter.
As small groups formed, you could hear stories being told, memories
being recalled and people laughing. And there were tears when people
told each other how it felt to say goodbye. Each person, as they left
the party, received a rose. It was an evening without embellishment,
without droning pep talks or explanations why the reorganization had
to happen.*

*In the weeks that followed, employees expressed how important
the 'party' had been for them. Many had assumed that "nobody wants
something like this anyway", but the evening proved that to be false. It
delivered a kind of catharsis. Farewells had been said, received and the
memory of the ritual provided peace and something real to hold on to.*

In many change and loss situations, there is rarely a ritual goodbye. How
does someone say goodbye to their familiar workspace when their boss has
decided to make it into an office garden? How do you say goodbye to a
computer numerical control (CNC) machine that's been a part of your life for
twenty years, that you know like an old friend? Even when changes appear
minor, saying goodbye can still be hard.[48]

*Everyone in this department of the bank was used to their own forms
for filing customer data. In a quality improvement project, the management decided on a standardized procedure in which everyone would
use the same forms. In a team meeting, the employees were introduced
to the new system. During an interim evaluation, a few months later, it
turned out that almost every team member had stuck with their own
forms. After a couple of weeks, the team leader invited everyone to a
meeting and asked that each bring copies of their own forms. Everyone
was given a few moments to say why they were so attached to their
form. Next, all the forms were put in a basket and the whole team went
outside together to ritually burn them. It caused a lot of amusement and
laughter and – as the team leader said to his management team – it did
feel a bit excessive. But, after the old went up in smoke, the new were
finally accepted.*

It helps to linger with things that are coming to an end and to look back on a
period that has passed. Expressing positive and negative feelings has a purify-
ing effect, as long as people do not get stuck in feelings of resentment, guilt
or anger. Clarity and truth are important here, however hard that truth might
be. During reorganizations, mergers or compulsory redundancies, much is
glossed over via woolly language, slick presentations and vagueness about
the full scope and impact of the measures. This always leads to uncertainty,
anger and loss of trust. No matter how distressing the truth might be, it is always better for people to hear it; to know where they stand.

Equally important to the credibility of the farewell ritual is remembering and commemorating. In addition to looking forward, the New Year's address should include looking back by naming those who have left the organization. This commemoration not only forms the foundation of remembering, it also provides recognition of the loss and permission to grieve at work. This recognition is important in order that people can give meaning to the work and experience it as a meaningful part of existence. Not only for those who left, but especially for those who remain.

There is no sustainable way to bypass discomfort

In the event of major changes at work or saying farewell to a job, whether forced to or not, it is important to reflect on this episode within whatever framework is possible. Even, perhaps more so, for people who would really prefer not to do this. It is important that a proverbial point is made, one that negates the risk that someone is still present energetically, still affecting day-to-day processes while physically they have long been employed by another company, or are sitting at home.

With organizational change – of any size – employees are often asked to shortcut, to skip over parts of the Transition Cycle. Then they don't get a chance to really say goodbye, to grieve what has ended and give meaning to their loss. They are expected to cheerfully welcome their new situation and their new colleagues and to embrace their new conditions. In the end, forcing a shortcut just makes the journey longer. People have much more difficulty adjusting to the new, if one foot is trapped in the old.

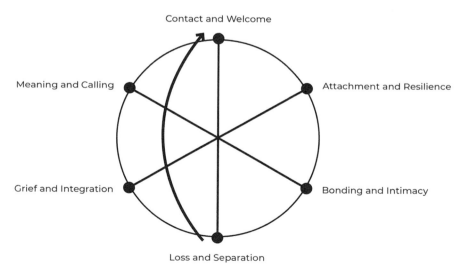

Figure 7.1 Shortcutting the Transition Cycle.

One of the people affected in the reorganization we talked about above – the one with the farewell party – was furious about how he was treated. He had been a sales representative for five years and had brought in a lot of business. He couldn't accept that he had been fired. "They can't do without me, and they'll soon see that for themselves". The person planning the farewell ritual listened respectfully, and then invited him to come to the farewell event, saying he could come when he wanted, and leave when he wanted. "I can't", he said. "I just can't do that". Six months later, he calls. "Could we meet up sometime, there's something I'd like to share with you". During their meeting he begins to choke up. He has a new job, back with a competitor where he worked previously. "I feel wretched that I did not come to the farewell. I had a good relationship with many colleagues and I didn't see any of them before I left. I have only been to the office once since then, when it wasn't busy. I notice, in everything I do and think, that I am still so bonded to that time in my life. Sometimes, with my 'new' clients, I accidentally use the name of my old employer, not my new one. Obviously I feel embarrassed, but more importantly, I blame myself for this. Had I come to the meeting and felt my sadness, let it show alongside my stubbornness and anger, I would have had the opportunity to say goodbye. How could I be so stupid? I notice that talking about this with you gives me a feeling of space. Apparently I needed to do this".

Resistance

Resistance arises from holding in the feelings, thoughts and needs surrounding the end and farewell (of a part) of an organization, by avoiding that place of difficulty within yourself. However, it isn't about resistance to the change itself, but resistance to the pain of the change, and resistance to surrendering your 'safe' position. By looking at resistance differently, by seeing the loyalty and bonding employees feel for the old familiar situation and giving employees the opportunity to actually say goodbye to it, space is created for new bonds. Ones that cannot be forced, but to which people can be invited in a dialogue, between individual and organization, about vulnerability and reticence on both sides.

Ron had founded the institute and put a lot of time, energy and love into making it a success. A few years before he retired, he began handing over responsibilities to his successor. But Ron held onto a few tasks because "I'm so good at them". As a result, he didn't really leave, he just had a smaller role. Exactly who was actually running the business became increasingly unclear to the employees and to Ron. He was still there and he wasn't. Discussing this with his successor, Ron realized he wanted to have a leaving party, a celebration. He wanted to be remembered as the founder of this wonderful institute and stand in the light one more time. His successor was delighted to 'offer' him this honor.

With every change where insufficient opportunity is provided to say goodbye, some employees will remain 'behind' in the old situation. Seen from the outside they might appear to cooperate in the new setup, but emotionally and psychologically they are not able to bond. With each change, there is risk of losing the commitment of more employees. An accumulation of losses occurs, comparable to the deposition of sedimentary rock: layer upon layer. In a cross section of the workforce, the 'organizational geologist' or 'organizational archaeologist' might uncover all the failed changes of the past being carried by employees as bands of solidified organizational grief.

The peak-end rule

Research by Daniel Kahneman and others shows that people value past events or time periods based on two specific experience-points: the memory of a 'peak moment' during that period, irrespective of whether a high or low point, and the memory of the end point, the conclusion of the episode. This outcome is known as the *peak-end rule*.[49]

The peak is the memory of the most intense event and can be either positive or negative. In the individual's evaluation, the experience of the peak and the end drown out, as it were, memories of other experiences during the episode. On the one hand this is because the brain tends to remember emotionally charged experiences better, on the other hand because more-recent experiences are more easily accessible.

This rule holds an important lesson for leaders and organizations: whereas you can't really influence the peak, you can influence the end. Usually, the employee determines what counts for him as his peak during his employment. But, as a leader, you can (and should) influence the shape of the farewell, if there must be one, regardless of the cause of the farewell: takeover, merger, reorganization, redundancy or dismissal. By creating a conscious leaving ceremony and designing it well, the organization can influence how the employee evaluates and remembers his career and the organization. From the point of view of being a good employer, it should be no more than normal to say goodbye properly. From the point of view of being a good businessman, it pays to say goodbye properly. Surely you would want all employees – past and present – to be ambassadors for your organization and always to talk positively about your company and their time in it.? It turns out that it really does matter how the farewell is designed. If the farewell, despite the reason, is a positive final experience, then it will be valued.

Important insights to take away

- Loss manifests in many, various ways and layers on a daily basis, both business and private.
- Avoiding (or wanting to avoid) separation is an important (mostly unconscious) driving force for certain behaviors.

- Trying to shortcut, or avoid, saying goodbye, ultimately hinders your ability to bond again. Resisting change is a way that unsaid farewells ask for attention.
- Your brain can learn to disconnect the intense emotions that go with an experience from the experience itself, so that new perspectives become possible. In this way you learn to take ownership of your story.
- Rituals are necessary to mark important transitions. They provide solid ground and reduce difficulties when change does occur.

Questions for self-reflection

1. What did you learn from your parents or educators about loss? What of that is helpful to you? What isn't? Why?
2. What losses were there in your life? What was or were the most impactful or painful for you? Why? How have they shaped you in your leadership?
3. In what ways did you actually say goodbye to these losses? How did you do that? Who was present?
4. What loss is currently playing out in your life or is imminent? What does it bring up in you?
5. What losses has your organization or team faced? How did it/they respond to them? How did you react to them? Did you/everyone say goodbye?
6. Do you avoid farewells or do you make sure that farewells are recognized?
7. Do you see separation as something negative or as a new opportunity?
8. Is there hidden grief in your life?
9. Is there hidden grief in your organization or team?
10. What are you afraid of losing in your life?
11. What risks do you avoid in your life because you're afraid to lose (someone/something)?
12. What loss is playing in your intimate relationships? How does that affect these relationships? Are you bonding and sharing this with your partner?

Questions for you to ask of the people around you – your person effect

1. What has ever been lost between you/any of you and me? Do you/any of you feel that we are (have been) sharing about that?
2. What is the most disappointing thing that has taken place between you and me? What has that meant to you?
3. Looking back on your work for this organization, what do you feel you have lost during your time here? How does that impact your bond to the organization? Do you feel like I give enough attention to you/that?
4. How does the team deal with saying goodbye? What do you see me doing in this? What is the effect on you of how I act in this? What is the effect on the sense of safety in this team?

5. Which goodbyes do we need to shape in this team or in this organization? How will that help us as we move into the future?
6. What do you see me doing when I experience or see loss and painful emotions? How can I (further) develop myself in this?
7. What loss helped shape you? What lessons did you learn from it? Would you tell me a little bit more about that?
8. What loss or (imminent) farewell are you dealing with at the moment? What can I do to help you with that?
9. If this were the last time we would see each other, what would you say to me? What else would you like to ask me?

8 First the Pain Then the Gain
Grief and Integration

About grief and integration

To grieve is to include in your life that which otherwise threatens, locked away, to disappear. To grieve is to take your whole life story, every part of it, large and small: the joy, sorrow, pain, abandonment, despair, happiness and desire. Don't gloss over the dark pages; they are a part of your story too. In the process of grieving you orient yourself to the past and the future, travelling back and forth between them. You reexperience the fractures in your attachments and are invited to heal, to reconnect them. As this chapter will show you, grieving is about integrating, putting the separate pieces back together into one, new whole. Grief is essentially a process, of connecting life as it was with life as it can be, or will become.[1]

> *Dick, a department head in a chemical company, had a new, very earnest young woman under his care, who was keen to learn. A special 'master-apprentice' relationship developed which Dick enjoyed and valued. It gave an extra dimension to his work to mean something important to the new generation of employees. After two years, he was told that the young woman had chosen to accept a job elsewhere, effective immediately. She hadn't even said goodbye. Dick was surprised at how much it affected him. He was angry, sad, confused and felt abandoned. An HR manager, with whom he had a good relationship, put words to his feelings. "It looks like you are grieving". He had never imagined grieving the departure of an employee. The conversation with his colleague revealed how he had spent years working toward a position in which he could pass on all that he had learned. It had given him a special sense of self-worth.*

Dick and the young employee had built a bond together. The abrupt, unexpected departure, without a farewell, felt almost like a stab in the back. He had invested in the young woman, felt that he meant something to her. He'd expected, and almost unconsciously assumed, that the young employee would stay for longer, to learn all he had to pass on. At least confide in him

DOI: 10.4324/9781003409922-8

when she left. He is grieving not only the lost relationship, but also the loss of trust and the loss of his belief that he meant something to her. As we can see here, sometimes one loss triggers other losses; you'll hear these called secondary losses. This can make grieving even more confusing and unpredictable. Like Julia Samuel puts it, when we try to navigate grief, we must face the paradox of finding a way of living with a reality that we don't want to be true.[2]

Grieving in the context of work

In your work you might be confronted with many kinds of loss that you can grieve. For example, you could grieve people you've lost through death or through (temporary) separation. You could grieve the loss of work, of familiar patterns, of a leader moving on, of a workplace, of the company name following acquisition, or even of trusted and familiar practices and programs. You might even grieve for a project that didn't work out as you had hoped. While there is a certain risk in comparing different kinds of losses[3] with each other, research shows how similar the emotional responses to loss in the organizational context are to the grief that results from the loss of an important relationship (through death or some other form of separation) in one's personal life.[4] Perhaps the term grief is a word you don't expect in a business context. Perhaps you experience it as 'heavy'. But denying reality does not change it. In other words, grief exists, it is real; it walks with you every day, even if you prefer to use other words for it. Of course, in the end it is not important which word you use, but whether you are able to see what wants to be seen.[5]

Johan runs a department in a provincial-government HQ. He talks to his colleague Matt about the terminal illness of their director, Maurice. "Of course the news hit everyone enormously hard. Me for sure: I can hardly concentrate, the simplest tasks just drag on and on. And I have become rather emotional, at home and at work. My wife isn't very understanding. I guess she thinks I'm making a drama of it; but it's not about me. Or is it?" Matt suggests they talk about it soon. At their next meeting, Johan recalls the death of his father, who died after a long illness while Johan was still in high school. Johan realizes that Maurice's impending death is confronting him with how – as an adolescent boy – he dealt with his father's death. In a way, he had not given it much attention. He says "There was so much going on in my life at that time. Looking back now, I see that I often felt guilty to be asking for attention. But I also realize now that with Maurice I always feel welcome and seen. With him I experience the respect of an older man, which I missed so much after the death of my father. At the time I found it very difficult to be with my grief, to let it show. It feels like I'm making up for that now".

Grieving as a social process is not limited to the private sphere.[6] The team as secure base is an important support in grieving.[7] This was already evident when we wrote about psychological security in Chapter 5. When a team or organization grieves together, it builds (and restores) trust. Not being able to grieve as a team has the unavoidable consequence that feelings are internalized, and then find other ways to make themselves seen in the organization. They can come to the surface when you least expect it, sometimes years or even decades later. As a leader, you have an important role to play, in and for your team, by taking the lead in recognizing and embracing grief. This applies both to events that occur in the team as a result of working together – or not-working together – and to events that affect individual members who then return to the team carrying their grief.[8] David Kessler sees the need of a community when we grieve, because we are not meant to be islands of grief. We heal as a tribe.[9]

> *On the first day of work after her maternity leave, with her infant son having died just before birth, the entire team was waiting for her. They had reserved a room and took time together to listen to her story. Her tasks were then shared among the team, so that she could do her work, but also so that she could pause or stop at any time if she found it no longer possible. On the second Sunday in May, she received messages from her teammates letting her know they were thinking of her, on her first Mother's Day.*

The team can be a secure base for a team member who has suffered a loss. In turn, the team also can suffer a loss that it must deal with as a team, while each team member will respond to this in their own way. The extent to which team members are able to shape grief in their own way, is also a good measure of the psychological safety within a team.

> *The IT project team had been working intensively for a year and a half to replace the outdated financial system with a new custom application. Soon after the merger, however, management shelved the project and implemented a system from the new 'owner' company.*
>
> *All the creative energy that the team had put into the project together was wiped out at a stroke. There was tremendous disappointment. The only work left was to move the old data into the 'new' system. However, this task was given to a team from the new company. With nothing to show for 18 months of committed, hard work, everyone was looking for a way to be useful again and make a tangible contribution. Only when the manager gave the team a day off and sent them on a 'team-building' day – that they would have had anyway, if the original project had been completed –was there room to express to each other how much pain the abrupt termination had caused them. This recognition enabled everyone to begin orienting themselves to the remainder of the implementation.*

Teams have their own dynamics in how they learn to collaborate, with changes in composition due to leavers and joiners having an impact on the team.

> When a team at a chip manufacturer was changed without consultation, removing two experienced advisers and adding three new ones, it took quite a while before the team could get going again. The existing structure had been broken and everyone had to find their own (new) place in the new whole. Existing arrangements were regularly challenged and tension increased. There were gaps in the planning, because certain tasks had no specified owner and nobody else took them on. Team members started to behave differently towards each other and conflicts arose. The team, that had worked harmoniously for a long time, couldn't handle this discord. Increasingly, product deadlines were not met: Sabine, the team leader, called a team meeting to discuss the deteriorating situation.
>
> During the meeting everyone was given the opportunity to say what they thought was the problem. At first people were hesitant, but soon anger was expressed about the change in the make-up of the team. That there had been no warning that it would happen. That there had been no discussion. The 'old team' members made it clear that they no longer had confidence in the team and that they felt unsafe if decisions could be made in that way. Sabine was shocked by the intensity of the emotions and spoke honestly when everyone else had had a turn to speak. She said she was sorry she had not involved the team in her deliberations, and that this had, unintentionally, contributed to the current atmosphere. She indicated that she wanted to create space for everyone to deal with this and that at the same time they, together, had a responsibility to deliver products on time, as planned. Those two realities existed side by side. Then she asked everyone to indicate what they thought they needed in order to be able to deal with both these realities within the new team composition.

Grief and attachment

A loss always starts from a basis of attachment, as you read in Chapter 5. A secure attachment provides a firm foundation for coping with grief. This does not mean fewer emotions, nor does it safeguard against grief and the pain that comes with it.

People who are securely attached are more able to regulate their emotions and know they are not alone. They can ask for and accept support from others. While someone with an insecure attachment style is more of a 'do-it-yourselfer', who takes care of everything himself and hardly ever asks for or accepts support; or, just the opposite, appeals too much and too often for help and clings to others. When faced with stress and emotion, our initial response, at least if the environment is sufficiently safe, is to call on what Porges calls the *social involvement system*.[10] This system helps regulate emotions and reduces stress, contributes to a calm state of mind and inhibits unnecessary defensive responses. It requires the proximity and presence of others, of secure bases such as trusted colleagues and leaders.[11] But when there are no secure bases available, people switch seamlessly to a more 'primitive' response: fight or flight. Or they freeze and are no longer in touch. We'll come back to that later in this chapter when we talk about the window of stress tolerance. So being able to stay open and present with the, sometimes intense, emotions of your team members is an important leadership quality.[12]

Grief is an attachment reaction. You are grieving for something or someone to whom you are attached and with whom you feel bonded or with whom you would have liked to feel bonded. Because if you are not attached – which, by the way, is not synonymous with having a good relationship – then you don't need to grieve. To love always means to be vulnerable, as C.S. Lewis puts it beautifully: love anything and your heart will be wrung and possibly broken. If you want to make sure of keeping it intact you must give it to no one.[13]

What Lewis describes is how you shut out vulnerability when you avoid attachment; when you become a hardened leader, unreachable by your employees. But, as Brené Brown writes, vulnerability demands courage, the courage to show that you are not in control of the outcome. Otherwise, you stop growing as a leader. When the armor has become so thick that you no longer feel anything as a leader, you have more or less died inside. Every successful leader must accept the risk of disappointment, failure, loss and heartache.[14] Only then may you step in and join the conversation. Brown refers to Theodore Roosevelt's quote, about the strong man standing in the arena, when he says that if you have not also had the courage to stand in the arena and take the blows, he is not interested in your feedback.[15]

Mistakes, failure and loss can cut deep. Often people stumble around aimless and bewildered after a loss.[16] They don't know where to turn with their feelings. Building up your capacity to be kind to yourself – which consists of acceptance, forgiveness and compassion towards yourself – is a fundamentally necessary quality. Combined with a growth mindset, the realization that failure is an inextricable part of your learning process – during school, training, sports, work or any other endeavor in your life – will significantly improve your sense of wellbeing.[17] Like Michael Jordan, who confessed to have missed more than 9000 shots in his career, to have lost almost 300 games and to have been trusted twenty-six times to take the game-winning shot and missed. He has failed repeatedly in his life, he says, and that is why he succeeded.

By grieving, people face the change, confront the losses and deal with them. People must take on their grief, perhaps not immediately, but it is essential that at some point, they do. Grieving happens not only via emotions (sadness, pain, anger, fear, confusion), but also in thoughts (how could it happen like this), in the body (fatigue, illness), in the perception of the world around them (so much is the same and yet everything seems different) and at the identity level (who am I without her, who am I without my teammates).

> *An old financial services provider had been up for sale for some time and was finally taken over by its major competitor. There was a great deal of unrest and, in an initial telephone call, the HR director said, "Some are ducking and diving, others are fighting and still others are working so hard as if, somehow, this will keep things as they were". Four large meetings were organized for all the leaders of the organization to discuss the emotions involved in radical change.*
>
> *At one of the meetings, a man in his late fifties, sitting at the back of the room, is invited to tell his story. "When I was a little boy, I often went boating with my friends here in this town. We had a small boat. When we sailed past this building, I would point up and say, "That's where I'm going to work. And that's what happened. I have been working here for forty years and the idea that the name will soon disappear from the building fills me with anger and sadness. I can hardly find the will to come to work anymore". There is silence in the room for a moment. It is emotional: people share their experiences, also in smaller groups. The sessions are very moving, those present find they share common ground. There are many conversations between leaders and employees and a sense of trust begins to be restored, bonds begin to form.*

Grieving is learning to land in the flow of the new reality. This is true at the level of the organization as an entity and at the level of its employees and leaders. Examples at the organizational level might include:

- Who are we as a group, now that our competitor has taken us over? What remains of our original culture of warmth and involvement?
- How do we survive in the new market while dealing with this crisis?
- With much fanfare the logo was taken off the wall. That was two years ago. But, internally, most people still use the old name. This is hindering true integration.
- Our director was killed in an accident. He was seen as the father of the company. How do we get through this together?
- The team has disintegrated after an intense conflict. It has driven a wedge between a number of people who still need to work together. How do we deal with this?
- How do we get our organization and our people back on track following the industrial accident in which three employees died?
- There was a fraud case which ended with the CEO being fired. The remaining executives have had to endure an intensely emotional process in which they were vetted by the DM (district attorney). The trust seems gone, the ship adrift, rudderless.

- After six months of working on a bid, the multi-million-dollar order went to a competitor. What we were offering was unique. Who are we if we can't win such an order together?

At the level of individual employees, grieving opens a window to the future, without forgetting the past. People become able to start their 'new' life. You could also say that grief is a way to find yourself again, to reinvent yourself perhaps. Each time you grieve, your identity changes, bringing questions such as:

- How should I relate to my colleagues who, till recently, I was leading?
- How do I see myself after my burnout?
- Will I still be suited to lead after being demoted?
- They say I should be glad I still have my job, after more than half my colleagues have been laid off. But I feel guilty and miserable. Is that crazy?
- Should I call myself a widow, even though I have a new boyfriend?
- Do people now see me as a pathetic divorcé abandoned by his partner, or am I now an attractive bachelor?
- Am I still a father now that my only child has died?

Does someone feel like an unemployed person when he loses his job? A patient when he becomes seriously ill? A refugee when he is a Syrian living in the Netherlands for five years? A psychiatric patient when he is suffering from depression? It takes time to answer such questions.

> To grieve is to learn to land (again) in life,
> *with all its fault lines.*

This means that there is an important task contained in grieving loss. Grieving is not optional, nor does it necessarily happen automatically. Grieving is an act of leadership by which you grasp the wheel of your own life, giving the people you lead the example and encouragement to do the same. Gianpiero Petriglieri and Sally Maitlis, professors at INSEAD and Saïd Business School respectively, list three basic attitudes a leader can adopt that help grieving employees:

1. In the void: be present.
2. In the absence: be patient.
3. In the new beginning: be open.[18]

Grief is the ultimate way to prevent yourself being held hostage by circumstances, of not becoming a victim of them. Grief always forms a turning point in the transition, through which, by trial and error, you learn that when all is said and done the future is more important than the past, but not separate from it. In the end grief turns out to be an enormous source of power, connecting you to your full potential. This can be a long, hard road, though.

Leaders are willing to face their own history and how it impacts their leadership. Willing to include those chapters from the book of life that they'd rather not remember. Losses are a part of life, no matter how much our culture of social engineering might suggest you can erase them. You might use different words and you might prefer to talk about pain rather than grief, about disappointment rather than loss. But what happens happens: it is a fact, even when you have denied it all your life.

In the jargon of psychology, the term *processing* is often used. "That happened long ago, hasn't he processed it yet?" As if grieving has a clear cutoff point. In particular with cases of profound loss, of long-and-strong attachments, when you had a special bond with or loved the person you lost, the loss stays with you forever. It makes you who you are.[19]

The concept of processing something fits well in a production environment, but in the context of grief we prefer to use *integrate*. That you weave your experience of loss into the tapestry of your being. You often don't see the frayed knots of life until you look under the rug. And sometimes, without warning, when a current event sparks old losses into flame, the underside rises to the surface.[20]

She is an HR (human resources) manager at a large NGO (non-governmental organization). When one of her team members says he can no longer find any meaning in his life, his colleagues are shocked, and she is called in to take care of the team member and to ask for help if needed. She does this well enough, but the following week she notices she has lost a lot of energy and feels alone and sad. Talking with her coach, she remembers the suicide of her sister when they were both teenagers. She recalls how everything revolved around her sister and her parents; there was hardly any time, space or attention for her. She was left alone with her grief. The work issue is pulling her back into that teenage experience. The team member received lots of care and attention, but no one asked her how it is for her. No one could know that the past was here in her present, or how intense the experience was.

Her coach instructs her to go back to her leader and tell him how hard this has been for her and that she needs his support. To her surprise, he listens, giving her all the time and space she needs. He even thanks her, because he realizes this is an important lesson. For her it is a healing experience: there is someone who understands what the process has brought up for her.

Although we might assume that social support around loss is primarily provided outside of work, Joyce Neijenhuis' research shows that fifty percent of grieving employees experienced colleagues as an important source of support. Similarly, forty-five percent of this group experienced the leader as an important source of strength. People from the work environment scored higher, as a source of strength and support, than people in the 'acquaintances' category.[21]

The myth of resistance to change

Much change literature holds grimly to the misconception that 'resistance' is a natural reaction of employees to change. 'Managing' that resistance is seen as a fundamental part of change planning. Of course, change brings up emotions in the employees. To label these emotional reactions as 'resistance to change', however, ignores the deeper origins of these emotions. If resistance really is an obstacle to implementing change, it is because employees have not been given the opportunity to say goodbye to the old, familiar situation. The emotions that surface are often dismissed as unnecessary and undeserving of attention.[22]

> *Bert was an experienced change manager in a financial institution, tasked with leading the major reorganization of a very large department. He was shocked by the grim and bitter atmosphere he found there. "People seemed extremely tense and even everyday exchanges quickly turned personal and nasty. Reproach, rebuke, reprimand was how things were done. Despite the fact that I 'felt' we were talking honestly with each other, the planned changes simply didn't happen. As a last resort (that's how I felt it at the time) we brought in an external consultant. To our amazement, during the sessions he conducted with managers and staff, we mainly looked back on where we had come from as an organization. This made painfully clear the extent various groups from earlier mergers were still influencing behavior. How employees had been walking around for years frustrated and misunderstood, with the feeling that their rich history had been squandered by a succession of interim managers. It turned out that resentment ran deep, and much came to the surface. Although I was shocked, too, by the sheer emotional charge, giving attention to this pain led to tangible relief. The change wouldn't have succeeded without these sessions".*

Leaders often feel trapped, held hostage in limbo between commands "from the top of the organization" and complaints "from the bottom". The pressure that leaders feel, trying to convince a board of directors that everything is under control, too often translates into attempts to convince employees of the same rather than getting them fully on board. This ignores how emotionally employees respond to change, and that they feel not taken seriously. Trapped between the hammer and the anvil, leaders find it difficult to let their own vulnerability show. Honestly expressing that they don't exactly know either, and also find it a difficult process, doesn't seem allowed. Faced with this illusion of control and mastery, as the tools for the social engineering of change processes, employees sometimes expect too much from leaders.[23] They do not have superhuman qualities and capacities; as people themselves, they, too, are not insensitive to the consequences of change.

> *In the run-up to a major reorganization in which a third of the employees had to leave the organization, the management team attended a preparatory two-day workshop on Shaping Transition. This included extensive consideration of leaders' emotions surrounding separation and loss. This immediately raised many essential questions. "Why is it necessary? What is the point of it? Surely the reorganization is no more than a business decision that we just have to put into effect?" The prevailing thought was to send the redundant employees to an appropriate (re)training course.[24]*
>
> *Leona explains. "However, by considering our experiences of loss, both personal and professional, we noticed how much we got from reflecting on seemingly simple and obvious questions such as 'What helped you through that profound change?' My previous experience of being laid off resurfaced. I was surprised at how much it affected me again. The personal stories of my colleagues also touched me. But what it gave us, especially as a team, was an awareness of what the employees were going through during an already uncertain period. And not only an awareness, but also an understanding of how this uncertainty manifested in their reactions. And, for the management, a new perspective on how to deal with these issues.*
>
> *Certain consequences of the changes were already noticeable in the organization, such as increased absenteeism and a bitterness that colored many meetings. We realized that we could not innocently hide behind the fact that the reorganization was a financial necessity. I'd done that before, used the 'it's essential for the future of the business' as a shield to hide behind. In my role as director I also had to take responsibility for the decision and acknowledge my culpability in it. Only by showing my emotions about how painful I had found the decisions I'd had to make, could I bond with the employees again. I was sure they weren't expecting that from me. It really was a result of the workshop, and we were all pretty amazed by how it worked. We truly experienced the positive effect of letting our own vulnerability show".*

Grief and transition

Grief is inescapable in the transition period from the moment of separation to the beginning of a different future. We say it earlier in the book: *a transition is not the same as a change*. A change is situational and discrete: you face a merger, your colleague retires, the production line is changed, your relationship founders, your partner gets a terminal diagnosis, the company goes into receivership. Transition is the emotional layer: it is what people go through when they let all the consequences of the new situation penetrate them wholly, feel what it means to them, and accept it all. Transition is change at the level of identity.

Loss means leaving the old behind. The way it was is gone and will never return. Your life is changing and it needs you to accept the loss, let it go and (preferably ritually) bring it to a close. This does not mean that nothing is left. You still have your memories; something or someone can still 'feel' present, but "life knows no way back".[25] However, the emerging future is not yet clear and, at best, just a vague shape on the horizon. You find yourself in a kind of no man's land – a desert for some – between the old and the new. You have to deal with uncertainty, as you can't know what is coming, and you have to deal with the realization that you cannot return to your old life. It's a lot to bear. You have to oscillate between *getting by through carrying on* and *getting whole by going through*.[26] Sometimes the new has something good in store for you, but you can't sense it in no man's land. Moreover, even if something good does come along – such as an interesting new colleague, a system improvement, a competent interim manager, brand new offices, new sales opportunities – you should still grieve what has been. In this phase, people are often simply surviving day to day. There is nothing wrong with that, often there is no other way. Avoidance, not daring to look at the loss, is also a normal part of this. What is important is whether there is movement; that you're not stuck. That avoiding the loss gradually transforms into integrating it into your life, so that what was is no longer separate from what is.

This movement can be imagined as a pendulum, swinging between engaging in loss and engaging in recovery. Sometimes you are able to choose where to put your attention, to focus consciously on the loss or consciously on the recovery. In time, however, you might also be tossed back and forth between an intrusive loss that suddenly demands attention and a life that keeps on going, making demands on you. At home the children have to eat, the laundry has to be done, the house tidied up and the garbage taken out. You are expected to be at work, deadlines must be met, products must be launched.

Grief requires you to relate proportionately to this duality. You move between the poles of loss and recovery, ensuring that both receive your attention.[27] Integration, then, is inexorably bringing these two extremes, bit by bit, closer together. The wounds you have suffered do not have to disappear; they become part of who you are. You don't let the pain guide you anymore. Instead of moving away from it, you lean in, no matter how difficult that may be. The loss is always present because the future contains the past. It remains a part of your personal life and your career.

Shaping transition: everyday life

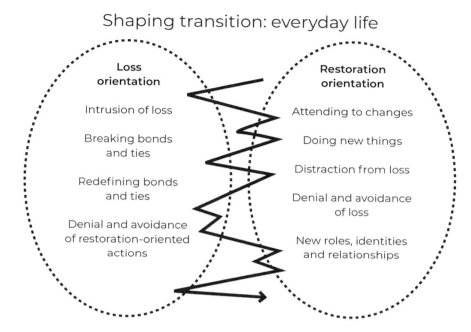

Figure 8.1 Shaping transition in everyday life, based on The Dual Process Model by Margareth Stroebe and Henk Schut, courtesy of SAGE Publications.

Avoiding painful feelings

It is human nature to try and avoid pain. By pretending it isn't there, by finding distraction, or even a 'cause' to focus on, we avoid what is inevitable: feeling our deepest pain. Avoidance is a survival strategy we use to keep putting one foot in front of the other. Even with seemingly small daily losses, we often use these strategies, especially when they touch on another and/or older loss.

The directors of a large insurance organization have put a lot of money and time into an energy-management program for the staff, to ensure greater effectiveness, perhaps more vitality and improved performance. This has borne fruit, except in one department. Here there is frequent absenteeism, a 'heavy' feeling in the office and around the people, and most of the staff have problems in their private lives. Angela, the department leader, concludes that the timing of the program for her department, must have been wrong. She sees that moving on cannot take place without first spending time on what is happening now. And that means attending to the personal losses of the staff. Angela engages in conversations with each of the team. A mountain of challenging situations comes to the surface: caring for aging parents; a child who is a smack addict; a sick partner; a struggling relationship and so on.

A plan is made to suspend the program for her department and focus on how to make her people feel welcome in the workplace with everything that is going on in their lives. And to support them to identify what support they need. A month or so later, you can feel the space this has given and how the prevailing energy in the department is now warm and positive.

Survival strategies

It is precisely in loss situations that you come up against your survival strategies and those of your employees. This is a chance to gain vital insights, because 'just' surviving prevents you from accessing your full potential. Survival strategies block your heart, your greatest source of energy, by preventing you from grieving what you have lost. The fear that you will not be able to bear the pain ensures that the door to the painful emotions remains locked.[28]

It's not that survival strategies are always bad. After a major loss situation, they protect you so that you can, more or less, continue to function and not collapse. We've all seen it, the employee who just lost his partner is back at work after a week; the team leader, diagnosed with a serious illness and sent home, continues to work from there; and the employee working out his notice diligently finishes her current project. In the Route Planner you read about the Transition Cycle and its themes of interpersonal relationships. When you address those themes, you are working to integrate the loss so that you can grieve in a healthy way. However, the pain can be unbearable and you begin to employ avoidance strategies: you no longer move toward the pain, but away from it. Thus, each theme has its shadow side, which we represent in the Cycle of Stalled Transition.

Isolating or retreating

Isolating is the shadow side of making contact. The withdrawal movement and no longer making contact are recognizable here. You avoid meeting colleagues in both the business and the social spheres: "I'm too busy." "It's not convenient." "I don't feel like it". "There's no time".

Detaching or clinging

You are there but at the same time you are not there. You avoid help or questions from others and solve everything on your own. Or you stop the other from letting go and cling excessively or in panic. You ask too many questions and too often seek the help of the other.

Avoiding bonding and intimacy

This shadow side is powered by fear of being hurt or disappointed. Or it arises because you never had an experience of intimacy in your family of origin or in previous relationships or groups. Also, intimacy can rub up against the pain of loss too much and so you avoid it.

Denying loss, not saying goodbye

Loss and separation can evoke fear of abandonment, loneliness and not being able to handle your emotions. You might also hold onto the illusion that it did not happen, or that it didn't mean all that much: "I was already prepared for it". "Our relationship was no big deal anyway". "This job didn't really suit me after all".

Not feeling, resisting

Because there is fear of the pain or because the emotions are too intense, you unconsciously suppress your feelings. It leads to emotional numbness. Resisting is a protective mechanism to keep pain out, because you do not yet have enough strength to grieve or you do not yet experience enough safety. In this way you keep others at a distance.

Meaninglessness, cynicism, lack of focus, calling out in the desert

Resentment and revenge are effective mechanisms for keeping grief out. You spend your energy getting 'justice', expressing anger, sulking. You can't accept what happened so you don't put time into recovery activities. You

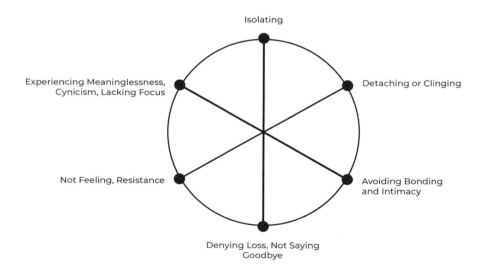

Figure 8.2 Cycle of stalled transition.

experience chaos, can no longer set goals, and are unable to 'make sense' of life anymore. Your past has become more important than your future.

When my then ten-year-old daughter was diagnosed with a life-threatening autoimmune disease, I still went to work. Some of my colleagues thought that was strange, others had tears in their eyes when they talked to me. That really frightened me. Was it that bad for my child? I was so in denial that work seemed like a safe place where the loss could not touch me. After all, wasn't everything the same there? I realized later that it was the same strategy I had employed when my father was dying. Like my brother and sisters, I often sat at his deathbed working on something. It had been instilled in us with a sense of humility. Hard work can keep grief at bay.

Riet

Survival mechanisms are, basically, varieties of avoidance: suppressing feelings with food, drink, sex, porn, gaming, internet shopping, medicines or narcotics. But also, more socially accepted ways such as hard work, intensive sport or caring for others. The latter ways are rarely seen as survival strategies and are usually encouraged. You also see ways such as perfectionism and control (usually combined), acting as if nothing is wrong, clowning around, diverting or downplaying attention from oneself. Every person has their own arsenal of approaches.

When Teun unexpectedly reappeared on the shop floor soon after a serious industrial accident, his colleagues were surprised. Didn't he need more time to recover? Teun waved them all away and picked up his work enthusiastically. He worked even harder than before, but avoided any conversation about the accident. He did not speak with his colleagues, his leader or the HR manager.

Miriam slowly returns to work after the loss of her husband. It is noticeable that she isn't really on top of things, whereas before she was a stickler for details. She doesn't look well and it seems she's not getting enough sleep. When a friendly colleague drops by, unexpectedly, on her day off, he finds she's a little bit drunk. This is how she deals with her feelings.

Xander is the life and soul of the department. He is always ready with a joke or a funny story. Things seem to be going well in his life, so everyone is surprised to hear that his relationship has ended and his wife has left with the children. Xander denies that it is serious, "I felt nothing for her for quite a long time anyway", "long live freedom" and more of the same. But everyone knows how much he loves his children and really cannot live without them. But as the department 'clown' he laughs away the pain.

The more pain that is hidden, the greater the survival mechanisms manifest; one mirrors the other, as it were. They jump in between the person and their pain like a bodyguard and so it stays bearable. In the beginning this is a blessing, but over time this way of surviving turns against you. It prevents you from truly bonding. By blocking not only the pain but also the joy in life, they make it impossible to live to your full potential. And they block grieving.

Survival strategies ensure that the loss does not become a coherent experience, and thus that integration is not possible. They don't work for free: they use up valuable energy which is needed for all the positive demands of life. You could liken grieving to a power station that produces lots of energy. You must be constantly alert to make sure no painful feelings 'escape'. When you can relax out of this constant alertness, much energy is released and recovered.

Because the loss and pain are not allowed to belong and are hidden, they lurk everywhere and can be triggered unintentionally at any moment. Leading to behaviors that those around you cannot link to the context of the moment. Even seemingly insignificant incidents can trigger memories of painful losses.

> *Marnix has not worked in the department for very long. He is motivated and talented; a young powerhouse. One day, an important client comes to discuss an ongoing project with the director. Marnix sees the man arrive and hand his coat and hat to the secretary. He is then upset for hours, cannot concentrate and feels tears welling-up behind his eyes. Only when his close colleague takes him aside and asks what is going on, does Marnix realize that his father, who died when Marnix was a teenager, had exactly the same hat. For a moment, the sadness was all there again.*

When you prefer to look away from the pain, you often lose connection with its origins, like Marnix had. Only when the right person, the right moment and the right way combine to bring you into contact with the pain, do you become aware of it. And the awareness sets free the grief or the other emotions that go with the particular memory. And that is precisely what is needed: to look directly at the place you'd rather avoid, so that you come out of isolation and regain access to your feelings.[29] There is, literally, more air and space, the fight-and-flight response recedes and rigidity is replaced by motion. If you do not share what is going on, keep on denying and hiding your pain, then a part of your life story stays hidden, frozen in time. As Edith Eva Eger describes, she could not find freedom by running away from her past, from her fear. She turned her fear into a cell and kept it locked by keeping silent.[30] Integration is not possible and there is not enough continuity, so that pieces of the life story are missing.[31]

When we engage wholeheartedly with grief, it can be integrated into the life story, creating new space for people (or objects, places or goals) to become secure bases (again). Your deep pain is both your Achilles heel and your greatest source of strength.[32]

Coping by fragmenting

Unexpected losses can be too big to comprehend (even when there was advance notice of the change, or the outcome of a fatal illness was already known), especially when they are experienced as too abrupt, too intense, too painful, too fearful or too lonely. In order to deal with such an experience, a standard human mechanism comes into play.

Fragmentation can feel like not being whole anymore, being broken into pieces, unable to pull it all/yourself together. In order to avoid feeling this – often intense – pain, you chop events into manageable pieces, into sizes that are easier to handle and less in your face so to speak, so you can continue your daily life, care for your family and go to work. The particularly painful pieces of the event then go behind lock and key.[33] Kind of like *put it in a cell, lock it, bolt it, forget everything and move on*. Inside you emerges a trinity: the painful events are exiled from daily life as much as possible, stored behind lock and key; there is a part that functions as a gatekeeper, that takes care of that exile (the survival strategies) and a mature, healthy part remains that uses your qualities and secure bases to deliver good work, to think clearly and reflect on your actions, and to be bonded with others.[34]

Healthy functioning

While an internal struggle is taking place to keep the painful feelings under lock and key, there is also the part in you that makes sure you continue to function healthily. The part that makes sure you get the kids to school on time, go to work, to the golf course, start the new project, maintain friendships, put dinner on the table, and take care of the practical matters related to the change process.

Healthy functioning often provides the foundation to bear the loss. From here you can think, feel, reflect and act. It forms a base for enduring the struggles in the other parts of the team and coming to realize that the initially helpful survival mechanisms are now counterproductive and hindering. Using secure bases, you are able to get past the gatekeepers of survival and give the closed-off painful feelings more and more space, allowing them to belong. When you regain access to these feelings, there is more space, more relaxation, you become softer without losing resolve. You start moving again. By locking the cell door, you give yourself time to recover and to build up the strength needed to look the monster in the eye. In the words of Edith Eva Eger: the key to change is in your pocket.

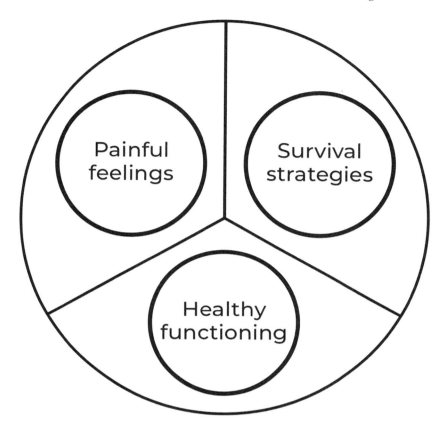

Figure 8.3 Fragmentation (caused) by loss.

Grief and resilience

You just saw how healthy functioning is the basis for dealing with adversity and loss in life. The foundations of resilience are laid in attachment, and that resilience is strengthened or weakened by grief. When painful feelings are cocooned and locked away, your life energy stagnates and you become increasingly stiff. Rigidity is the opposite of resilience. Stepping into your painful feelings, and then, sometimes, literally shaking the tension and fear out of your body, like a dog does when it has had a shock, keeps you from becoming rigid and keeping your body in some kind of traumatic state.[35] If you learn in life that painful experiences are part of the game, that you can ask for support from your secure bases, then you can develop a resilient nervous system. This offers you possibilities to deal with difficult situations and radical change. A helping perspective is the concept of the *window of stress tolerance*, which we'll look at in the following section.[36]

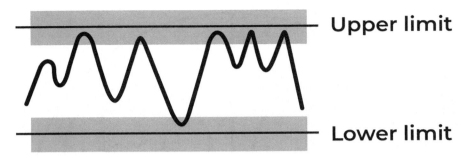

Figure 8.4 Window of stress tolerance: optimal stress level.

Optimal stress level

The brain is part of your central nervous system. Another part, the autonomic nervous system, governs action, energy, lust for life: when you have your foot on the gas pedal you use fuel and, like a car, your tank needs to be filled up regularly. You do that (recharging) by putting on the brakes, refueling; so that you can relax, rest, digest and recover from events.

Between the upper and lower limits is the window within which you can live and work optimally. In this window you have access to your thinking, feeling and reflecting and can take action. This is where the comfort zone is and where healthy functioning resides. There is a constant wave motion of charging and discharging. From activity to rest and vice versa, the way a spring can be stretched and springs back. At the gross level you see this in the rhythm of the day: you're active during the day and you rest at night.

However, this fluctuation is also necessary throughout the day itself. You can work harder – physically or mentally – when you take regular coffee breaks as moments of rest, perhaps a lunchtime walk or a power nap, then back to work refreshed. It is this healthy fluctuation that keeps you resilient. As a leader, you need to be seen taking a rest now and then, as this gives your employees 'permission' to do the same.

Stretching the envelope of stress

It can be exciting out at the edge, where you are challenged to go the extra mile, take a little more risk or make a significant change in your working methods. It is in the growth zones (the shaded areas around the upper and lower limits) that you need to get more out of yourself and to stay engaged. When you manage moderate, predictable stress, and have a positive experience (e.g., whatever you did was a success) this usually leads to a larger stress envelope and thus to greater resilience.

As a leader, you are dynamically working between these poles: you provide safety and trust (caring), so employees feel accepted, supported and

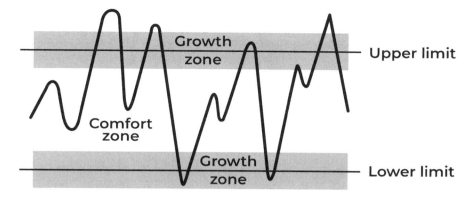

Figure 8.5 Window of stress tolerance: stretched stress level.

experience a comfort zone. And you invite your employees, from their safe space, to step out of their comfort zone and stretch their envelope, their window of growth. There is more stress in these growth zones, but it can be endured. As a secure base leader, when you dare, you challenge your colleagues to step up and take risks in the growth zones.

Employees learn from these experiences when they are back in the comfort zone and bonded to you as their leader. You learn when you can ask for just that little bit more and when you shouldn't ask too much. You see when there is enough daring, and so give the employee the space, if needed, to step back into the comfort zone for recovery and reflection. Caring like this, you prevent employees from becoming demotivated or suffering from burnout. In these movements of exploration, your employees grow their resilience.

Mindset determines the effect of stress

The way you **think** about stress appears to be important for how you **experience** stress – physically too. People who have gone through stressful life events tend to experience their lives as meaningful. Also people who say that they are experiencing high stress levels in that moment, also rate their lives as more meaningful. If you think positively about stress, perhaps by training your perceptions to that end, then you will have a positive mental and physical experience. A second crucial factor is the degree to which you feel **bonded** to secure bases and are focused on others. This involves both asking for help and being of service to others or to a larger goal.[37]

When employees are dealing with severe personal or professional challenges or loss experiences they sometimes cross the line behaviorally. Then secure bases are needed to calm the nervous system back down and return to the comfort zone. This could be a conversation with you as a leader, sitting in a park with a colleague, going home an hour earlier, help from a loss and grief coach or, temporarily, a less stressful assignment.

In the face of personal loss, work can provide structure, ground, bonding and meaning. If an employee can pick up his work again and rejoin the team, exactly as they are, with all they are feeling and all they cannot yet show, then that is a blessing. It can help to get in contact with the employee and ask what he needs to be as present as he can be. Would he like to talk about it with his colleagues or does the workplace offer precious distraction from feelings of loss? If the latter, it is important to agree that you may return to this once in a while, to see how he's doing. People's needs can change, and this can lead to loneliness if everyone is carefully avoiding the subject of the loss.

Marjan lost her daughter in a major disaster. She works at a large non-profit that has maintained contact with her from the beginning. Together with her HR manager they discuss what would be the best way for her to return to work. They also offer to pay for a coach to support Marjan in her grieving and guide the process of returning to work. No pressure is exerted, not by her leader and not by the board. Marjan gets all the assistance she wants. With the help of the coach Marjan slowly but surely picks up her work again. She feels comfortable among her colleagues, carried by their warmth and care. Sometimes, still, her work is (too) heavy but, more often than not, it is a welcome distraction.

Unhealthy levels of tension

In times of transition, and when employees are experiencing a crisis situation in their personal lives, fear and panic are common. The high and low limits are breached. This happens especially with major, unpredictable stress which is (almost always) experienced as negative.

Triggered by this stress and fear, the body produces adrenaline, breathing and heart rate increase and the gas pedal hits the floor. You see behavior such as prolonged overwork, hyperactivity, fight-and-flight reactions as hormones race through the body. It might show as intensive, excessive sport and obsessive pursuit of a hobby. The hormone, cortisol, ensures that you can keep this up for a long time. You are fully 'on' and can no longer find the off switch.

If you are 'on', due to sustained high stress levels, a point comes when your nervous system can't manage this anymore and you crash. Even when you are experiencing a situation as (life) threatening (when, in reality, it isn't), you're no longer able to function: you go out of touch, collapse, are emotionless, exhausted, numb or frozen.

Unhealthy stress

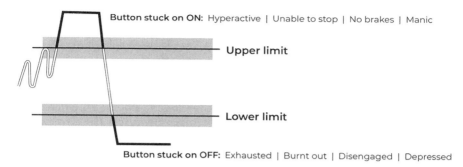

Figure 8.6 Window of stress tolerance: unhealthy stress level.

When the stress 'switch' is stuck – ON or OFF – and healthy alternation between tension and relaxation doesn't happen, your health suffers. Some employees work under constant pressure: because of a deadline, an assignment beyond their competence, fear they can't do certain work, or that they cannot keep up with their colleagues. They sit permanently above the top frame of the stress window, until they become so exhausted that they crash out of the bottom of the window into depression and/or burnout because they have no reserves left.[38] This also happens with persistent stress and anxiety in personal life. The consequences of sustained negative stress should not be underestimated, as it leads to increased deaths from heart attacks in particular.[39] And males are twice as likely as women to develop heart disease and live an average of seven years less than women – excluding death from war and famine. Many studies show that men bond substantially less than women, have more-unhealthy lifestyles, take greater risks and talk less about emotions and emotional challenges. And, strange as it may seem, although women are more prone to depression, men are much more likely to commit suicide.[40]

Mental health through integration

When loss experiences compromise people's mental health, grief – however difficult it might be – is the answer. And it involves integrating both the upper and lower brain, and the right and left brain to give the painful experiences and feelings a place, to make them belong again. And, finally, integrating your orientation to loss and restoration via the pendulum of alternately engaging with loss or recovery.

You read in Chapter 5 how the brain forms from the bottom up. The neocortex, the thinking part, only starts to participate around eighteen months of age. During puberty the upper brain undergoes significant expansion and it is only around the age of twenty-five that this development is more or less complete.[41] Most people would say, whether leader or 'follower' that at that age they are able to think well. This is true in principle, but at the same time, major change and drastic loss experiences can sometimes overwhelm this earlier integration. That's because when there is great stress, the reset switch is flipped and you suddenly find yourself back in 'factory-default' mode, as if life hasn't taught you anything yet.

> *Suddenly there is angry shouting and doors being slammed. When the department manager arrives to see what's going on, one of his employees is standing in the middle of the office, totally bemused. It seems one of his colleagues totally lost it when he, apparently, did not react appropriately or fast enough.*

According to psychiatrist Bessel van der Kolk, adults revert to 'Neanderthals' when overstressed.[42] The button of the thinking brain goes off and we react from our primitive lower brain like other mammals and reptiles. Sometimes, just a look or particular tone of voice is enough to trigger this. In the case above, the colleague is clearly not reacting from in the *here-and-now*, because nothing is actually going on; he is somewhere in the *then-and-there*. Perhaps back with his father who would look at him in the same way. Logic does not help here, but staying calm and composed does.

The body is your life's filing cabinet, and it is important that all the drawers, from top to bottom are accessible. Each part of the brain performs its own tasks and yet they are interconnected. The upper brain monitors the actions of the lower brain and regulates the strong reactions, impulses and emotions that arise there. But conversely, the lower brain is an important link between the body and the upper brain. Important decisions in the upper brain cannot be made without the input of emotions, needs and physical sensations. These function as a compass, guiding you.

In addition, the right hemisphere of your brain is focused on nonverbal communication, sensory perception, atmosphere and environment and regulates your emotions, so it plays an important role in social interaction.[43] When you are very young, words don't matter that much, but the way they are pronounced, tone, rhythm and sound is incredibly important, as are eye contact, smell and touch. The left hemisphere develops later. That's where things like language, facts and analytical skills are located. Both parts of the brain are important for your functioning. Experiences from the first years of life, when only the right hemisphere was available to you, are stored in your body, and make themselves heard when you are in situations that link back to those early years.

> *Gerda's boss is a competent woman, but Gerda doesn't feel comfortable with her. When in contact with her, Gerda gets an unpleasant gut feeling that can even manifest as real intestinal pain. She talks about this with her sister, who encourages her to continue. Gerda tells her that,*

*although her leader seems to be talking **to** her, it always feels as if she is looking **past** her, not making any real contact. Gerda says she remembers her mother doing this. She was there physically, but mentally she was mostly somewhere else. So she couldn't be a secure base for Gerda. They never spoke about it, but the experience of not being seen or heard is stored in every cell of Gerda's body and is being triggered into action by events in her workplace.*

Gerda is no longer a defenseless child with minimal options. After talking to her sister, she realizes that she needs to have a conversation with her leader to tell her what bothers her about their contact.

When the two hemispheres of the brain are not well integrated, specific problems occur. Experiences are 'felt' on one side only. If you are a predominantly left-brain leader, you hardly have any feeling for the emotional aspect and the personal experiences when in contact with someone. Your employees probably see you as competent, but also as cold, businesslike and distant. An unapproachable leader who has difficulty bonding. And, naturally, they will be less likely to speak out or turn to you with their questions and feedback. Predominantly right-brain leaders tend to be experienced as humane, warm, approachable, but insufficiently forceful, businesslike and goal-oriented. They often struggle to impose order, structure and logic.[44]

When stress is high, most people fall (temporarily) out of balance. A tsunami of stimuli originates from the right brain and overwhelms the processing capacity of the left brain. People with a secure attachment are better able to self-regulate, actively seeking out a secure base in order to stabilize their brain. People with attachment problems have much more difficulty doing this. As a leader, the levels of responsibility you carry can cause you to feel tremendous pressure. Securely attached leaders are better able to continue effectively, under stress, without losing bonds with others.

It is critical to understand that, at times when deep pain is touched in a person – whether in a personal or professional situation – only right brain to right brain communication works. We need to communicate as we would to a very young child, but in an adult way. It is about pitch, intonation, tone of voice, sound, silence, soft words, eye contact and touch. This is the only kind of contact that makes a person feel seen in their pain, comforted and safe enough to stay bonded and, in that bond, to find their way back to themselves.

Daniel Siegel is an expert in this field and at using simple language to articulate what happens in the brain.[45] His advice is to first calm the other down, sometimes by quietly listening to them, sometimes by holding them for a moment (if that's appropriate); in short, mainly by being completely present for them. That's right-brain communication. As a leader, you wait until the other person is calmer, and then engage your left brain by giving words to what is happening: "That customer contact didn't work out; so you might feel ashamed to face your colleagues. Does that sound right?" In Chapter 5, you can find Siegel's process for calming an employee; a step-by-step way for them to be able to use both hemispheres of the brain again.

Integration via the 'key'

According to Kohlrieser, Eger and Kets de Vries, grief can be a great source of strength. But you cannot use this strength if your grief is locked up in a cell. Keeping it locked up is the only way you can mask your pain. So the key is to integrate your grief by looking from your healthy functioning state for the key – that is always in your pocket – to slowly but surely open the cell door.

You give your survival strategies an honorable 'part-time discharge', so they no longer have to keep the cell door hermetically locked. They were once very helpful, when you were young and had no other options, or older and dealing with a major loss situation. But in the long run they become a hindrance. With the use of secure bases, you can make sure that you fall back on your survival strategies less often. And we say 'part-time' because they do not have to go forever; there will always be moments when you need them again. And within them are qualities, resources that will always be useful. Because, if the 'department clown' never made a joke again it would be boring; if the hard-working man didn't step up a gear every now and then when needed, that would be a shame. But certain qualities should remain in check in the event of a painful experience, to avoid turning them into pitfalls. But you still have to be able to protect yourself, that's always so.

> *Richard is in a relationship crisis at home. The once amiable employee no longer talks to his colleagues, takes lunch alone and avoids any contact that's not work-related. As a result, the others feel left out and the atmosphere in the department changes. The leader decides to have a chat with Richard. They agree that it can't continue like this. Richard decides to make it clear that he does not want to talk about his personal situation with everyone at work, but that he will share with certain people and he will make those choices himself. That it has been spoken about, and then spoken out, gives the department some breathing space: Richard is now frequently sharing lunch breaks with one or two close colleagues.*

The wall Richard put up to protect himself became an invisible boundary to others. They could see Richard but they could not reach him. Following the leader's intervention, people could talk again without being afraid that Richard would be hurt or that he would explode. According to Brené Brown, vulnerability still needs a boundary, some kind of protection. Because if you let everything come in unfiltered, the hurt can become so great that you develop more armor, becoming more and more unreachable.[46]

The gift of forgiving

Grief and forgiveness go hand in hand and yet are not natural friends. Forgiveness is one of the most difficult areas of leadership. As Gandhi stated, the weak can never forgive; forgiveness is an attribute of the strong. Forgiveness could be seen as the deepest step you can take as you dive fully into grief. An example that has captured the imagination of many is that of Nelson Mandela. After spending nearly three decades in captivity, his first words were of forgiveness and reconciliation. He had every right and reason to leave prison bitter, cynical, soured and without focus, but he chose a different path.

If you read Mandela's life story, you will see that what made forgiveness possible for him was found, among other things, in his ability to turn enemies into friends. For example, he bonded strongly with the guards on Robben Island. In addition, he maintained bonds with secure bases, including a poem by William Ernest Henley, *Invictus*, which gave him strength in difficult times.[47]

Forgiveness is the core leadership trait that is about daring to be great but not at the expense of others, being able to see past mistakes, again and again, without denying or ignoring them and continuing to challenge each other to achieve the maximum.

Anthony, in his mid-fifties, is head of facilities management at an academic institution. He has worked there for about twenty-five years and has made his way from the bottom up. He is participating in a leadership training course in which the works council, which he has been in for seven years, is also present. During the pre-training interview Anthony says that his work has become routine. He has concentration problems and often thinks about "the years until I retire". A day or so in, they are in a session about loss and leadership. Anthony shares about a violent incident, ten years ago. "That was, excepting my sister's death, the most terrible thing I have ever experienced. I was home for about three months. I received good counseling, but during that whole period I had no contact with my boss". Anthony turns red when he talks about it and his face is a mix of anger and tears. "I don't understand it. I felt abandoned, not seen. Something really closed up during that time". The trainer asks Anthony if this incident influenced his decision to join the works council. "Without question!" According to Anthony's colleagues on the council, he is constantly looking for confrontation which, in their opinion, makes productive consultations with the director very difficult. The trainer asks Anthony if he has discussed his painful story with the current director. Anthony says he thinks that would be pointless. At the invitation of the trainer, Anthony writes a letter to the former director about the incident. He asks a good friend to help him compose the letter. He also begins a dialogue with the current director.

After three months, it's time for the second module of the training. Anthony tells the group how intensely emotional writing the letter was, and especially sharing with the friend. "I didn't know it could be so deeply hidden away. I feel liberated. I also wrote in the letter that I am not yet able to forgive completely, but that I want to walk in that direction. That man moved on a long time ago. He has no idea about the impact he had on me and it's me holding myself hostage with this". The conversation with the current director had been enlightening, he says. More than a few pennies dropped for Anthony. "We were also able to share a laugh about it together". His colleagues in the works council, and in his own team, experience Anthony as being much more relaxed and approachable.

Forgiveness begins with an active decision of will. You no longer will allow yourself to be held hostage. As Nelson Mandela says in the movie *Invictus*, forgiveness liberates the soul; it removes fear and that makes it such a powerful weapon.[48] But just making the decision does not establish forgiveness, for it is not an action, but a process.[49] It goes step by step, bit by bit. It is practicing, over and over again. Coming back to a piece again and again, encouraged by your secure bases. It cannot be forced, it is a practice of free will.

The biggest misconception about forgiveness is that you do it for another person. Forgiveness is something you do for yourself; the other person need never know. Forgiving, by acknowledging the hurt and injury, is finally letting go of the hope that you can make the past better than it is. Not forgiving, bearing a grudge endlessly, is like drinking from the poisoned chalice yourself and expecting the other person to die. Forgiveness, then, is the final step from victim of the situation to freedom from it. It is also very good for your brain. People who develop forgiveness have greater control over their emotions, are significantly less angry and hurt and much healthier. Forgiveness changes the brain positively.[50]

Although forgiveness is a singular process, conducted internally and alone, it can pave the way for restoration of a relationship. Forgiveness recognizes that what happened is not forgotten, but stops the pain and anger around the event from poisoning the bond.[51] Forgiveness is a gift to yourself, as Edith Eva Eger puts it.

Sometimes the move towards forgiveness occurs in a tension-filled relationship, where you feel a need for justice and retribution. Grieving a loss can become complicated when you feel that someone else is, in some way, guilty of causing your loss. The call for justice for the victim becomes an obstacle to working through the grief and hinders much-needed meaning making[52] Forgiveness is a deliberate choice, the Dalai Lama states in conversation with Desmond Tutu. They feel sometimes people misunderstand and think forgiveness means you accept or approve of wrongdoing, but that is not the case they argue. There is an important distinction to be made: between the actor and the action, between the person and what he has done.[53]

Without forgiveness, full integration just cannot happen. In a way, grief stagnates and solidifies, creating rigidity when what is needed is movement.

Bear in mind that the word emotion literally means *an outward movement.* Rigidity blocks creativity and inspiration, which irrevocably affects how you as a leader find inspiration and, in turn, inspire others. Forgiveness, then, is the step of breaking free from being held hostage by the past, by a situation, by another.

By forgiving, you avoid *unfinished business.* This term was introduced by the famous American-Swiss psychiatrist Elisabeth Kübler-Ross, a pioneer in the field of living, dying and grieving. It means that there is unfinished business lying around, somewhere, simmering, often unconsciously. Some of those examples we have already looked at in this book. That you still have something incomplete with one of your parents. That you still have to face your guilt. That you still have to discuss with your boss the hurt he caused you.

Feeling some space again

When you have truly grasped your loss and looked grief in the eye, you tend to experience some form of relief. It is as if a heavy stone has been lifted off your back. Many people know the exact moment that such a change occurred. Frans Rasker, a film and television producer, lost his wife and was left with two young children. He remembers the exact moment of a change in the way he grieved. Flying back to the Netherlands after a stay in Spain, he flew over Paris, France, and could see the city clearly in the late evening sky. The incredible beauty of the city struck him and a thought came: we're going to move! Six months later he moved there, and it was like a burden fell off his shoulders. Finally he felt he could move on.[54]

Because humans are intrinsically social, and spiritual, beings, once enough time has passed, space emerges for new bonds. You have less of a tendency to defend yourself and you focus more on the positive. You look more to the outside than the inside. There is room to work with and from a vision, to set new goals for yourself and the organization, to gather new courage and to reconnect with the ability to inspire others.

Your heart is open again for the next, and very important, step: creating meaning in a world of change and, from your calling, leading that change. Your journey as a hero continues. Your world is no different than that of others, but you choose to respond differently to that world. So you cross the bridge, stepping firmly towards your calling.

Important insights to take away

- Grief also affects thoughts, physical sensations and behavior. You can grieve the loss of tangible and intangible things, with which you have a meaningful relationship, alongside grieving the loss of people from your life.
- How you grieve reflects your attachment style. A secure attachment allows you to reach out for support and help with grieving. A safe social

environment helps regulate emotions and mitigate stress. Giving shape to grief is an act of leadership, grieving becomes the turning point in your transition where you choose no longer to be held hostage by the past.

- To grieve you need other people.
- Resistance to change is a misnomer for how people behave when they are suffering the pain of separation that is inherent in change.
- You can think of grieving as a pendulum swinging between dealing with loss and dealing with restoration. Both sides require attention and you have to attend to this duality.
  Integrating the loss into your life story, bringing loss and restoration closer together, requires integration at the brain level. When you are not really aware of the pain of loss, you run the risk of inner fragmentation, where survival behaviors increasingly prevent you from feeling joy. For optimal performance, it is important to stay within the window of stress tolerance.
- Forgiveness is a step towards freeing yourself from being taken hostage. As we've seen, you don't need to tell the 'other', but it can help to share this step with secure bases.

Questions for self-reflection

1. How do you grieve a loss? How might those around you notice you're grieving?
2. Which events in your lifeline have you grieved? How does that affect your leadership?
3. Which events on your lifeline do you not really care about grieving? How does that affect your leadership?
4. How do you balance the duality pendulum as it swings between paying attention to the loss and focusing on restoration?
5. What aspects of grief – emotional, physical, cognitive and spiritual – get lots of attention or very little attention from you?
6. What is the most important thing you have learned about yourself from intense losses in your life?
7. What 'old grief' do you encounter in your organization or team? How does it manifest?
8. Which survival mechanisms do you find yourself going to first?
9. How do you organize support for your grief?
10. How do you organize support for grief in your team or organization?
11. What situations make you stretch the window of stress tolerance?
12. What helps you stay within the window of stress tolerance?
13. How do you support others in their grief? How might they notice?
14. How does grief play a role in your current family (and your family of origin)? How does that affect the bonds in your family (of origin)? And between you and your partner?
15. What is the most painful thing that ever happened at your (previous) job? How did it affect you?

16. What is the most painful thing that ever happened between you and your (ex) partner? How did (and does) that affect you?
17. Who have you been able to forgive in your life? What did you have to put in place for that? What or who helped you do that?
18. From whom have you been able to ask forgiveness in your life? How did you manage to do that? What or who helped you?
19. Who would you like to forgive? And from whom would you like to ask forgiveness? How might that help you in your leadership?

Questions for you to ask of the people around you – your person effect

1. Would you tell me how you do it: how you grieve?
2. What is most painful for you/all of you in this situation? What do you/you all, need from me?
3. Do you/you all feel that I respond empathetically to the pain and discomfort of others? If so, how do you notice that? How are you affected by seeing me like that? If you feel I don't respond empathetically, how does that affect you?
4. What do you need from me when you are overwhelmed or paralyzed?
5. How are you integrating this loss into your life?
6. What do you see me doing to pay the right balance of attention to loss and restoration? How would you evaluate the relationship between the two right now?
7. What in my behavior shows that I am grieving a loss or a failure?
8. Do we, as a team, pay sincere and sufficient attention to what is going wrong and what hurts? Do we try to learn as much as possible from these losses and failures?
9. What is the most painful thing that has ever happened between you and me? What impact did that have on you?
10. Are you good at forgiving? Why (or why not)?
11. In your opinion, am I able to forgive? Have you seen me forgive? And what stood out for you about that?
12. What could/should I forgive you for? Why is that important to you?
13. What could you forgive me for? What would that mean for you? And for me – in your opinion?

9 The Key to Real Change is in Your Pocket
Meaning and Calling

About meaning and calling

Derek has worked at the bank for many years and he has enjoyed dedicating himself to the organization. His career path has been steep and he received a nice promotion during the recent reorganization. In his current position, however, he hasn't been able to get any traction and this is clearly evident in his department's results. After six months, his manager calls Derek and tells him he has no confidence in his ability to do the job. He intends to let him go and wants to discuss how best to share out his workload.

"I was shocked. My job was everything for me. It was so unexpected. It made me think. How could I not have seen this coming? Why isn't this role working out for me?" He realizes that through the (many) reorganizations he lost sight of his career path and has drifted away from the core of who he is. Each reorganization brought opportunities, took him a step higher, but it also meant that it was no longer him that was thinking about what he wanted. Where had his passion gone? He was shocked by this discovery. "How did I get here? Where, when did I stop leading my own life? And what does that mean for where I am now and for the direction my life is taking?" As he asks himself these questions, he realizes that the arrival of his son also shifted his attention somewhat. He realizes that his career has become less important. That his original career ambitions no longer give him satisfaction. He decides to take a sabbatical to explore his feelings: "Who am I? What do I want to do in this life? What is really important to me?"

Derek is stopped in his tracks by the news that he will be fired. A drastic event that acts as his wake-up call. Confronted by his life and with the fact that everything is finite, Derek decides to investigate. His journey of discovery leads him, among other things, back along past experiences. In contact with secure bases, under the guidance of a coach, he examines the meaning of these events in the light of what is happening now. What signals has he

DOI: 10.4324/9781003409922-9

missed? Who is he really, and what does he want to contribute to the world? What is it that is calling him? These questions of meaning and calling are the subject of this final chapter.

Meaning

No event in your life makes sense or has meaning in or of itself. This is true of both positive and negative experiences. Sense-making is the act of assigning meaning to the experiences that life brings you.[1] You could say that it is a calibration and appraisal of events all along the lifeline: past, present, future. The process is both active – you do something for it, go in search of it, get moving and inactive – it takes place, it 'happens to you', it arises in time and space. Meaning is a complex happening involving head, heart and hands. Viktor Frankl calls the search for meaning and values the primary motivating force of human beings.[2]

Meaning requires examining and weighing-up events, assigning value to them and answering the question of what they mean for the path of your life. How have those events shaped you? How do they influence the way in which you experience yourself and the world around you? How do you let the various events in your life inform and guide you and your choices? Meaning is then also a process of learning and development.

The dance between meaning and learning is a key pillar in the development from perfectionism to excellence.[3] The perfectionist will not experience true joy or live the full potential of their calling because 'never enough' and 'never good enough' get in the way.[4] The perfectionist is looking for approval. He is repeating old patterns where he did not get any approval from those with whom he had meaningful relationships, or from those with whom he longed to have a meaningful relationship. Perfectionism is, as it were, a persisting conversation in the inner theater of the leader where self-criticism always has the last word.[5] It is the quicksand that can sabotage calling, the perfectly hidden depression and burnout.[6] Perfectionists cannot yet be a secure base for themselves, because they have not yet learned to bond sufficiently, while in their vulnerability, to external secure bases.[7]

Leadership begins with leading your self. There, in the face of uncomfortable, fearful, shameful, or painful experiences – where unmet needs seem to be calling the shots – you explore what you feel when you focus on the question: *What can I discover here? What can I learn? What can I improve?*[8] Thus, the lifeline becomes more and more a journey of meaningful experiences. Peter Senge calls this the personal mastery of the leader. The leader knows how to influence himself, and so knows how to lead and enable a learning organization.[9] Meaningfulness is thus linked to focusing the mind's eye on what can be discovered and learned: excellence.

Changes you experience can lead to a feeling of being broken, shattered into pieces. In the transition process, you pick up the shards and start gluing until a new image emerges, a different, meaningful image, that includes the brokenness and the pieces you cannot find. We can call this Kintsugi (or Kintsukuroi) which means "golden connection" or "golden repair".

Kintsugi is a Japanese art in which broken ceramics are repaired using gold or silver paint. According to the Japanese tradition, the objects become more beautiful than they were before. Often, from the new wholeness, that includes and celebrates the old, something emerges that is valued and makes life fuller and richer. In the new bowl, the shape of the old remains deliberately visible.

Losses occur in your personal life, but also in your working life. Suffering is an unavoidable part of being human and, therefore, cannot be avoided in the organizational context. However, when efficiency, efficacy and results demand so much energy and attention and exist alongside the equally human anxiety around disappointment, loss and existential stress, work does seem to be a place where suffering is less readily recognized or accepted. From the perspective of meaning, however, 'organizational' suffering offers as great an opportunity for personal and spiritual growth as personal suffering.[10]

Meaningfulness is coupled to your ability to see and experience beauty. The following excerpt from Eger's book, *The Choice*, demonstrates this powerfully. To see the beauty, while deep in the pain, takes practice, especially when that which is dear to you, that which gave you joy, is taken away from you. Loss tests your ability to see beauty by challenging you to dive down into the deepest layers of your authenticity and identity. To discover what is at your core. Who are you in the soul of your being when important relationships are broken and you are facing loss? What were you holding on to – perhaps wrongly or against your better judgment?

Edith Eger and her sister Martha lost their parents on the first day of arrival at Auschwitz. After being shaved bald, the two sisters emerge from the showers. Martha asks Edith to tell her truthfully what she looks like. Edith thinks her sister looks like a mangy dog, a naked stranger, but she cannot bring herself to say this to her. She decides to try and find a truth that doesn't hurt. When she stares into the proud blue eyes of her sister, she realizes that, even for her pretty sister, asking "How do I look?" is extremely brave. In an environment without mirrors her sister asks Edith to help her find and see herself. So Edith tells her the only truth she can say and tells her how beautiful her eyes are and how well they can be seen now, no longer covered by all that hair. For Edith it is the first time she experiences that people have a choice: pay attention to what you have lost, or pay attention to what you still have.[11]

American psychologist and philosopher Emily Esfahani Smith distinguishes four pillars of meaning:[12]

1. The feeling of being bonded.
2. Living with a purpose.
3. Sharing your life story with others.
4. Experiencing transcendence.

The feeling of being bonded

First, it is important for everyone to feel that they belong somewhere, to be able to relax into a comfort zone. The desire for bonding is one of the reasons people form relationships. Ultimately, bonding is the reason you are here, it gives meaning and purpose to your life, says Brené Brown.[13] The feeling of being part of something also contributes to finding a sense of meaning in life. By the way, it is not only about long-term relationships, but also about any *quality interaction* such as meeting a stranger on the plane with whom you suddenly have a deep conversation, before going your separate ways.

In his famous speech in *Any Given Sunday*, Tony d'Amato (played by Al Pacino) gives his players the choice to *either heal, now, as a team, or to die, as individuals.*

The brain is programmed to bond with other brains: *Neurons that fire together, wire together.*[14] In and through interaction with the group, meaning arises and healing takes place. This applies as much to an individual going through radical change as it does a team or group as a whole. Regularly feeling you are part of a greater whole is the most effective way to combat loneliness. Not only is loneliness one of the biggest causes of mental and physical ill-health, it is one of the main causes of death.[15]

During the coronavirus crisis, it became clear how important it is to feel bonded to others. Despite all the limitations of masks and distancing, people still want to meet each other face to face, speak to each other and look each other in the eye. Video calling proved to be an important tool to experience the feeling of being bonded to each other.

Living with a purpose

Second, Esfahani Smith mentions living with a purpose. Everybody talks about *purpose*, but not everyone means the same thing. Esfahani Smith, just like Victor Strecher[16], speaks of *purpose* as what you want to do in the world, the goals you pursue in your life. You could say that purpose is about a destination, the bullseye on the big dartboard of your life that you aim your 'darts' at.[17] Purpose gives focus. Viktor Frankl who, like Edith Eger, survived the Nazi concentration camps, discovered the power of focus and the pursuit of (larger) goals in finding meaning.[18]

In the camps, Frankl had noticed that it was not the physically strongest people who survived. He observed that the difference between wanting to stay alive and giving up came from having a goal and being able to keep believing in it. For some prisoners, this made life meaningful, in the midst of the daily atrocities, and gave them the 'strength' to endure. People without a purpose or unable to sustain their belief in one, died "before their time". They had given up. The question was no longer about the meaning of life, it was about how each person related to the trials and tribulations that life brought every day. This made the question of meaning very concrete. When life brings suffering your way, you give up or you deal with it. Suffering, per se, is not meaningful but, in recognizing suffering as a personal task, a responsibility that no one can absolve you of, or do for you, lies your opportunity and your choice. For Frankl himself, this became his life's work, documented in a manuscript he was working on that got lost in the camp. Following his release, he set himself the goal of writing that (lost) book, about what he came to call *logotherapy*. That was reason enough to want to stay alive. Edith Eva Eger would meet Frankl later in life. She attributes her own healing to his teachings and shares her own experiences and lessons in turn with the world. In her words, she made Auschwitz her classroom.[19]

It is not only big and noble goals that enable you to bear suffering, find meaning in it and make choices. Goals can be very 'everyday', such as being a good father or contributing to social cohesion in your neighborhood. Purpose is a guide that motivates you and acts as an organizing principle in your life. Living with goals in mind will lead you to make a difference and contribute to something larger than 'just' you. It enables you to experience an increase in existential meaning, leading to greater resilience and motivation.

After a profound loss, people often lose their sense of purpose and with that the meaning in their lives. They are faced with finding the meaning of life again, of taking it in anew, as it were. By finding 'new' meaning, the story of their lives takes on a different color. The narrative of their life has changed, for themselves and others. The third pillar mentioned by Esfahani is about sharing your story and finding meaning in telling it (over and over again).

An example is Azim Khamisa (see box). Azim's son Tariq was murdered. Azim was naturally stricken by deep grief. But he also quickly had the understanding that there were "victims" at both ends of the gun.

Forgiving the murderer of your son

Azim Khamisa, a Sufi Muslim and banker, finds a business card on his doormat one morning, from the San Diego Criminal Investigation Department, with these words on it: *We are trying to reach Tariq Khamisa's family.* His twenty-year-old son Tariq was murdered by Tony, a fourteen-year-old gang member, while delivering a pizza. Intense grief followed. Azim chooses a courageous path. Encouraged by two secure bases – his spiritual leader and the Quran – he resolves not to lose himself in grief. He decides to forgive Tony and, together with Ples Felix, Tony's grandfather and foster father, establishes a foundation in honor of his son. The Tariq Khamisa Foundation is dedicated to showing and teaching young people the power of forgiveness, and continues to help to stop children killing children. In November 1995, the two men came together to share their story with the world. Through school visits and online videos they have encouraged millions of young people to choose a peaceful life of nonviolence and forgiveness.

It was during the period of grief that Azim realized that his path to liberation had led him to forgiving Tony. Forgiveness is not an easy process though. It requires going through and beyond anger to embrace it. The more you hold back anger, the more attention it demands. Forgiveness also invites you to look at and feel how **you** have hurt people in life. I find that, as the years go by, forgiveness becomes easier, but needs constant practice.

Azim developed a deep friendship with Tony; not only did he petition for him to be released early, he also offered him a job with the Tariq Khamisa Foundation.

Still, Azim would like his son to walk through the door, he says. But he also wants to be honest and say that it is through Tariq's death that he has found his calling and is truly alive. And he would never want to miss that either.[20]

Sharing your life story with others

The impulse to make a story out of the events in your life comes from a deep-seated need in humans: the need to make sense of the world. And that means getting to know that world better and better. Or getting to know it again and again, in the aftermath of radical change. You want to create order in the chaos, you are constantly busy trying to imbue bits of information with meaning. Otherwise, you wouldn't be able to function. Stories help you give meaning to the world and see your place in it, to understand why things happen as they do. There is a pattern in the way people, who experience their lives as meaningful, interpret and describe their experiences. They tell stories of catharsis or stories in which there is a sudden transition from a negative to a positive situation or perspective. They talk about suffering being overcome. The hero makes a journey. There is a pivot in their life story, where a positive event springs from a negative one and gives their suffering a degree of meaning. Loss becomes a source of inspiration. The opposite of this is what Esfahani Smith calls a "depressing story". This is when people can only see their lives, or events in their lives, as going from bad to worse.

And so there are multiple kinds of stories: stories of action, transformation, loneliness, love and so on. The narrative you tell about your life reveals how you understand yourself and how you interpret the way your life is unfolding. Telling these stories is telling the meaning of life. They are the thread of existence. And in the face of brokenness and fragmentation, this is of extraordinary importance, because in telling you can find healing.

Experiencing transcendence

The experience of being part of something greater, something that transcends you, is an experience that touches a longing in the deepest part of human nature. It is the feeling of the light touch of the mystery, a sense of spirituality, whether that is a religious experience, looking up at a starry night sky, standing in front of a magnificent work of art, or watching your child playing with a friend. In such moments you can experience something of the power of transcendence, which literally means *going beyond*.

In a transcendent experience, you have the feeling that you are rising above everyday reality, experiencing a higher reality, becoming part of something bigger than yourself. Because Azim decided not to be overcome by hate after his son's death, he was able to forgive Tony and set up a foundation, and to become a significant voice in the larger movement against armed violence.

Work, in part because of its central place in adult life and how much of most lives it occupies, is an ideal place for people to experience meaning. This opportunity exists in the work itself (the tasks and activities performed), the meaning of the work (the impact on others), the meaning of the workplace (the relationships), the leadership, and the meaning for society as a whole.[21]

Esfahani Smith's four pillars of meaning show the importance of meaning in life and the value of searching for it along your lifeline. Meaningfulness opens the gateway to further growth. By allowing ourselves to grieve our sorrows, wounds and disappointments, Edith Eger says, we can find freedom in accepting what has happened. And freedom means gathering the courage to break down our prison, brick by brick.[22]

Let's talk about your calling

On your path from origin to final destination, as a leader you encounter your *calling*.[23] Using the word calling is already an act of bravery.[24] Because calling evokes something of the tension between autonomy and surrender. It is, perhaps, the invitation that life makes to you, and so is of vital importance. Calling is the question of who you are at the deepest level of your identity.[25] It is not easy to identify, know, be certain of your calling. In fact, most people confuse the question of their *calling* with what they *do* in life, with a role they play (leader), or a skill they practice (accountant). Try this. Ask someone in your neighborhood to say what is their calling and you will hear, in the vast majority of cases, something about an activity, a role or a purpose. Being a good father, climbing mountains, giving refugees a new home, seeing your family have fun and be healthy, being a teacher, making your organization successful, going on that world tour, making the world safe and just, increasing respect for nature and sustainability, bringing people to God. These 'answers' provide, possibly crucial, information about their roles, about a mission to which they have committed, about their purpose . . . but they say nothing about their calling.

But what then is your calling? We see it this way; your calling always has two parts: *Who am I? and What am I setting in motion in the world?*

The first question is linked to your identity. Who you are is determined by all the experiences and events on your lifeline – experiences of loss, success, events from your youth back to infancy. And even long before you were born, in the experiences of the previous generations that live on in you, how you have given meaning to them and by the patterns of your life that have been shaped by them. Your identity develops in contact with the world around you, through the roles you play and on the basis of the unique talents you have. This determines your *being energy*.

The second question is linked to the impact you want to have and are having on the world around you, what you want to set in motion, through the goals you are pursuing (your purpose). This determines your *doing energy*. Your *being and doing energies together form your calling* and enable you to live your full potential in service of yourself and others.

> *During his sabbatical, through intensive sessions under the guidance of a coach, Derek discovered the meaning of various, recent and earlier, events in his life. By going back to early, sometimes traumatic child-hood events, by dwelling on different experiences of loss, success and failure, he came to understand that he had developed patterns that made him successful in his role as an executive at the bank. At the moment he was told that he was no longer trusted, he had to face the fact that what had made him successful up to that point – the trust of others – was no longer present. The trust and challenge he had felt from his bosses in previous positions meant that he had been able to bring about impactful change in his teams. He realized how he had ended up in a role where his supervisor, employees, and the financial team were waiting for him. They expected Derek to take the initiative and now, this paralyzed him.*
>
> *This discovery brings him back to his father, from whom he learned to be a team player; "together you achieve more than alone". And how, together, they were always improving things. From upgrading the lawn mower to optimizing the morning bread-making process. And every time they succeeded, they set themselves a new goal. He realizes that his calling is to be a creative innovator, bringing beauty and progress to the world through trust and challenge. Not too long after, Derek accepts two new positions. He becomes manager of the finance department, at a home-care organization with a big change agenda, and he becomes coach of his son's soccer team.*

Once you have found your calling, the challenge is to live it in the roles you already have in life. A calling found and lived translates into several different roles:

- personal
- organizational
- social
- professional.[26]

Derek (from the case study) lives his calling in his role as a father and partner (personal), as a manager (organizational), supervisor of the soccer team (social) and as a financial expert (professional). Overidentification with one role means less focus on the others. This imbalance irrevocably leads to 'hassle' in the form of, for example, (continuous) struggle in and between the various roles and employees, or teams and departments that are underperforming. In addition, an internal imbalance (in the leader/Derek) in and between the different roles can lead to physical/mental illness, burnout, relationship problems, loneliness and not being able to experience success or joy.[27]

The window of leadership and calling shows, among other things, the interaction between roles and calling. For some people, their calling is fairly clear from an early age, though they might not know how to articulate it right away. There is a connection between growing up with many (strong

Figure 9.1 The window of leadership and calling.

relationships with) secure bases and knowing your calling, consciously or unconsciously. For others, finding one's unique calling is a great search, and challenge.

Your calling has been with you all your life, though its form or fulfillment may vary over time. If you haven't found your calling yet, your roles can also provide clues, signs and give words to it. Living and leading from your calling requires focusing your mind's eye, making positive choices, excelling. Living and leading from a calling provides clarity, focus and the confidence to act. However, it is not always the easy path. Living your calling is not without consequences, it requires you to make choices and sacrifices in all the roles you have.

In the context of organizations, this means leaders must be aware of their calling and lead their employees from there. It makes the difference between transactional leadership (getting things done) and transformational leadership (bringing out the best in people). Transformational leaders work – even if they may not yet put it quite so literally – from a deeper place, from their calling.

People who can express their calling in their work score higher on their commitment to and meaning of their work, in addition to higher scores on general satisfaction with their lives. Here it is important to note that having a calling is not enough. It is about actually being able to live your calling. Having, or being aware of, a calling without being able to give it form has a more detrimental effect on people's wellbeing than not having or knowing your calling.[28]

The relationship between meaning and calling

It's remarkable: the residents of the Japanese island of Okinawa are, on average, among the oldest on earth. Okinawa has the most centenarians per 100,000 inhabitants in the world. Francesc Miralles and Héctor García investigated why. And soon in their research they came across the Japanese word *ikigai,* which can be freely translated as "the happiness of always being busy". According to the Japanese, everyone has their ikigai, their raison d'être. For the Japanese, it is the reason why they get up in the morning. Living in a community and having a clear ikigai turn out to be the key elements for a life in which one keeps busy and feels no wish to retire.[29]

As you have seen, giving meaning to experiences on your life's journey requires that you relate these experiences to your calling. Because your calling is always with you, the question is whether you are aware of it, so that you can also use it consciously when you have choices to make. When you are in a flow,[30] experiencing the joy of play, transcending time and space, everything seeming to happen by itself, feeling completely you, this is a powerful sign that you are living and leading from your calling. When you know how to give words to your calling, you are already a step ahead. However, your calling is much more and much bigger than those words. They act as a key, unlocking the door into the space from which you can start living this calling. Your calling is unique because you are the only one who can do it your way. No one else can do it for you or in your place.

> *As the marketing manager for a major electronics company, Jeremy was the numbers man. No detail escaped him. He was guided strictly by the data he meticulously collected and with his analytical approach he was usually ahead of the curve. He lived for his work and left the housework, family care and social contacts to his wife. What he did not see coming was that his wife was leaving him for someone who would give her some attention. What followed was an acrimonious divorce over the division of the estate, because Jeremy knew no other way than a strictly numerical approach and was unable to allow any emotional bonds. His wife recognized this and it was precisely at this stage that she became desperate. The struggle also alienated him from his two daughters. To his own surprise, the divorce also affected his work. He began to overlook things, make simple errors. The data that had always made sense to him became steadily incomprehensible.*
>
> *For the first time in his life Jeremy worked with a coach, and being questioned about his calling struck him deeply. He had never looked at himself that way. In the chaos that he was experiencing in his life at that moment, he understood instinctively that he indeed needed something to hold on to other than numbers and data. With the coach, he reflected on his personal values as the basis of his calling. 'Caring' scored high on his list. For the first time he saw the imbalance between his serious approach to his work and the lack of attention for his social environment. Although dwelling on his own emotional life and that of others caused him discomfort, Jeremy took on the responsibility of fulfilling his personal roles – based on his calling – in addition to his professional and organizational roles.*

You know when you are following your calling, because then you know how to give meaning to the challenges that come on your life path. If you have learned to separate what belongs to your wounds from what belongs to the fruit of those wounds. Your calling works for you in all aspects of your life, personal and business: in relationships, hobbies, sports and work. It ensures you don't fall into *impostor syndrome*,[31] the constant, undermining fear that others will find out that you neither know nor can do anything. Finally, your calling ensures that the fire of your curiosity is rekindled. At the foundation of your calling lie your personal values. Living and leading from your calling promotes a life of satisfaction, because it enables you to interpret those values to the max.

Bonding with others is an essential part of being able to give real form to your calling. It becomes more difficult if you experience yourself as a voice in the wilderness, or feel that others see you that way. Sometimes it can take a while for you to realize you really are a voice in the wilderness. But if you notice that despite your best intentions, your message or behavior is having no effect, it is time for self-reflection. Your (if it's your business) website or your organization's might say "It is my mission to . . ." beautifully, inspiringly and elegantly. But, if you don't succeed in living this mission in the world, you can become just another lone, unheeded voice, and run the risk of starting to behave like a modern-day Don Quixote. However noble the cause, and however principled your ideals, when your belief that you are right is greater than your connection with the world around you, then you have lost touch with reality. The cause might not lie in the nature of your calling. More likely, you are out there shouting in the wilderness because you have lost connection with your surroundings and are confusing having a mission with having a calling.

Don Quixote is the archetype of the foolish hero. Enthused by reading chivalric stories he believes he is a knight-errant (a medieval term for *wandering*). His 'tilting at windmills', which he sees as giants, has become a proverb for fighting imaginary danger, for trying to change what cannot be changed.[32] Completely in his own imagined reality, Don Quixote travels through Spain on his horse Rocinant, an old peasant's workhorse. He is accompanied by Sancho Panza, a farmworker who knows for sure that his master has lost his 'way'. Sancho Panza, however, keeps this opinion to himself. He prefers to think of his master as "the tragic knight" in the hope of the reward his master has promised. Don Quixote fights against all forms of (what he believes to be) injustice and wrongdoing. He hopes to achieve fame through his good deeds and thus win over his unattainable love, the princess Dulcinea. Like his knighthood, however, the princess is a product of his confused mind. In reality, she is a peasant's daughter from the neighboring village. Don Quixote not only mistakes windmills for giants, but also inns for castles, clergymen for villains and a flock of sheep for an army.

To truly live your calling, like setting out to Ithaka, is taking the long road, full of adventure, full of discovery. With Ithaka always in your mind, arriving there is what you're destined for, but the journey should not be hurried.[33] To truly live your calling is also an irrevocable choice: once made, there's no going back. It is also a leadership challenge to learn to understand the signs that confirm you are living your calling, or that you're straying from the path. To notice the signals no matter how faint or in what form.[34] For living and leading from your calling will cause you to be tested, just as the hero is tested on his journey, as you saw in Chapter 3. After all, the flip side of the gift is the task. Setbacks, experiences of loss can help you become aware of your calling, but your calling will not protect you from new setbacks, from new trials. Just the opposite. Standing up for your calling can evoke resistance in those around you, in people who know you and don't like the change or seem to begrudge it. Or inner resistance: when the loyalty that binds you to your past pulls you back like a rubber band, preventing you from fully embracing new things. You always have to take account of where you have come from and accept what you were given there, in order to choose to follow your calling again and again. Living your calling confronts you with the reality that up until now you might have been trying to find grip in the wrong places.

Leading from your calling is never static. It is a journey. It always requires homework, taking stock and, above all, staying bonded. It requires the persistence and perseverance,[35] that comes from a deeper knowing that *this is right*. But always bonded and checking with others. Asking for and receiving feedback on your person effect, to make sure you're not heading towards the desert, losing troops with every step. If this is my calling, and these are the roles I fulfill, how might others see that I am living my calling in these roles . . . or not?

On the hero's journey, secure bases are indispensable as support and inspiration. So you must be able to accept support and guidance, take direction from others. Be able to trust and commit to a leader or guide in order to move forwards on your own path, to your Ithaka. For existing secure bases, it can be a challenging task to support you in your calling, especially when you have to make new choices. Secure bases prove true when they can go through that development and that journey with you, even when they too are being tested by it. You always have the chance to find additional secure bases from within your calling. And if it proves necessary to say goodbye to existing secure bases in order to remain true to your calling, that is part of the hero's journey.

Calling as the journey to the second mountain

David Brooks calls finding and living your calling "climbing the second mountain".[36] The first mountain is built by finishing school, going to college or university, your early employment, starting a family, making a career; doing what is, more or less, expected of you. This is the mountain of *competence, happiness and competition.* You choose a profession, identify with it, become good at it and achieve something in it. Your goals on the first mountain are about the things everyone wants: a nice family, a fine house, a new car, exotic vacations, good food and drink, good friends around you. And while you're busy climbing this first mountain – possibly you've even reached the top – something happens. You may begin to wonder if this is all there is. You question whether climbing this mountain is fulfilling enough for you. Whether success on the first mountain will provide the deeper satisfaction that you now feel a longing for. But it is also possible that life, mercilessly, throws you off your first mountain. Perhaps you fail somewhere, or you find yourself in a crisis and the way forward is no longer the way up. Or you are confronted with major difficult events: loss, illness, a life-changing experience that was not in your original plans. Suddenly you find yourself in the dark valley between the mountains. This can happen to you at any time in your life. The valley can make and break you. Here you are confronted with your ultimate vulnerability and you will probably find yourself looking for new answers, because the old ones don't work anymore. You are no longer your old self. All alone it seems, you have to reinvent yourself, create a new self for your new reality. How do we turn a crisis into an opportunity for personal development? Reconnect with our life track, with ourselves, the meaning of our existence?[37] When you start looking for new answers, you've left the darkness of the valley and started up the second mountain.

> *Ton Kosteljk graduated as a physicist and received his PhD from the Technical University Eindhoven where, in addition to a good job at Philips, he also taught. He saw himself as a "super-techie". In recent years, however, as he has developed personally, he has become more interested in the emotional/physical side of humans. Now he is a body-oriented therapist. He took quite a financial hit, but not as bad as he would have expected. It gives him a lot of satisfaction to see people he treats really settle down and take control of their lives.*[38]

Dusting yourself off, in the valley, at the bottom of the first mountain, you realize you have been given the opportunity to build a life that can transcend your old one. You reject the easy option, of going back up the first mountain to recapture what you once had. You choose to start up the second mountain in search of who you might be when you bond to others, from out of your new self, and the experience of vulnerability down in the valley. The second mountain is about *calling, joy and service.* With the retrospective realization that the first mountain was not the ultimate goal, you can, enriched by the experience of both climbing the first mountain and your time in the dark valley, ascend the second mountain by pursuing higher goals, and living your calling in relationship with others. This does not mean you 'throw the baby out with the bathwater'. The invitation is to bring everything of value into the calling, all your knowledge and experience. You might continue to do the same work, maintain the same relationships, but you will notice that when you start living and working from your calling, everything will, somehow, be different. Experiences will be richer, relationships more intense. You find a deeper joy in all you do.

Not everyone climbs the second mountain. Not everyone is willing to make hard choices and sacrifices. Those who don't, for whatever reasons, will never climb out of the valley and up the second mountain. They will continue to seek short-lived moments of happiness on the first mountain, rarely experiencing true joy and not living their calling to the fullest.

Finding and formulating your calling

> *As a child, he was always building tree houses. He dragged all kinds of materials to the grove behind his parents' house. He constantly had new ideas to make the huts even better, sturdier and more beautiful and to erect them in the most unusual places in or among trees. He always*

took friends along to give him a hand. His favorite moment was always at the end of an afternoon, when they would sit together in a half-built hut, hanging out and discussing new plans. They would also make up stories and dream about the adventures they would have when they were older. High above the ground, they made their own world. During his high school years and at university, he returned to his tree house regularly. It always helped him clear his head.

Now an executive, he notices that his management team is so fixated on the content that they have no real vision. It seems as if the right perspective is lacking, the team cannot take the necessary distance. As an inspiration he decides to take them to the forest. Under the watchful eye of a forest ranger, they build a platform among the trees and hold their awayday up high. The new collaboration, the physical challenge and the new perspective work wonders. Ideas begin to flow. He realizes that his calling might be to lead people looking at challenges, literally and figuratively, from a different perspective.

Finding and giving words to your calling requires the will to look back on your life: to make connections between what you find there, with what is here in the present, and with your emerging future. The life you have led so far is a rich source of learning that gives you the language and symbols that give form and content to your calling, to who you are and what you want to set in motion in the world.

As you begin the search for your calling, we want to offer you a roadmap, to help you orient yourself on the path to calling. Along that roadmap we distinguish several sources that are essential to finding and formulating your calling. As we lead you along these sources, we will ask you questions that enable you to complete the puzzle, piece by piece. As you travel along these sources and reflect on the questions we ask you, you might want to write down your ideas, thoughts, inspirations and discoveries.

PART I

Joyful childhood experiences[39]

Think back to one or more moments in your (early) childhood when you experienced real joy. Moments when you were totally 'lost' in something. Write down as much as possible about them, with as much detail as you can.

- What books did you read?
- What series did you watch?
- What activities/sports did you do?
- What pursuits and hobbies did you have?

- What secure bases were present? Parent(s), siblings, friends, a sports coach, a (music) teacher, a pet etc.?
- What thoughts were you having at those times or moments?

Describe them in as much detail as possible.

- What feelings did you have at those times or moments?

Describe them in as much detail as possible.

- What physical sensations can you recall?

Describe them in as much detail as possible.

Sources of inspiration

Everyone has one or more activities, occupations, elements or objects in their lives that they have a special feeling about, that inspire them. Things that make their energy flow. These sources of inspiration determine to a large extent who you are. They give you the feeling of being alive.

- What sources of inspiration did you have in the past?
- Where do you draw inspiration from right now? What do you like to do?
- What does this source(s) bring you?
- What energy does it provide? How does it make you feel? What thoughts and emotions are present?

Transition moments[40]

When you look at your lifeline, you see several highs and lows. Moments when something happened that was impactful. Moments that profoundly shaped you and that affect you to this day with all the pain (if they were 'negative') and all the joy (if they were 'positive') that accompanies them.

We call these moments, these experiences and events, *transition moments*. They are turning points, when your life changed for the better. You might not always have realized it at the time, but looking back, these moments have strongly influenced your view of yourself and of (your) reality. The integration of all these moments has made you the person you are today.

We would like to ask you to reflect on the following questions:

- What highs and lows do you see when you look back at your life?
- How have they affected you?
- What transition moments require your attention again? Dwell on this question for a few moments: What did I lose here? And, what did I gain here?

- What leadership qualities have you developed as a result of these transition moments? What strengths, what motivation, what talents have blossomed thanks to these moments?
- What leadership challenge have you developed? Based on all of the transition moments, what remains a permanent point of attention? What do you find difficult or a struggle in your (personal) leadership?

Patterns of leadership[41]

In your life you have experienced success at different times, in different situations and roles. In these successes you have shown yourself and others what you can do, you have done something that others – and perhaps yourself – did not think possible. These are moments when you rose above yourself, got the best out of yourself and experienced joy and pleasure. These success experiences are an important source of information. You could say that was you leading at your best.

We invite you to reflect on moments in your life when you have experienced 'flow'. Situations in which you experienced that your talent came into its own, that you achieved results beyond expectations. Situations in which you experienced leading not only successfully, but brilliantly.

Consider the following questions:

- How did the process develop, who was involved (people in authority, peers, subordinates, family, friends)?
- What were the ups and downs, the challenges?
- In the end, what exactly was the success?
- And what did you do to achieve that success? What added value did you bring? What talents did you bring to the table?
- What circumstances contributed to your success?

When you experience success and flow in your life, there will also be moments when you feel disappointed in yourself. Moments when you feel you failed.[42] We invite you to reflect on these too.

Consider the following questions:

- How did the process develop, who was involved (people in authority, peers, subordinates, family, friends)?
- In what aspects did you feel you failed?
- What or who was missing in these situations, and how did that keep you from being successful?

Looking at both your successes and moments of failure, what common thread can you discern? What patterns become visible in your leadership? And what clues does this give you about your calling?

Now take stock: look at everything you wrote down. Then really take your time and see if you can complete the following sentence for yourself.

I am . . . (being energy)
who . . . (doing energy)
through which/so that . . . (impact on the world)

Take Derek, with whom we started this chapter:

I am *a creative innovator, offering trust and challenge, making beauty and progress visible in the world.*

For inspiration, a few more examples.

I am *a buddy* **who** *will adventure together with you on the road to surrender.*
I am a *fiery woman* **who** *shines, bringing light to dark paths.*
I am *an awakener* **who** *lovingly loosens stuck potential* **so** *that it can be fully lived.*

PART II

Now that you have an initial formulation for your calling, have put words to it, we invite you to hone it further with the following exercise.

As described earlier, your calling influences the roles you can and will fulfill in your life. But in order to gain (deeper) insight into your calling, you can 'look from the other side' and use the roles as a source of information. We would like to take you through an exercise that you can do alone or with someone you trust.

- Find a quiet place.
- Close your eyes and breathe in and out quietly.
- Place four chairs in the room in a circle. Each chair represents a type of role.

    - Personal (e.g. mother, spouse, brother)
    - Organizational (e.g. owner)
    - Social (e.g. sports coach/choir leader)
    - Professional (e.g. consultant)

- Take time to sit in each of the chairs. Then ask yourself these three questions:

    - What roles do I fulfill in this place?
    - How do I shape my calling in these roles?
    - What new information do these roles give me regarding my calling?

- You now have tried all four chairs (and thus all the types of roles). If you now look again at the answers you gave above, how does your calling now look, feel and sound?

I am . . . (being energy)
who . . . (doing energy)
Through which/so that . . . (impact on the world).

The calling of an organization

Like people, organizations have a calling too.[43] Brian Robertson, the man behind *Holacracy*,[44] uses the phrase "evolving purpose" – we would call it *destiny* – to show that each organization and every employee have a calling.[45]

What is the organization's identity? And what does it want? The appropriate metaphor is that of the journey of parent and child: we recognize that our child has her own identity and her own path and her own purpose. And while I might be delighted if my child becomes a doctor, it doesn't mean I'm going to project that onto my child. If I do that, it's harmful and it makes them dependent. We have learned as parents that healthy parenting is a journey of differentiation and that, ironically, that differentiation between parent and child gives each the space to more fully experience their own autonomy and identity. Which, in turn, gives space for a more conscious integration where we relate and bond to each other, but it is a relationship of equals.

As humans we can align ourselves with the evolutionary purpose of an organization. But the key is to keep the identities apart and find out "What is the calling of this organization?". Not, "What do we want to use this organization – our asset – for?" but rather, "What is the creative potential of this piece of life, of this living system?" This is what we mean by evolutionary purpose: the deepest creative potential to bring something new into the world, something with energy, something with value for the world. It is to that creative impulse, to that potential, that we want to tune in, independent of what we ourselves want.[46]

The calling of an organization is formed by its identity and the purpose it pursues. That purpose is the calling that wants to be made manifest in the world. The founders, from their own calling, have (or had) a goal in mind with which they want(ed) to enrich the world, a product or service that is of value to others. At the base of every organizational calling, therefore, lies the calling and soul of the founders. Leaders know that calling, they can commit to it, use it as a source of inspiration for themselves and their employees. The calling forms the basis of the *corporate story*: a meaningful theme that is presented in a distinctive way.[47] Every organization already has a story ready with its own history of origin.[48] It is important that organizations translate the founder's original, inspirational story into the 'organizational soul', into the mission, vision and values.[49] The corporate story can emerge as a dialogue within the organization. By connecting the deeper motives of the organization with the pride of employees within the organization, the story can unfold.[50]

Corporate storytelling, just like your personal life story, is about shaping coherence, but from within the context of the whole organization. Whereas on the one hand the organization is larger than the sum total of the employees, buildings, machinery, equipment and products. On the other hand, a good corporate story makes the organization recognizable in the form of the brand, brings it close, makes it 'small'. So that everyone, not only existing and prospective customers, but also anyone who has an interest in the organization – such as potential suppliers, partners and staff, as well as competitors – can easily recognize and bond with the organization. This involves shaping an identity for the organization that today's society can relate to. If that identity is meaningful to people, employees and customers will naturally want to bond with the organization's calling.

> *The Dutch funeral organization, Dela, was founded in 1937 with the motto "Carry Each Other's Burden". Over time it has become: "DELA – for each other". A few years ago they started a campaign called "Dear . . ." and invited people to share their feelings about each other, to say what they want to say to each other now, in the present. This was followed by the campaign, "Why wait to say something nice when you can say it today". These campaigns are in line with each other, yet clearly refer back to the founding goal of the company.*
>
> An organization that continually reconnects with its calling, and invites its employees to do the same, enjoys the benefits of this every day, in many ways. In 2020, DELA was selected as the best employer in the Netherlands, according to *Great Place to Work*.[51]
>
> What is important about the corporate story is that it is shared, that it continues to be told and is passed on. This establishes continuity, because, as the story is told and retold, it brings past, present and future together. Now, and again, and again.

In conclusion

William Bridges sees the journey to one's calling as the basic thread around which the fabric of one's entire life is woven. So it was never only about your profession in the narrow sense of the word. It is about how life calls you – in the broadest sense – to contribute to the task of doing the work of the world.[52]

The greatest regret, of people at the end of their lives, is not the things they have done, but the things they have not done.[53] The (also emotional) risks not taken, the desires and dreams not expressed and followed, the help not sought at moments of pain, doubt and loneliness, the gratitude not expressed, the forgiveness not given, the conflicts avoided.[54] Rarely do you hear someone on their deathbed say that they would have liked to work more: more likely they'll speak of wishing they'd spent more time with their loved ones.

Being able to live life fully requires equal measures of reflection and action. According to the Greek philosopher Socrates, the unexamined life, for a human, is not worth living.[55] According to Henri Nouwen, the greatest joy of life is not caused by the life we lead. It is caused by the way we think about the life we lead and the way we experience this life. This is also true for the greatest pain in life.[56] This "thinking and acting" is the leadership journey of finally daring to come home to who you truly are.[57] It is important to search for your true identity, and equally brave to fully embrace it, once found.[58]

And after this searching and, hopefully, finding, we will bid you farewell. We began this book by exploring the difference between change and transition. We could not have done so without standing on the shoulders of William Bridges. After decades of his pioneering work with organizations and their leaders, he was faced with the biggest change and loss in his life: his wife's death. It led him to apply to his own life all the lessons he had taught to others. He fought every step of the way to recover from that profound personal loss. Eventually, the loss and restoration process opened, in him, areas of creative insight and spiritual growth. He discovered new meaning in retelling the story of his life path and career. He discovered how that which is most fixed, set in stone, namely the past, is truly alive and growing. As the past changes, it paves the way for a new future. He discovered that he wants to show people how to find the value hidden in their life stories and the transitions they went through.

We have taken you through the book along the major themes of leadership as we represent them via the Transition Cycle. It's time to leave you, to let you continue your own journey. And we trust that we will meet again. And then, we'll ask you about your calling, and the joy it has brought you. Until then: stay curious. For, the day you stop being curious is the day you stop being a leader.[59] And trust that *the best is yet to come*!

Important insights to take away

- No event is meaningful in itself. Meaning is not given in advance. Assigning meaning to experiences and rewriting your life story is an active and conscious process.

- You always have freedom of choice. Even though you cannot always choose the circumstances, you can always choose how you relate to the circumstances. Your purpose in life, a mission that you experience and roles that you fulfill in your life, are not your calling. What you do, and undertake, is not who you are.

- Your calling answers the questions *"Who am I?"* and *"What, in life, do I set in motion?"* and forms the foundation for the various roles you fulfill: personal, professional, organizational and social. Your calling is an expression of your true identity. It will not change, but your roles certainly will.

- Your calling has been with you all your life. In reflecting on joyful childhood memories, inspirations, wounds, moments of transition, patterns of leadership, and the roles you fill, you can clarify your calling and begin to live it to the fullest.
- Living your calling requires bonding with your secure bases: accepting support, understanding the signs you are given and being willing to do whatever is necessary.
- When you are living your calling, you are climbing the second mountain. The mountain where the focus shifts from me to the other and from I to we. Where you commit to something bigger than yourself.

Questions for self-reflection

1. You should now be familiar with the first mountain. Think about your first mountain:

   - What talents and competencies have you been able to develop?
   - What accomplishments are you proud of?
   - What competition have you embraced in your life, and what have you avoided?
   - What are your answers, to the previous questions, when you apply them to your four distinct roles: personal, professional, organizational, social?

2. And now to the second mountain. When you think about your second mountain:

   - What valleys of pain do you recognize in your life and, looking back, what is the essence of what you learned there?
   - At what moments are you able to surrender to something greater than yourself, without negating your self?
   - How much are you in service to others?
   - What big dream in your life gives you an uneasy gut feeling?
   - What are you most afraid of?
   - Are you fully experiencing joy in your life?

What are your answers, to the previous questions, when you apply them to your four distinct roles: personal, professional, organizational, social?

1. In Chapter 3, we asked you about your calling. We are also curious about how your calling is developing during your current journey. From where you are, right now in your life journey, how would you formulate your calling?
2. How does your calling translate into the four roles: personal, professional, organizational and social?

3. What values do you strive for? How do they relate to your calling and then to your organization's calling?
4. What meaning have given to the life transitions in your personal and professional history? How has that meaning evolved over time?
5. What does that meaning bring to your calling?
6. Describe those times when you experienced the flow of living and leading from your calling?
7. What sacrifices are you prepared to make in order to fully live your calling? And what will you not sacrifice?
8. What secure bases are essential if you are to live your calling?

Questions to ask of the people around you – your person effect

1. Would you tell me your calling? How do you lead from your calling?
2. What obstacles do you encounter in leading from your calling? What could I do for you in that?
3. What has been one of the most meaningful moments in your life? Why?
4. What did you experience as one of the most meaningless events in your life? How has this affected your leadership?
5. Do you feel able to fully express your talents? What talents do you think need more development/What do you need for this development to happen?
6. What does the word success bring up in you? What are you successful at?
7. What do you find me successful at? Why? How do you feel when you see me being successful?
8. What do you think is our organization's calling? How do you experience our loyalty to that? How not? What is the effect – of both your answers – on you and on how you bond to this organization (this team, this board)?
9. Do you feel that we sufficiently reflect with each other on why we do things the way we do? How do you think your answer affects our team?
10. May I share my calling with you? What happens to you when I tell you the meaning of my calling?
11. How do you recognize my calling in my behavior? What do you see me doing? What, in my behavior, inspires you?
12. When do you see me acting contrary to my calling? What, then, do you see me do and avoid? How does that affect you and our relationship?
13. In which role – personal, professional, organizational, social – do you think I need to grow in how I lead from my calling?

Behind the Names: About Jakob

Personal Roles
Son of Peter and Marijke;
Brother of Karin;
Husband of Svetlana;
Stepfather of Vika

Professional Roles
Coach;
Educator and
Trainer;
Author

Calling

Organizational Roles
Partner at
The School for
Transition;
Affliliate of the
Portland Institute
for Loss and
Transition

Social Roles
Member of a choir;
Contributor to (national) media

Calling
I am a friend and father who helps calling to be found
and lived, on the path to healing

The front

Given name: Joost Peter Jakob van Wielink
Called: Jakob
Born: October 21, 1974 in Eindhoven

The back

My father and mother chose to raise me in the Catholic faith, which is strongly embedded and gives me my roots. Belief in the Resurrection is the most powerful guide in my life. It continually stirs up the passionate desire in me to be working with people and to take steps in my life towards healing what is broken.

The first books I disappeared into were atlases and my parents took my sister and me to beautiful places in Europe. Thus was born an almost insatiable interest in other cultures and customs and what is enriching in them.

At an early age, I was captivated by the told and untold stories of the Shoah. They made me curious about the motives of people and the role emotions play in their behavior. My choice to study and follow a (first) career in international law were a response to that curiosity.

In my international work with executive leaders and in training professionals, I am shaping the destiny that began so early in my life. I experience this as living my name, as climbing up and down my ladder, as the journey of my leadership. I discovered in my work that we all have a unique calling that is often hidden in the unexplored roots of leadership. I believe that leadership is about standing up, stretching away from what terrifies us, and living our calling in all the roles we are invited to fill in our lives. This belief also led to my founding The School for Transition.

I have been fortunate to meet many inspiring leaders, guides and trainers at home and abroad. The fundamental turning point in my life came through and after my marriage to Svetlana. I decided to do everything in my power to take risks in my new (family) life, my friendships and my work in order to reap the success that waits there to be harvested. That was also the moment I began learning from and working with George Kohlrieser and Bob Neimeyer. Their impact on the journey to my heart and my calling, through their support, faith and encouragement has been immense. And I celebrate, too, my wonderful fellow authors Riet and Leo, who are there in all the roles of my life as friends and witnesses on my journey.

Naturally, I am aware of my struggles with the emotions that affect my behavior. They emerge in full force around a trio of fierce experiences. Bullying in elementary school in particular, my parents' divorce when I was 19, and not becoming a biological father myself are wounds that demanded understanding and explanation. The effect of these experiences on my behavior was that they hindered my ability to trust myself in a group, or the group itself. While researching this issue, I kept coming across the fracture lines and pain in my relationships with my parents. I discovered how – in addition to the love and care I definitely received – I had missed support, emotional bonding and encouragement at key moments. Facing grief was an important part of my journey. In the process, I began talking more and more with my parents. The fruits of my wounds eventually led me to my calling.

And my calling takes me to many places. Above all, however, every journey always brings me back home, completing a new cycle every time. At home – with Svetlana and Vika and my friends – I can recharge. In this way I integrate what I have learned and, as friend and father, I pass it on in joy.

Jakob

Behind the Names: About Riet

Personal Roles
Daughter of Jan and Barbara Jaspers;
Sister of Mart, José, Ankie and Wilma;
Mother of Hanneke and Renske;
Grandmother of Joris, Mats
and Guus;
Committed to Jan

Organizational Roles
Affiliated with:
The Centre of
Expertise in Coping
with Loss;
The Publication Agency
In the Clouds;
Circle Publishing

Calling

Professional Roles
Coach;
Grief and trauma
therapist;
Educator and trainer;
Author

Social Roles
Member of a poetry group;
Former local government officer;
Board member Mourning;
Support Fund Foundation

Calling
I am an anchored, devoted wife, a beacon
of support who weaves fault lines back into life again

The front

Given name: Maria Josina Martina Fiddelaers-Jaspers
Called: Riet
Born: July 19, 1953 in Budel

The back

Looking back on my life, I realize it is no coincidence that I have made the themes of loss and grief my field of expertise. For years I had no suitable answer to the recurring question of why this so interested me. Only when I realized that loss manifests in so many areas did it become clear to me that my personal loss has always been there. My arrival in the world was not accompanied by applause, and I missed the welcome, warmth and security that every child so desperately needs. My response to this was a firm line of defense that resisted bonding and intimacy.

My father came from a working-class family and was born after two stillborn brothers. My mother was one of the oldest members of a large farming family; she was scarred by the loss of her youngest sister and was not looking forward to having children herself. Emotions were repressed; hard work and getting on with life was my parents' answer. Thus the seed was planted for my later work: I unconsciously breathed in their sadness and my not (yet) being welcome. Soon I filled the void and, as the oldest, became a secure base for my parents and my siblings.

My parents also gave me beautiful life gifts, positive baggage. My mother sang with us and encouraged us to read. We read every book in the library, received more books as gifts, and listened to radio plays together. My father took me on the road both for his work and for pleasure trips in the car. Thus, my view of the world expanded, my imagination and creativity were engaged, and I longed for more. Although my parents wanted us to 'learn', their horizon did not extend beyond middle school, for which we only had to walk down the garden path. I complied, but woke up just in time to realize my dream: education. My father gave me an impossible choice: "Study, or your boyfriend". Looking back, I made an important decision there that determined the course of my life. I chose to develop myself, through study and education, to give a voice to children who have to live with the fault lines of their lives.

The search in my life for appreciation, welcome, safety, bonding and intimacy led to my calling. The road sometimes went through deep valleys, especially where I no longer felt welcome in an important relationship and had to let go. By working on, and with, my life themes I continue to meet the other at ever deeper levels. I learned to be present, even in the deepest pain, trusting in the resilience of the other. I have known many teachers and I am grateful to them all and, although I sometimes took new paths, seeds were planted. Wibe Veenbaas, Piet Weisfelt, Franz Ruppert, Stephan Hausner and Bessel van der Kolk are the ones I would like to mention.

To Jakob I am grateful for his generosity in sharing the contacts he has with international masters; thus my world became even larger. Leo I got to know as one of my students, but has gone far beyond this stage. He is a faithful fellow traveler and, like no one else I know, able to visualize the ideas we have as authors. And perhaps I have learned the most from my clients: about trust and welcoming myself and that bonding with my loved ones is the most important thing in my life.

In the meantime, I have reached retirement age and I am taking care of securing my life's work. So that the invitation to weave fault lines into life continues.

RIET

Behind the Names: About Leo

Calling
As guide I'll lead you to the top of your mountain, so that you
can experience, celebrate and share your success

The front

Name: Leonard Wilhelm
Called name: Leo
Born: November 17, 1966 in Amsterdam

The back

When I became a father, the desire to lead arose in me. Before that I had always consciously chosen to work in IT. But when Elise, our first daughter, was born, it was as if a switch was tripped. I wanted to experience that special feeling I had at home when taking care of our daughter, at work too. The feeling of being responsible for someone else. Originally, I had no ambition to be a manager. It felt like stepping into the unknown, away from the safe and manageable world of IT for which I had studied.

In retrospect, I can see that bringing the energy of a young father into caring for my employees also cost me a lot. At a reorganization, I tried to protect my employees from any uncertainty, yet, in my position, I could not provide the clarity they were asking for. I actually wanted to ensure they felt no discomfort, but still had to learn that I could not take that away from them.

My first few years as an executive brought me to the brink of burnout twice. Without wanting to admit how I was doing, I did tell people at home about my work with tears in my eyes. My initial reaction was to stop talking about my work. This was followed, shortly after, by wanting to stop being a manager. Asking for help and saying how difficult it was for me was new. The fact that my management team wouldn't just let me leave was a comforting sign of trust. However, the fact that they called me out was not easy.

With the birth of Joy, our second daughter, I experienced the vulnerability of seeing that new life isn't, naturally, guaranteed to survive. Within days of the birth, we were back in the hospital with a sick child. This also confronted me with my inability to deal with goodbyes and loss. Fortunately, Joy quickly recovered, but I had further work to do on myself in the area of dealing with loss. So I started volunteering at the Jakob hospice, where I learned to be present with people who were terminally ill and their loved ones. Here I became aware of the inadequacy of language, because what do you say in such a situation? And it made me experience how meaningful it is to be near, to have someone near, to be together when it is difficult. Just being there was more important than what I said or did.

To learn more about this, I went into training with Riet and Sabine Noten. Looking through the lens of loss, I also began to see the discomfort people at work had in such situations. So I started working with these themes at work, within my leadership and coaching roles. First by supporting loss in the death of colleagues, but soon also from loss experiences through change. This was what brought Jakob and I together, resulting in a long and deep friendship.

I had to turn thirty to find out that I would like to have children, the greatest gift granted me. At forty, I found out – as a rational and somewhat detached person – that I am not only a child of my father. I also appear to be – emotionally involved and bonding – a child of my mother. I have desirable and undesirable qualities from both, and am challenged to bring it all together into who I want to be. For example, I now face, at fifty, my tendency to adapt to the other. To elevate the other above myself, at my cost. On the way to my second mountain, I let go of much of what felt – and turned out – not to be mine. In doing so, I also chose the painful and ulti- mately inevitable path of ending my intimate relationship. So I am writing a new chapter in my life, saying goodbye to how I expected my story to un- fold. As a climber and bouldering instructor – which I first encountered as a student, and which helped shape me as a person – a new route thus presents itself for me. With my calling as direction and friendship as support, I dare to start a new climb.

Leo

The Shoulders On Which We Stand

Words of thanks

With this book, we set out on a largely unknown road, certainly not a paved path through the land of leadership. We brought courage, bags of experience and ideas, a clear vision and, above all, real dedication. And sometimes, when we came to crossroads, we stayed awhile, spending time with people who inspired us, who pointed the way, so that we, recharged, could continue our journey. We are grateful to many people for their inspiration and encouragement. A complete list of those who inspired us can be found in the endnotes. However, at this point, we would like to mention a few extra-special people. We stand on their shoulders; they are both our secure bases and valued sources of inspiration.

In May 2014, we were invited by George Kohlrieser, whom we knew from his books, to attend as *observational guests* at the *High Performance Leadership Program* – a globally renowned, international leadership program – where he works with leaders from around the world on themes of attachment, bonding, loss, grief, conflict and dialogue. It was the beginning of countless meetings and adventures together. We are forever indebted to his insight and the transformations his teachings made possible in our lives.

Of indescribable influence has been Edith Eva Eger. Jakob – together with Klaartje van Gasteren and Marnix Reijmerink – met her in 2018 in her hometown, La Jolla (San Diego). At the request of The School for Transition and the Expertise Center for Coping with Loss, she came to the Netherlands in May 2019 to give a masterclass. An event that touched many people deeply. These meetings, and her book *The Choice,* were an important source of inspiration and we are very grateful to her for the inspiring and moving words she wrote for our book.

Robert Neimeyer has an unparalleled knowledge of the language of transition. His are the essential, the core teachings in working with meaning in profound life transitions. His work via the Portland Institute for Loss and Transition has shown us the way.

That we never got to meet William Bridges is of profound regret. We encountered his sincere and relevant work shortly after his death. He was one of the first to engage with and write about the themes of loss, grief, transition and leadership. We offer him a great deal of posthumous thanks and reverence. The Transition Cycle, that helps structure this book, takes its name from the privilege of being inspired by and drawing from his work.

Nick Craig inspired us, through his work on leading from purpose, to expand the theme of Meaning on the Transition Cycle to embrace Calling; this evolved directly from Nick's work. Having translated his book into Dutch, we followed up by interviewing him.[1]

Klaartje and Marnix made an important contribution to the content of Chapter 9 in the form of the roadmap for orienting yourself to your calling. In addition, as co-readers they were part of the journey and constantly invited us to look deeper and make improvements. We are enriched by their friendship and the joy of shaping this beautiful work together.

Marcel, Martijn and Michiel also read along: leaders who know the territory. Marcel van Wersch is a leader at Solid Professionals, specialists in finance and risk. Michiel Soeters was a leader in various organizations and is the face behind No Man Overboard (geenmanoverboord.nl). Martijn van Lanen comes from the education sector and is a team leader at the HAN University of Applied Sciences. Both gave valuable feedback from their own leadership practice. Thanks to Frances Jonkers and Anne Verbokkem-Oerlemans who critically read our biographies.

Our editor for the Dutch edition, Hester Bruning, sharpened the original text, saved us from unintended repetition and kept an eye on the manuscript's storyline and continuity.

Hanneke Fiddelaers, at Circle Publishing our original publisher in the Netherlands, had to take a deep breath. It took a long time before our full manuscript landed on her desk. We are indebted to her patience and her confidence in us, especially when our changes must have seemed endless.

James Campbell took on the task of translating the manuscript from Dutch to English. Feeling personally at home with the central themes of the book, which was a great help, he did a masterful job. Not only was it a pleasure working with James, given his commitment, he also totally met our needs, given the emphasis on the importance of language when dealing with transition, the core theme of this book.

We are particularly grateful to the team at Routledge, especially Zoe Thomson, for warmly accepting our proposal and making its publication possible.

This book would never have existed without the countless individual clients and participants in our education and training programs who entrusted us with their – often acutely vulnerable – stories of transition. They are our true teachers. They show us the landscape in which leaders must shape their transitions. Through the trust they give us, we emerged and found new direction and course together. Working with them is an inexhaustible source of inspiration, learning and growth; each lifeline a unique and precious gift.

The combination of our eagerness to learn, willingness to travel and curiosity has, for many years, taken us to places, at home and abroad, where we have met inspiring masters and colleagues: in collaboration, intervision, supervision and training. We are grateful to them for the questions they ask and how they help us to find our way.

And, of course, we stand on the shoulders of our parents. In Chapter 4, in particular, we describe how important the system of one's family of origin is in the shaping your leadership. Naturally, this applies to us and we acknowledge it in our brief biographies. Our parents point the way; we choose the route.

The main obstacle in writing this book was to combine the call of the book and the way it filled our schedule, with staying bonded to our environment. That was a big focus and a big task. At times it demanded a lot from the people with whom we have relationships, especially in the final writing stage of the book. Thank you for giving us that space and trusting that we would return to you after this intense journey. This book is important. You are more important.

Notes

1. Welcome to The Language of Transition

1 Daniel Goleman and Richard Boyatzis (2008). Social Intelligence and the Biology of Leadership. *Harvard Business Review*, September.
2 William Peace (2001). The Hard Work of Being a Soft Manager. *Harvard Business Review*, December.
3 Holly Weeks (2001). Taking the Stress out of Stressful Conversations. *Harvard Business Review*, July/August.
4 Compare Jeanie Daniel Duck (2001). *The Change Monster: The Human Forces That Fuel or Foil Corporate Transformation & Change*. New York: Three Rivers Press.
5 See also Lennette Schuijt (2008). *Met Ziel en Zakelijkheid: Paradoxen in leiderschap (With Soul and Business: Paradoxes in Leadership)*. Schiedam: Scriptum.
6 Jakob van Wielink and Leo Wilhelm (2020). (Re)discovering Calling in the Wake of Loss through Secure Bases. *AI Practitioner*, May.
7 Roger Nierenberg (2009). *Maestro: A Surprising Story About Leading by Listening*. New York: Penguin.
8 Anselm Grün (2016). *Omgaan met conflicten: Moeilijke situaties onder ogen zien en oplossen (Dealing with conflict. Facing and resolving difficult situations)*. Utrecht: Ten Have.
9 Margareth Heffernan (2015). *Beyond Measure: The Big Impact of Small Changes*. New York: Simon & Schuster.
10 Jakob van Wielink and Leo Wilhelm (2017). Secure bases als bedding voor talent (Secure bases as a bed for talent). *MD – tijdschrift voor talent- & managementontwikkeling*, June.
11 Walter Mischel (2015). *The Marshmallow Test: Why Self-Control Is the Engine of Success*. New York: Little, Brown Spark.
12 Roy Baumeister and John Tierney (2011). *Willpower: Rediscovering the Greatest Human Strength*. London: Penguin.
13 Angela Duckworth (2016). *Grit: The Power of Passion and Perseverance*. New York: Scribner Book Company.
14 Erin Meyer (2016). *The Culture Map: Decoding How People Think, Lead, and Get Things Done Across Cultures*. New York: Hachette Book Group.
15 Geert Hofstede, Gert Jan Hofstede and Michael Minkov (2016). *Cultures and Organizations: Software of the Mind*. New York: HarperCollins.
16 Erin Meyer (2017). Being the Boss in Brussels, Boston and Beijng: If You Want to Succeed, You'll Need to Adapt. *Harvard Business Review*, July/August.
17 Stephan Poulter (2006). *The Father Factor: How Your Father's Legacy Impacts Your Career*. Buffalo: Prometheus; Stephan Poulter (2008). *The Mother Factor: How Your Mother's Emotional Legacy Impacts Your Life*. Buffalo: Prometheus.

18 Peter Lovenheim (2018). *The Attachment Effect: Exploring the Powerful Ways Our Earliest Bond Shapes Our Relationships and Lives*. New York: TarcherPerigee; Kate Murphy (2017). Yes, It's Your Parents' Fault. *The New York Times*, 7 January.
19 Edith Eger (2018). *The Choice: Embrace the Possible*. New York: Scribner Book Company.
20 Klaartje van Gasteren, Marnix Reijmerink and Jakob van Wielink (2019). Ik heb Auschwitz veranderd in een klaslokaal (I turned Auschwitz into a classroom). In conversation with Dr. Edith Eva Eger. *Tijdschrift voor Coaching*, March.

2. Route Planner

1 The cycle came our way in a number of steps, through the work of George Kohlrieser, Wibe Veenbaas, Piet Weisfelt and Riet Fiddelaers-Jaspers. The cycle has a number of different versions in its genesis, with names like contact, connection or attachment cycle and loss or grief cycle. Transition forms a cross-cutting understanding of all topics on the cycle.
2 George Santayana (2011). *The Life of Reason or The Phases of Human Progress: Introduction and Reason in Common Sense*. Cambridge: The MIT Press.
3 For a detailed introduction we would like to refer you to Chapter 4 'The Power of *secure bases*' in George Kohlrieser (2006). *Hostage At The Table: How Leaders Can Overcome Conflict, Influence Others, and Raise Performance*. New Jersey: John Wiley & Sons Inc.
4 See also: Lisa Feldman Barrett (2017). *How Emotions are Made: The Secret Life of the Brain*. London: Pan Books.
5 Gemma Boormans and Esther Cohen (2020). *Huidhonger: Als je alleen bent na scheiding of verlies van je partner* (*Skin Hunger: When you're alone after separation or loss of your partner*). Amsterdam/Antwerp: Publisher De Arbeiderspers.
6 Irvin Yalom (2009). *Staring At The Sun: Overcoming the Terror of Death*. San Francisco: Jossey-Bass.

3. Every Change Begins with an Ending

1 Anders Ericsson, Michael Prietula and Edward Cokely (2007). The Making of an Expert. *Harvard Business Review*, July/August; Warren Bennis and Robert Thomas (2002). *Crucibles of Leadership*. Harvard Business Review, September; Olivia Fox Cabane (2012). *The Charisma Myth: Master the Art of Personal Magnetism*. London: Penguin Books.
2 Tim Ferriss (2016). *Tools of Titans: The Tactics, Routines, and Habits of Billionaires, Icons, and World-Class Performers*. London: Vermillion.
3 Interview by Coen Verbraak in *In de beste families* (*In the Best Families*), NTR, July 31, 2019.
4 Joseph Campbell (2008). *Hero With a Thousand Faces: The Collected Works of Joseph Campbell*. Novato: New World Library; Robert Quinn (2010). *Deep Change: Discovering the Leader Within*. San Francisco: Jossey-Bass.
5 Compare Robert Anderson and William Adams (2016). *Mastering Leadership: An Integrated Framework for Breakthrough Performance and Extraordinary Business Results*. Hoboken: Wiley.
6 Miloe van Beek in collaboration with The Hup and De School voor Transitie (2019). *Vertrouwen, verbinden, groeien. De winst van een secure base organisatie* (*Trust, connect, grow. The benefits of a secure base organization*). Heeze: Circle Publishing.
7 Richard Boyatzis, Melvin Smith and Ellen Van Oosten (2019). Coaching for Change: How to help employees reach their potential. *Harvard Business Review*, September/October.

8   Warren Bennis and Robert Thomas (2008). *Crucibles of Leadership: How to Learn from Experience to Become a Great Leader*. Boston: Harvard Business Review Press.

9   William Bridges with Susan Bridges (2017). *Managing Transitions: Making the Most of Change*. London: John Murray Press. See also Riet Fiddelaers-Jaspers and Jakob van Wielink (2017). *Aan de slag met verlies: coachen bij veranderingen op het werk (Getting started with loss. Coaching with changes at work)*. Utrecht: Ten Have.

10 Jeffrey Pfeffer (2015). *Leadership BS: Fixing Workplaces and Careers One Truth at a Time*. New York: HarperCollins.

11 Anand Narasimhan and Jean–Louis Barsoux (2017). What Everyone Gets Wrong About Change Management. *Harvard Business Review,* November/December; John Kotter (1997). *Leading Change*. Boston: Harvard Business Review Press; John Kotter (1995). Leading Change: Why Transformation Efforts Fail. *Harvard Business Review*, March/April; Bert Cozijnsen and Jakob van Wielink (2012). *Over de rooie: Emoties bij verlies en verandering op het werk (Going ballistic: Emotions in loss and change at work)*. Alphen aan den Rijn: Vakmedianet.

12 Jean-Francois Manzoni and Jean-Louis Barsoux (2007). *Set-up-to-Fail Syndrome: Overcoming the Undertow of Expectations*. Brighton: Harvard Business Review Press.

13 Warren Berger (2014). *A More Beautiful Question: The Power of Inquiry to Spark Breakthrough Ideas*. New York: Bloomsbury.

14 William Bridges with Susan Bridges (2017). *Managing Transitions: Making the Most of Change*. London: John Murray Press.

15 Interview by Coen Verbraak in *In de beste families (In the Best Families),* NTR, July 31, 2019.

16 George Kohlrieser (2018). The importance of the person effect on your leadership: 4 reasons why our person effect is one of our most important leadership tools. *IMD Research & Knowledge*.

17 David Marquet (2016). *Turn the Ship Around!: A True Story of Building Leaders by Breaking the Rules*. London: Penguin.

18 Ivan Pavlov – who became famous for his experiments with drooling dogs – was the first to talk about the person effect. Horsley Gantt, a student of Pavlov, took the research further by examining the interactions between people. William Horsley Gantt, Joseph Newton, Fred Royer and Joseph Stephens (1966). Effect of Person. *Conditional Reflex: A Pavlovian Journal of Research & Therapy*. Volume 1.

19 James Lynch (1979). *The Broken Heart: The Medical Consequences of Loneliness*. New York: Basic Books.

20 Compare the stories of (physician) Gor Khatchikyan (2020). *De Coronacrisis: Verhalen van de frontlinie (The Corona crisis: Stories from the frontline)*. Nieuwegein: Gor Khatchikyan. Also Sander de Hosson (2018). *Slotcouplet: Ervaringen van een longarts. (Final couplet: Experiences of a lung specialist)*. Amsterdam/Antwerp: Publisher De Arbeiderspers.

21 Julianne Holt-Lunstad, Timothy Smith, Mark Baker, Tyler Harris and David Stephenson (2015). Loneliness and Social Isolation as Risk Factors for Mortality: A Meta-Analytic Review. *Perspectives on Psychological Science*, Vol. 10(2).

22 Olivia Fox Cabane (2012). *The Charisma Myth: Master the Art of Personal Magnetism*. London: Penguin Books.

23 Edgar Schein and Peter Schein (2013). *Humble Inquiry: The Gentle Art of Asking Instead of Telling*. San Francisco: Berrett–Koehler Publishers.

24 Paul Zak (2017). *Trust Factor: The Science of Creating High-Performance Companies*. New York: American Management Association.

25 Marco Iacoboni (2009). *Mirroring People: The Science of Empathy and How We Connect with Others*. London: Picador.

26 The ever-faster changing world we live in has been given the acronym VUCA, for Volatility, Uncertainty, Complexity and Ambiguity, by Judith Stiehm and Nicholas Townsend. The term VUCA comes from the US military, where it was used in the doctrine of the 1990s, after the end of the Cold War, to denote the increased complexity of the world. Today's world is often referred to as a VUCA world, in which the increasing speed of developments and changes causes certainties to disappear, stability to decrease, and anticipation to become increasingly difficult. Judith Stiehm and Nicholas Townsend (2002). *U.S. Army War College: Military Education In A Democracy*. Philadelphia: Temple University Press.
27 Rudolf Erich Raspe (2008). *Adventures of Baron von Münchhausen*. London: Forgotten Books.
28 Anders Ericsson and Robert Pool (2017). *Peak: Secrets from the New Science of Expertise*. Boston: Mariner Books.

4. From Kitchen Table to Conference Room

1 Richard Francis (2012). *Epigenetics: How Environment Shapes Our Genes*. New York: W.W. Norton & Company. See also: Nessa Carey (2012). *The Epigenetics Revolution: How Modern Biology Is Rewriting Our Understanding of Genetics, Disease, and Inheritance*. New York: Columbia University Press.
2 Tessa Roosenboom and Ronald van de Krol (2010). *Baby's van de hongerwinter: De onvermoede erfenis van ondervoeding. (Babies of the Hunger Winter: The unsuspected legacy of malnutrition)*. Amsterdam: Augustus Publishing House.
3 Rachel Verweij and Bea van den Bergh (2015). Emoties van moeder beïnvloeden ontwikkeling van het kind (Emotions of mother influence child development). *Tijdschrift voor Verloskundigen*, No. 5.
4 Caroline Leaf (2018). *Think. Learn. Succeed: Understanding and Using Your Mind to Thrive at School, the Workplace, and Life*. Michigan: Bakerbooks.
5 Edward Tronick and Jeffrey Cohn (1989). Infant-mother face-to-face interaction. *Child Development*, 59.
6 Vivian Broughton (2019). Lecture on May 19 at the book launch. *Coachen waar het pijn doet. (Coaching where it hurts)* (Ien van der Pol). Amsterdam: Boom.
7 Edith Eger (2018). *The Choice: Embrace the Possible*. New York: Scribner Book Company. See also Jakob van Wielink in conversation with Edith Eger (2019). *I Turned Auschwitz into a Classroom*. youtube.com.
8 The foundations for systemic work were laid by Bert Hellinger. He developed the 'laws' for the system. See among others *No Waves without the Ocean: Experiences and Thoughts* (2006). Heidelberg: Carl Auer International. Later, this systemic look was also applied to organizations.
9 Siets Bakker and Leanne Steeghs (2016). *Systemisch wijzer: Kennis uit opstellingen die je iedere dag kunt gebruiken (Systemically Wiser: Knowledge from constellations that you can use every day)*. Zaltbommel: Thema.
10 Interview by Coen Verbraak in *In de beste families (In the Best Families)*, NTR, July 31, 2019.
11 Jan Hoedeman (2020). Zonder werk kan ik niet. (I can't live without work). *Eindhovens Dagblad*, May 23.
12 Tijsse Klasen (2020). *Slimmer met het systeem: Een nieuw perspectief op complexe organisatievraagstukken (Smarter with the System: A new perspective on complex organizational issues)*. Avenhorn: Het Noorderlicht.
13 Anderson Cooper (2019). *Stephen Colbert on overcoming grief and loss as a child*, August 17, 2019: edition.cnn.com/videos.
14 Tijsse Klasen (2020). *Slimmer met het systeem: Een nieuw perspectief op complexe organisatievraagstukken (Smarter with the System: A new perspective on complex organizational issues)*. Avenhorn: Het Noorderlicht.

15 Chris Argyris (1960). *Understanding Organizational Behaviors*. Homewood: Dorsey Press.
16 Michael Wallin (2007). *Managing the Psychological Contract: Using the Personal Deal to Increase Business Performance*. New York: Routledge. Denise Rousseau (1995). *Psychological Contracts in Organizations: Understanding Written and Un-written Agreements*. Thousand Oaks: SAGE Publications.
17 James Surowiecki (2005). *The Wisdom of Crowds: Why the Many Are Smarter Than the Few*. London: Abacus.
18 Amy Edmondson (2018). *The Fearless Organization: Creating Psychological Safety in the Workplace for Learning, Innovation, and Growth*. New York: Wiley.
19 Jakob van Wielink and Leo Wilhelm (2019). Developing Psychological Safety in Leaders and Organizations. *Coaching Perspectives*, January.
20 Lauren Joseph (2016). *Is your team in 'psychological danger'?* Genève: World Economic Forum. weforum.org.
21 Laura Delizonna (2017). High-Performing Teams Need Psychological Safety: Here's How to Create It. *Harvard Business Review*, August.
22 George Kohlrieser, Susan Goldsworthy and Duncan Coombe (2018). *Care to Dare: Unleashing Astonishing Potential Through Secure Base Leadership*. New Jersey: John Wiley & Sons Inc.

5. In Your Vulnerability Lies Your Strength

1 Mario Mikulincer and Phillip Shaver (2016). *Attachment in Adulthood: Structure, Dynamics, and Change*. New York: Guilford Publications. See also Jakob van Wielink, Leo Wilhelm and Denise van Geelen (2019). *Loss, Grief, and Attachment in Life Transitions: A Clinician's Guide to Secure Base Counseling*. New York: Routledge.
2 John Bowlby (1988). *A Secure Base: Parent-Child Attachment and Healthy Human Development*. London: Routledge.
3 Piet Weisfelt (1996). *Nestgeuren: Over de betekenis van de ouder-kindrelatie in een mensenleven (Nesting smells: On the meaning of the parent-child relationship in a human life)*. Amsterdam: Boom.
4 Ivan Boszormenyi-Nagy and Geraldine Spark (2014). *Invisible Loyalties. Reciprocity in Intergenerational Family Therapy*. New York: Taylor & Francis Ltd; Riet Fiddelaers–Jaspers and Sabine Noten (2019). *Herbergen van verlies: Thuiskomen in het Land van Rouw (Harboring loss: Coming home in the Land of Grief)*. Heeze: In de Wolken.
5 George Kohlrieser (2006). *Hostage At the Table: How Leaders Can Overcome Conflict, Influence Others, and Raise Performance*. New Jersey: John Wiley & Sons Inc. *See also*: Melanie Green and Timothy Brock (2002). In the mind's eye: Transportation-imagery model of narrative persuasion. In: Melanie Green, Jeffrey Strange and Timothy Brock (red.). *Narrative Impact: Social and Cognitive Foundations*. Road Hove: Psychology Press.
6 Mary Main (1996). Introduction to the special section on attachment and psychopathology: 2. Overview of the field of attachment. *Journal of Consulting and Clinical Psychology*, Vol. 64(2).
7 Anders Ericsson, Michael Prietula and Edward Cokely (2007). The Making of an Expert. *Harvard Business Review*, July/August.
8 Daniel Goleman and Richard Davidson (2017). *Altered Traits: Science Reveals How Meditation Changes Your Mind, Brain, and Body*. New York: Avery Publishing; Mark Williams, John Teasdale, Zindel Segal and Jon Kabat-Zinn (2017). *The Mindful Way Through Depression: Freeing Yourself from Chronic Unhappiness*. New York: The Guilford Press; Tara Bennett-Goleman (2013). *Mind Whispering: A New Map to Freedom from Self-Defeating Emotional Habits*. London: Rider.

9 Duncan Coombe (2016). See Colleagues as They Are, Not as They Were. *Harvard Business Review*, January 16.
10 Antoinnette Scheulderman (2020). Mijn jeugd werd een slagveld: Ik dwarrelde in stukken en stukjes uit elkaar (My childhood became a battlefield: I whirled apart in bits and pieces). *VK Magazine*, February 1.
11 Donald Winnicott (1951). Transitional objects and transitional phenomena. *Collected Papers: Through Paediatrics to Psychoanalysis*. New York: Basic Books Inc.
12 Kristie Rogers (2018). Do Your Employees Feel Respected?: Show Employees That They're Valued, And Your Business Will Flourish. *Harvard Business Review*, July/August.
13 Patrick Lencioni (2017). *The Five Dysfunctions of a Team: A Leadership Fable.* New York: John Wiley & Sons Inc.
14 Otto van Wiggen (2016). *Niemand is belangrijker dan het team: Een militaire visie op leiderschap. (No one is more important than the team. A military vision of leadership)*. Arnhem: White Elephant.
15 George Kohlrieser (2006). *Hostage At the Table: How Leaders Can Overcome Conflict, Influence Others, and Raise Performance*. New Jersey: John Wiley & Sons Inc.
16 Paul Zak (2017). *The Neuroscience of Trust: Management Behaviors That Foster Employee Engagement*. Harvard Business Review, January/February; Michelle Bligh (2017). Leadership and Trust. In: Johan Marques and Satinder Dhiman (ed.). *Leadership Today: Practices for Personal and Professional Performance*. Berlin: Springer.
17 Eric Berne (2017). *Games People Play: The Psychology of Human Relationships*. London: Penguin Books; Lieuwe Koopmans (2012). *Dit ben ik: Worden wie je bent met Transactionele Analyse (This is me. Becoming who you are with Transactional Analysis)*. Zaltbommel: Thema.
18 Compare also Martijn Vroemen (2017). *Handboek Teamcoaching: Helpen zonder bemoeizucht (Handbook of Team Coaching: Helping without meddling)*. Deventer: Vakmedianet.
19 Mario Mikulincer and Phillip Shaver (2017). *Attachment in Adulthood. Structure, Dynamics, and Change*. New York: Guilford Press; Philip Riley (2011). *Attachment Theory and the Teacher-Student Relationship: A Practical Guide for Teachers, Teacher Educator and School Leaders*. New York: Routledge; Manfred Kets de Vries (2007). *The Leadership Mystique: Leading Behavior in the Human Enterprise*. London: Pearson.
20 Sandra Donker (2020). Floris Kortie: 'Ik hoorde in Beethoven wat ik voelde; liefde, verdriet, onvermogen (Floris Kortie: 'I heard in Beethoven what I felt; love, sadness, powerlessness'). *Algemeen Dagblad*, January 18.
21 Fee van Delft (2015). *Overdracht en tegenoverdracht. Een therapeutisch fenomeen vertaald naar alledaagse psychosociale begeleiding. (Transference and countertransference. A therapeutic phenomenon translated to everyday psychosocial counseling)*. Amsterdam: Boom.
22 Louis Cozolino (2010). *The Neuroscience of Psychotherapy: Healing the Social Brain*. New York: W.W. Norton & Company.
23 Allan Schore (2012). *The Science of the Art of Psychotherapy*. New York: W.W. Norton & Company.
24 Manfred Kets de Vries (2016). *Mindful Leadership Coaching: Journeys Into the Interior*. London: Palgrave Macmillan. See also Jakob van Wielink and Sijtze de Roos (2015). No baby without a mother, no leader without context. *AC Global Bulletin*.
25 The terms upper and lower brain are derived from 'upstairs brain' and 'downstairs brain' as referred to by Daniel Siegel, professor of psychiatry and director

of the Mindsight Institute in Santa Monica, USA. Daniel Siegel and Tina Payne Bryson (2012). *The Whole-Brain Child: 12 Revolutionary Strategies to Nurture Your Child's Developing Mind.* New York: Doubleday. See also Dan Siegel (2012). *Flipping Your Lid: A Scientific Explanation.* youtube.com.

26 Marijke Baljon and Renate Geuzinge (2017). *Echo's van trauma: Slachtoffers als daders, daders als slachtoffers* (*Echoes of trauma. Victims as perpetrators, perpetrators as victims*). Amsterdam: Boom.

27 Jaap van der Stel (2013). *Zelfregulatie, ontwikkeling en herstel: Verbetering en herstel van cognitie, emotie, motivatie en regulatie van gedrag* (*Self–regulation, development and recovery: Improving and restoring cognition, emotion, motivation and regulation of behavior*). Amsterdam: Boom.

28 Phyllis Kosminsky and John Jordan (2016). *Attachment–Informed Grief Therapy: The Clinician's Guide to Foundations and Applications.* New York: Routledge.

29 Bruce Perry is an American psychiatrist who specializes in early childhood trauma. Among other books, he wrote the bestseller *The Boy Who Was Raised As a Dog. And Other Stories from a Child Psychiatrist's Notebook: What Traumatized Children Can Teach Us About Loss, Love, and Healing.* (2017). New York: Basic Books.

30 Marijke Baljon and Renate Geuzinge (2017). *Echo's van trauma: Slachtoffers als daders, daders als slachtoffers* (*Echoes of trauma: Victims as perpetrators, perpetrators as victims*). Amsterdam: Boom.

31 Daniel Hughes (2007). *Attachment-Focused Family Therapy.* New York: W.W. Norton & Company.

32 Manfred Kets de Vries (2012). *The Hedgehog Effect: The Secrets of Building High Performance Teams.* New Jersey: John Wiley & Sons.

33 George Kohlrieser, Susan Goldsworthy and Duncan Coombe (2018). *Care to Dare: Unleashing Astonishing Potential Through Secure Base Leadership.* New Jersey: John Wiley & Sons Inc.

34 Manfred Kets de Vries (2014). *Mindful Leadership Coaching: Journeys Into the Interior.* London: Palgrave Macmillan; Manfred Kets de Vries (2012). *The Hedgehog Effect: The Secrets of Building High Performance Teams.* New Jersey: John Wiley & Sons.

35 Mary Ainsworth designed the *Strange Situation Test* on which the attachment styles are based.

36 Nathalie Huigsloot (2017). Een borreltje op zijn tijd is het beste antidepressivum (A drink in its time is the best antidepressant). *The Volkskrant,* September 23.

37 Henri Nouwen (2012). *Can you drink the cup?* Notre Dame: Ave Maria Press.

38 Gary Marcus (2019). *Kluge: The Haphazard Evolution of the Human Mind.* Boston: Mariner Books.

39 George Kohlrieser (2017). De kracht van woorden: Woorden kunnen ons gijzelen of bevrijden (The power of words. Words can hold us hostage or liberate). *TA Magazine,* June.

40 Roy Baumeister, Ellen Bratslavsky, Catrin Finkenauer, and Kathleen Vohs (2001). Bad is stronger than good. *Review of General Psychology.* Vol. 5–4.

41 Anita Kentie (2019). *Vrijheid in Verbinding. Naar een lichter en liefdevoller leven.* (*Freedom in Connection. Towards a lighter and more loving life*). Groningen: Nobelman Publishing.

42 Renate Geuzinge (2014). Specific changes in the brain by the nonspecific factors of the psychotherapeutic relationship. *Journal of Client-Focused Psychotherapy,* Vol. 52(1).

43 This statement was first used in 1949 by Donald Hebb, a Canadian neuropsychologist. See also: Christian Keysers and David Perrett (2004). Demystifying Social Cognition: A Hebbian Perspective. *Trends in Cognitive Sciences,* Vol. 8(11).

44 Marijke Baljon and Renate Geuzinge (2017). *Echo's van trauma: Slachtoffers als daders, daders als slachtoffers* (*Echoes of trauma. Victims as perpetrators, perpetrators as victims*). Amsterdam: Boom.
45 David Wallin (2015). *Attachment in psychotherapy*. New York: Guilford Publications.
46 Judith Crowel, Dominique Treboux and Everet Waters (2002). Stability of attachment representations: the transition to marriage. *Developmental Psychology*, 38.
47 Daniel Siegel (2011). *The Mindful Therapist: A Clinician's Guide to Mindsight and Neural Integration*. New York: W.W. Norton & Company. Siegel explains the steps to calming the brain in the video named 'Connecting to calm'. youtube.com.
48 Sue Johnson during the EFT congress 'Creating Connections', in 2015 in Kaatsheuvel, The Netherlands.
49 Marijke Baljon and Renate Geuzinge (2017). *Echo's van trauma: Slachtoffers als daders, daders als slachtoffers* (*Echoes of trauma. Victims as perpetrators, perpetrators as victims*). Amsterdam: Boom.
50 Emily Werner (2005). Resilience and Recovery: Findings from The Kauai Longitudinal Study. *Research, Policy, and Practice in Children's Mental Health*, Vol. 19(1); George Bonanno, Maren Westphal and Anthony Mancini (2011). Resilience to Loss and Potential Trauma. *Annual Review of Clinical Psychology*, 7.
51 Carol Dweck (2018). *Mindset: Changing the Way You think to Fulfil Your Potential*. Boston: Little, Brown and Company; Jakob van Wielink and Leo Wilhelm (2019). Cultuurverandering door coaching (Culture change through coaching). *Tijdschrift voor Ontwikkeling in Organisaties*, March.
52 Caroline Leaf (2018). *Think. Learn. Succeed: Understanding and Using Your Mind to Thrive at School, the Workplace, and Life*. Michigan: Bakerbooks.
53 Klaartje van Gasteren, Marnix Reijmerink and Jakob van Wielink (2019). Ik wil mensen wakker maken (I want to wake people up). In conversation with Carol Dweck on the growth mindset. *Tijdschrift voor Coaching*, December.
54 Jennifer Lilgendahl and Dan McAdams (2011). Constructing stories of self-growth: how individual differences in patterns of autobiographical reasoning relate to well-being in midlife. *Journal of Personality*, Vol. 79(2).
55 Frederic Laloux (2014). *Reinventing Organizations: A Guide to Creating Organizations Inspired by the Next Stage of Human Consciousness*. St. Millis: Parker-Nelson Publishing.
56 Anders Ericsson and Robert Pool (2016). *Peak: Secrets from the New Science of Expertise*. Boston: Houghton Mifflin Harcourt; Anders Ericsson, Michael Prietula and Edward Cokely (2007). The Making of an Expert. *Harvard Business Review*, July/August.

6. First Bond, Then Lead

1 Amy Cuddy, Matthew Kohut and John Neffinger (2013). Connect, Then Lead. *Harvard Business Review*, July/August.
2 Compare David Bohm (2004). *On Dialogue*. New York: Routledge.
3 Marshall Rosenberg (2015). *Nonviolent Communication: Nonviolent Life-Changing Tools for Healthy Relationships*. Encinitas: Puddle Dancer Press. See also Jakob van Wielink and Leo Wilhelm (2015). Wil je me precies vertellen wat je voelt? Eerbetoon aan Marshall B. Rosenberg (Will you tell me exactly what you feel? Tribute to Marshall B. Rosenberg). *Tijdschrift voor Coaching*, June.
4 Stephen Covey (2020). *The Seven Habits of Highly Effective People*. New York: Simon & Schuster.
5 Erik de Haan and Anthony Kasozi (2014). *The Leadership Shadow: How to Recognize and Avoid Derailment, Hubris and Overdrive*. London: Kogan Page. Compare

also Manfred Kets de Vries (2007). *The Leadership Mystique: Leading Behavior in the Human Enterprise*. London: Pearson. Also Yvonne Burger (2013). *Spiegel aan de top: Over de praktijk van executive coaching (Mirror at the top: On the practice of executive coaching)*. Amsterdam: Mediawerf.

6 Based on the drama triangle, also known as the Karpman triangle. This has three positions: victim, accuser and rescuer. All three positions impact each other in a negatively reinforcing way, because there is no real listening and no connection is made. Original publication: Steve Karpman (1968). Fairy tales and script drama analysis. *Transactional Analysis Bulletin*, 7(26).

7 Aristotle (2012). *Nicomachean Ethics*. Chicago: University of Chicago Press.

8 Matthew Lieberman and Naomi Eisenberger (2009). Pains and pleasures of social life. *Science*, 323; Matthew Lieberman and Naomi Eisenberger (2015). The dorsal anterior cingulate cortex is selective for pain: Results from large-scale reverse inference. *Proceedings of the National Academy of Sciences of the United States of America*, 112.

9 Gabor Maté (2019). *When the Body Says No: The Cost of Hidden Stress*. London: Ebury Publishing.

10 Jason Kanov, Edward Powley and Neil Walshe (2017). Is it ok to care? How compassion falters and is courageously accomplished in the midst of uncertainty. *Human Relations*, Vol. 70(6).

11 Curtis Hanson and Michael Apted (2012). *Chasing Mavericks*. Fox 2000 Pictures. Based on the life story of legendary surfer Jay Moriarity.

12 Compare Alison Wood Brooks and Leslie John (2018). The Surprising Power of Questions: It goes far beyond exchanging information. *Harvard Business Review*, May/June.

13 Brené Brown (2017). *Braving the Wilderness: The Quest for True Belonging and the Courage to Stand Alone*. London: Ebury Publishing.

14 Based on George Kohlrieser, Susan Goldsworthy and Duncan Coombe (2018). *Care to Dare: Unleashing Astonishing Potential Through Secure Base Leadership*. New Jersey: John Wiley & Sons Inc.

15 Daniel Kahneman and Amos Tversky (2000). *Choices, Values and Frames: Evaluation by moments, past and future*. Cambridge: Cambridge University Press; Daniel Kahneman and Amos Tversky (1979). Prospect theory: An analysis of decision under risk. *Econometrica*, 47.

16 Daniel Kahneman (20123). *Thinking, Fast and Slow*. New York: Farrar, Straus and Giroux.

17 Based on the children's book of the same name by Eric Carle. London: Random House.

18 Riet Fiddelaers-Jaspers (2019). *De rouwende school (The grieving school)*. Heeze: In de Wolken.

19 Audrey Eger Thompson and Jakob van Wielink (2020). Leading in Unknown Terrain. Lessons from Adversity. *Kosmos Journal for Global Transformation*, Summer.

7. To Welcome is to Learn to Let Go

1 Denise van Geelen-Merks and Jakob van Wielink (2020). *Met zoveel liefde heb ik van je gehouden: Woorden bij persoonlijk verlies (With so much love I have loved you: Words to accompany personal loss)*. Antwerp: Witsand; Laurens de Keyzer (2004). *Afscheid nemen (Saying goodbye)*. Tielt: Lannoo.

2 Manfred Kets de Vries and Katharina Balazs (1997). The Downside of Downsizing. *Human Relations*, Vol. 50(1).

3 Richard Price, Daniel Friedland and Anuram Vinokur (1998). Job loss: Hard times and eroded identity. In: John Harvey (ed.) *Perspectives on loss: A sourcebook*.

London: Psychology Press; Nick Kates, Barrie Greiff and Duane Hagan (1990). *The Psychosocial Impact of Job Loss*. Washington DC: American Psychiatric Publishing; Richard DeFrank (1986). Job Loss: An Individual Level and Review Model. *Journal of Callingal Behavior*, 28.

4 Brigitte Ballings (2016). *Een stap terug? Ik denk er niet aan! Over demotie en remotie, een nieuwe start en meer geluk op het werk (Taking a step back? I'm not thinking about it! On demotion and remotion, a new start and more happiness at work)*. Antwerp: Witsand.

5 Marie Louise Schipper (2011). 'Weg jij!' ("Away you go!") Interview with Caroline Harder and Ciska Pittie. *De Volkskrant*, September 15.

6 Bert Cozijnsen and Jakob van Wielink (2012). *Over de rooie: Emoties bij verlies en verandering op het werk (Going ballistic: Emotions in loss and change at work)*. Alphen aan den Rijn: Vakmedianet.

7 George Bonanno (2009). *The Other Side of Sadness: What the New Science of Bereavement Tells Us About Life After Loss*. New York: Basic Books; Maren Westphal and George Bonanno (2007). Posttraumatic growth and resilience to trauma: Different sides of the same coin or different coins? *Applied Psychology: An International Review*, Vol. 56(3).

8 Richard Tedeschi, Jane Shakespeare-Finch, Kanako Taku and Lawrence Calhoun (2018). *Posttraumatic Growth: Theory, Research, and Applications*. New York: Routledge.

9 Sheryl Sandberg and Adam Grant (2017). *Option B: Facing Adversity, Building Resilience, and Finding Joy*. New York: Alfred A. Knopf.

10 Julia Obert (2016). What we talk about when we talk about intimacy. *Emotion, Space and Society*, 21.

11 Leona Aarsen and Jakob van Wielink (2018). Meeliften op de liefde (Hitching a ride with love). In conversation with with Kim Phuc Phan Thi, the napalm girl. *Tijdschrift voor Coaching*, September; Anselm Grün (2007). *Waar heb ik dit aan verdiend? Omgaan met leed en verdriet (What did I do to deserve this? Dealing with suffering and sadness)*. Tielt/Kampen: Lannoo/Ten Have; Fedia Jacobs (2012). *Pijnlijke Verrijking. Rouw en herboren relaties in de slagschaduw van oorlogsgeweld (Painful Enrichment. Grief and reborn relationships in the shadow of war)*. Amstelveen: Voetspoor / Totemboek.

12 George Kohlrieser (2015). *How to turn loss into inspiration*. TEDx. Lausanne. youtube.com.

13 Charles Dhanaraj and George Kohlrieser (2020). The hidden perils of unresolved grief. *McKinsey Quarterly,* September.

14 Shep Jeffreys (2005). *Coping with Workplace Grief: Dealing with Loss, Trauma, and Change*. Boston: Thomson Learning.

15 Jakob van Wielink and Leo Wilhelm (2015). Een nieuw begin: Over afscheid nemen in de praktijk van de professioneel begeleider (A new beginning. On saying goodbye in the practice of the professional counselor). *Tijdschrift voor Begeleidingskunde*, Vol. 4(4).

16 Regina Bento (1994). When the Show Must Go on. Disenfranchised Grief in Organizations. *Journal of Managerial Psychology*, Vol. 9(6).

17 Philippe Bailleur (2020). *Stuck?: Dealing With Organizational Trauma*. Independently Published.

18 John Bowlby (1988). *Separation, Anxiety and Anger: Attachment and Loss, Volume 2*. London: Pimlico, Random House.

19 Philippe Bailleur (2018). *Trauma in organisaties: Herkennen, aanpakken, voorkomen (Trauma in organizations: Recognize, address, prevent)*. Tielt: LannooCampus.

20 William Bridges with Susan Bridges (2017). *Managing Transitions: Making the Most of Change*. London: John Murray Press.

21 Jakob van Wielink and Leo Wilhelm (2015). Organisaties als veroorzakers van verlies. Reorganisaties, arbeidsverlies en de rol van de leidinggevende (Organizations as enablers of loss. Reorganizations, job loss and the role of the manager). In: Johan Maes and Harriëtte Modderman (ed.) Rouw, rouwbegeleiding, rouwtherapie: Tussen presentie en interventie (*Grief, grief counseling, grief therapy: Between presence and intervention*). Antwerp: Witsand.

22 Rachel Naomi Remen (2006). *Kitchen Table Wisdom: Stories that Heal*. New York: Riverhead Books.

23 Compare Charles Dhanaraj and George Kohlrieser (2020). The hidden perils of unresolved grief. *McKinsey Quarterly*. September.

24 Kenneth Doka (1989). *Disenfranchised Grief: Recognizing Hidden Sorrow*. Lanham: Lexington Books; Kenneth Doka (2002). *Disenfranchised Grief: New Directions, Challenges, and Strategies for Practice*. Champaign: Research Press Inc.

25 'When we lose someone dear to us, through death or divorce, grieving does not come automatically. In fact, in many people it doesn't come at all.' In: Darian Leader (2009). *The New Black: Mourning, Melancholia and Depression*. London: Penguin.

26 Mary Lamia (2022). *Grief Isn't Something to Get Over: Finding a Home for Memories and Emotions After Losing a Loved One*. Washington, D.C.: American Psychological Association; Daniel Schacter (2019) Implicit memory, constructive memory, and imagining the future: A career perspective. *Perspectives on Psychological Science*. Vol. 14(2); Daniel Schacter (1987). Implicit Memory: History and Current Status. *Journal of Experimental Psychology: Learning, Memory and Cognition*. Vol. 13(3).

27 David Noer (1993). *Healing the Wound: Overcoming the Trauma of Layoffs and Revitalizing Downsized Organizations*. San Francisco: Jossey-Bass.

28 By one of the actors in the 2009 film *Up in the air*, directed by Jason Reitman. Distribution by Paramount Pictures. A film about an outside consultant who is hired to fire people on behalf of companies who dare not do so themselves. youtube.com.

29 David Roelfs, Eran Shor, Rachel Kalish, and Tamar Yogev (2011). The Rising Relative Risk of Mortality for Singles: Meta-Analysis and Meta-Regression. *American Journal of Epidemiology*. Vol. 174(4).

30 Jakob van Wielink, Leo Wilhelm and Denise van Geelen. Lifeline and Memory Reconsolidation. In: Robert Neimeyer (ed.) (2022). *New Techniques of Grief Therapy: Bereavement and Beyond*. New York: Routledge; Bruce Ecker, Robin Ticic and Laurel Hulley (2012). *Unlocking the Emotional Brain: Eliminating Symptoms at Their Roots Using Memory Reconsolidation*. New York: Routledge.

31 David Kessler (2020). *Finding Meaning: The Sixth Stage of Grief*. New York: Scribner.

32 Bruce Ecker (2015). Memory reconsolidation understood and misunderstood. *International Journal of Neuropsychotherapy*, Vol. 3(1).

33 Compare also Stephan Poulter (2006). *The Father Factor: How Your Father's Legacy Impacts Your Career*. Buffalo: Prometheus. See also Alison Gilbert (2011). *Parentless Parents: How the Loss of Our Mothers and Fathers Impacts the Way we Raise Our Children*. New York: Hyperion.

34 Jakob van Wielink, Leo Wilhelm and Denise van Geelen-Merks. The Secure Base Map. In: Robert Neimeyer (ed.) (2022). *New Techniques of Grief Therapy. Bereavement and Beyond*. New York: Routledge.

35 Jan Hoedeman (2020). Zonder werk kan ik niet (I can't live without work). *Eindhovens Dagblad*, May 23.

36 Dennis Klass, Phyllis Silverman and Steven Nickman (2014). *Continuing Bonds: New understandings of grief*. London: Taylor & Francis.

37 William Worden (2009). *Grief Counseling and Grief Therapy: A Handbook for the Mental Health Practitioner*. New York: Taylor & Francis.

38   Jakob van Wielink and Leo Wilhelm with assistance from Joyce Neijenhuis (2015). *Rouwregels: Handvatten voor organisaties rond overlijden en terminale ziekte (Rules for grief: Tools for organizations around bereavement and terminal illness)*. Antwerp: Witsand.

39   Joel Brockner (1988). The effect of work layoffs on survivors: Research, theory and practice. In: *Research in organizational behavior*, Vol. 10. Greenwich: JAI Press.

40   Jakob van Wielink and Leo Wilhelm (2012). Transitie en de betekenis van werk: Loopbaanontwikkeling en veranderingsprocessen (Transition and the meaning of work. Career development and change processes). *LoopbaanVisie*, 1; Jakob van Wielink and Leo Wilhelm (2012). 'Pink Slip'. Tussen boventalligheid en ontslag. ('Pink Slip'. Between redundancy and dismissal). *P&O Actueel, 1–2*.

41   Michael Norton and Francesca Gino (2014). Rituals Alleviate Grieving for Loved Ones, Lovers, and Lotteries. *Journal of Experimental Psychology: General*, Vol. 143(1).

42   Roy Baumeister (1992). *Meanings of Life*. New York: Guilford Publications.

43   Klaartje van Gasteren, Marnix Reijmerink, Michiel Soeters and Jakob van Wielink (2020). Ik bouw met woorden huizen waarin mensen zich thuis voelen (I use words to build houses where people feel at home). In conversation with Anselm Grün on leadership and calling. *Tijdschrift voor Coaching*, March.

44   Daniëlle Braun and Jitske Kramer (2015). *The Corporate Tribe. Organizational lessons from anthropology*. New York: Routledge.

45   A check-in is an important way to create space at the beginning of a meeting or gathering to be able to land, to be truly present. For example, employees literally check in by all sharing something about the same question. Check-ins take many forms. They can range from more superficial to deep, from creative to more classical. The success and effectiveness of the check-in hinges on the sincerity of the leader and his group to shape it. Checking in "for form's sake" leads to the opposite effect.

46   Patrick Lencioni (2004). *Death by Meeting: A Leadership Fable . . . About Solving the Most Painful Problem in Business*. New York: Wiley.

47   Don Yeager (2016). *Great Teams: 16 Things High Performing Organizations Do Differently*. Nashville: Thomas Nelson.

48   Emma Bell and Scott Taylor (2010). Beyond letting go and moving on: New perspectives on organizational death, loss and grief. *Scandinavian Journal of Management*, 27.

49   Daniel Kahneman and Barbara Fredrickson (1993). Duration neglect in retrospective evaluations of affective episodes. *Journal of Personality and Social Psychology*, Vol. 65(1); Daniel Kahneman, Barbara Fredrickson, Charles Schreiber and Donald Redelmeier (1993). When More Pain Is Preferred to Less: Adding a Better End. *Psychological Science*, Vol. 4 (6); Daniel Kahneman and Amos Tversky (2000). *Choices, Values and Frames*. Cambridge: Cambridge University Press.

8. First the Pain Then the Gain

1   Riet Fiddelaers-Jaspers (2018). *De poort van mijn hart. (Over)-leven in 33 gedichten (The gate of my heart. Surviving in 33 poems)*. Heeze: In de wolken.

2   Julia Samuel (2019). *Grief Works: Stories of Life, Death, and Surviving*. New York: Scribner Book Company.

3   If people feel that they are not being sufficiently recognized in how profound the experience was for them, they often continue to seek recognition. For example, by telling the story again and again and in the same way. Or by comparing themselves to others. Or by looking for allies. This can create a dynamic in which their own rightness is contrasted with the wrongness of others. This 'suffering competition'

makes it harder to deal with one's own loss, as one's energy and attention are focused on other things. See: Jakob van Wielink, Leo Wilhelm and Denise van Geelen-Merks (2019). *Loss, Grief, and Attachment in Life Transitions: A Clinician's Guide to Secure Base Counseling.* New York: Routledge.

4 Lumina Albert, David Allen, Jonathan Biggane and Qing (Kathy) Ma (2015). Attachment and responses to employment dissolution. *Human Resource Management Review,* 25.

5 Adi Ignatius (2017). Above All, Acknowledge the Pain. A Conversation About Resilience With Sheryl Sandberg and Adam Grant. *Harvard Business Review,* May/June.

6 Compare Neil Thompson (2009). *Loss, Grief and Trauma in the Workplace.* Amityville: Baywood Publishing.

7 David Kessler (2020). Helping Your Team Heal: Leaders must recognize people's grief and assist them in finding meaning. *Harvard Business Review,* July/August.

8 Compare also Barbara Barski-Carrow (2018). *When Trauma Survivors Return to Work: Understanding Emotional Recovery.* Londen: Rowman & Littlefield.

9 David Kessler (2019). *Finding Meaning: The Sixth Stage of Grief.* New York: Scribner.

10 Stephen Porges (2017). *The Pocket Guide to the Polyvagal Theory: The Transformative Power of Feeling Safe.* New York: W.W. Norton & Company.

11 Jakob van Wielink, Leo Wilhelm, and Denise van Geelen (2019). *Loss, Grief, and Attachment in Life Transitions: A Clinician's Guide to Secure Base Counseling.* New York: Routledge.

12 Compare 'Emoties. De verborgen kracht van emoties' ('Emotions. The hidden power of emotions') in Jaap Boonstra (2013). *Verandermanagement in 28 lessen (Change management in 28 lessons).* Amsterdam: Business Contact.

13 C.S. Lewis (2017). *The Four Loves.* San Francisco: Harperone.

14 Interview by Loeka Oostra with Jakob van Wielink (2020). Waarom kwetsbaarheid voor managers veel oplevert (maar niet gemakkelijk is) (Why vulnerability for managers has a lot to offer (but is not easy)). *MT,* February; Interview by Miloe van Beek with Jakob van Wielink (2017). Weg met het pantser (Down with the armor). *Het Financieele Dagblad,* December 23.

15 Brené Brown (2018). *Dare to lead: Brave Work. Tough Conversations. Whole Hearts.* London: Ebury Publishing.

16 Riet Fiddelaers–Jaspers (2019). Met mijn ziel onder de arm. Tussen welkom heten en afscheid nemen *(Feeling lost. Between welcoming and saying goodbye).* Heeze: In de Wolken.

17 Serena Chen (2018). Give Yourself a Break: The Power of Self–Compassion. *Harvard Business Review,* September/October; Katie Gunnell, Amber Mosewich, Carolyn McEwen, Robert Eklund and Peter Crocker (2017). Don't be so hard on yourself!: Changes in self–compassion during the first year of university are associated with changes in well-being. *Personality and Individual Differences,* Vol. 107(1); Hans Schroder, Megan Fisher, Yanli Lin, Sharon Lo, Judith Danovitch and Jason Moser (2017). Neural evidence for enhanced attention to mistakes among school-aged children with a growth mindset. *Developmental Cognitive Neuroscience,* 24.

18 Gianpiero Petriglieri and Sally Maitlis (2019). When a Colleague is Grieving: How to provide the right kind of support. *Harvard Business Review,* July/August.

19 Lisanne van Sadelhoff (2020). Rouw heeft geen eindpunt. En dat is hoopvoller dan het klinkt (Grief has no end point. And that's more hopeful than it sounds). *The Correspondent,* June 25, 2020.

20 Riet Fiddelaers-Jaspers (2019). Met mijn ziel onder de arm. Tussen welkom heten en afscheid nemen *(Feeling lost. Between welcoming and saying goodbye).* Heeze: In de Wolken.

21 Jakob van Wielink and Leo Wilhelm with the cooperation of Joyce Neijenhuis (2015). *Rouwregels* (Rules for Grief). Antwerpen: Witsand.

22 Joop Swieringa and Jaqueline Jansen (2005). Gedoe komt er toch: Zin en onzin over organisatieverandering *(Fuss happens anyway. Sense and nonsense about organizational change).* Schiedam: Scriptum.

23 Boris Groysberg and Michael Slind (2012). Leadership Is A Conversation. How to improve employee engagement and alignment in today's flatter, more networked organizations. *Harvard Business Review,* June.

24 Compare Dennis Tourish, Neil Paulsen, Elizabeth Hopman and Prashant Bordia (2004). The Downsides of Downsizing: Communication Processes Information Needs in the Aftermath of a Workforce Reduction Strategy. *Management Communication Quarterly,* Vol. 17, No. 4; Kim Cameron (1994). Strategies for successful organizational downsizing. *Human Resource Management,* Summer.

25 Wilfried Nellis (2016). *Het leven kent geen weg terug; de fundamenten van het levens-integratie-*proces *(Life knows no turning back; the fundamentals of the life integration process).* Avenhorn: Het Noorderlicht.

26 Tanja van Roosmalen, Riet Fiddelaers-Jaspers and Machteld Lavell (2020). *Een pleister tegen tranen (A bandaid against tears).* Heeze: In de Wolken. In this book colleague Tanja van Roosmalen calls the pendulum movement of the Dual Process model 'living through' and 'living on'. On the one hand the change is tangible and on the other hand your life goes on.

27 Margaret Stroebe and Henk Schut (1999). The Dual Process Model of Coping with Bereavement: Rationale and Description. *Death Studies* 23; Margaret Stroebe Henk Schut (2010). The Dual Process Model of Coping with Bereavement: A Decade On. *Omega,* Vol. 61(4).

28 Riet Fiddelaers-Jaspers. The internal split in traumatic loss. In: Robert Neimeyer (ed.) (2022). *New Techniques of Grief Therapy. Bereavement and* Beyond. New York: Routledge.

29 Marie-José Geenen and Tijn Ponjee (2020). Uit de verstarring komen geeft ruimte (Coming out of rigidity gives space). In conversation with Margriet Wentink. *Tijdschrift voor begeleidingskunde,* Vol. 9(1).

30 Edith Eger (2018). *The Choice: Embrace the Possible.* New York: Scribner Book Company.

31 Barbara Barski-Carrow (1998). *Using Study Circles in the Workplace as an Educational Method of Facilitating Readjustment After a Traumatic Life Experience.* Dissertation submitted to the Graduate Faculty of the Virginia Polytechnic Institute and State University in partial fulfillment of the requirements for the degree of doctor of philosophy. Blacksburg, Virginia.

32 Interview by Dominique Haijtema with Jakob van Wielink (2017). Onze diepe pijn is onze achilleshiel en grootste krachtbron (Our deep pain is our Achilles' heel and greatest source of strength). *MT,* October.

33 Franz Ruppert (2012). *Symbiosis and Autonomy: Symbiotic Trauma and Love Beyond Entanglements.* Steyning: Green Balloon Publishing. The description of fragmentation in loss stems from the work of this German psychotherapy.

34 Compare also Margriet Wentink (2014). *Je verlangen: Dwaallicht of kompas? (Your desire: Wandering light or compass?).* Eeserveen: Akasha.

35 Peter Levine (2010). *In An Unspoken Voice: How the Body Releases Trauma and Restores Goodness.* Berkeley: North Atlantic Books. Levine produced groundbreaking work on how trauma remains trapped in our bodies and what we can learn from animals in this.

36 This window originated with Daniel Siegel who called it the *River of Integration.* It has been further elaborated and become known as the *Window of Tolerance* by

Kekuki Minton and Pat Ogden. Riet Fiddelaers-Jaspers and Sabine Noten called it the Window of Tolerance in their publication Herbergen van verlies (Inns of Loss). Heeze: In de wolken. (2019).

37 Kelly McGonigal (2015). *The Upside of Stress: Why Stress Is Good for You, and How to Get Good at It.* New York: Avery Publishing Group. See also her TED Talk ted.com/talks.

38 Cynthia Cordes and Thomas Dougherty (1993). A Review and an Integration of Research on Job Burnout. *Academy of Management Review*, Vol. 18(4).

39 Ahmed Tawakol, Amorina Ishai, Richard Takx, Amparo Figueroa, Abdelrahman Ali, Yannick Kaiser, . . . Roger Pitman (2017). Relation between resting amygdalar activity and cardiovascular events: a longitudinal and cohort study. *The Lancet*, January.

40 George Vaillant (2015). *Triumphs of Experience: The Men of the Harvard Grant Study.* Cambridge: Belknap Press; Marianne Legato (2009). *Why Men Die First: How to Lengthen Your Lifespan.* Londen: Palgrave Macmillan; Al Scaglione and Philip Shore (2006). *Why Men Die Before Women And How To Prevent It.* Bloomington: Xlibris; Michael Jan, Stephanie Bonn, Arvid Sjolander, Fredrik Wiklund, Pär Stattin, Erik Holmberg, Henrik Grönberg and Katarina Bälter (2016). The roles of stress and social support in prostate cancer mortality. *Scandinavian Journal of Urology,* Vol. 50(1).

41 Renate Geuzinge (2014). Specific changes in the brain due to non-specific factors of the psychotherapeutic relationship. *Journal of Client-Focused Psychotherapy,* Vol. 52(1).

42 Bessel van der Kolk in the integral interview accompanying the VRT documentary *If you only knew. February 2020; Bessel van der Kolk (2015). The Body Keeps the Score: Mind, Brain and Body in the Transformation of Trauma.* London: Penguin.

43 Allan Schore (2001). The effects of a secure attachment relationship on right brain development, affect regulation, and infant mental health. *Infant Mental Health Journal,* 22; Daniel Siegel (2015). *The Developing Mind: How relationships and the brain interact to shape who we are.* New York: Guilford Press.

44 Marijke Baljon and Renate Geuzinge (2017). *Echo's van trauma: Slachtoffers als daders, daders als slachtoffers (Echoes of Trauma. Victims as Perpetrators, Perpetrators as Victims).* Amsterdam: Boom.

45 Siegel explains in the video "name it or tame it" how the brain works when people are upset and what you can do to make them approachable again. youtube.com.

46 Brené Brown (2018). *Dare to Lead: Brave Work. Tough Conversations. Whole Hearts.* London: Ebury Publishing.

47 William Ernest Henley (1888). Last and best-known part of the poem was published in the *Book of Verses*; the title "*Invictus*" (Latin for invincible) was added when the poem was included in *The Oxford Book of English Verse*.

48 Clint Eastwood (directed) (2009). *Invictus;* distribution by Warner Bros. Based in part on the book by John Carlin (2010). *Playing The Enemy: Nelson Mandela And the Game That Made A Nation.* London: Atlantic Books.

49 Azim Khamisa (2005). *From Murder to Forgiveness: A Father's Journey.* Bloomington: Balboa.

50 Caroline Leaf (2018). *Think. Learn. Succeed: Understanding and Using Your Mind to Thrive at School, the Workplace, and Life.* Michigan: Bakerbooks; Robert Enright (2012). *The Forgiving Life: Pathway to Overcoming Resentment and Creating a Legacy of Love.* York: Maple Vail Books.

51 Klaartje van Gasteren, Marnix Reijmerink, Michiel Soeters and Jakob van Wielink (2020). Ik bouw met woorden huizen waarin mensen zich thuis voelen (I use words to build houses where people feel at home). In conversation with Anselm Grün on leadership and calling. *Tijdschrift voor Coaching*, March.

52 Jakob van Wielink and Leo Wilhelm (2012). Interne en externe zingeving bij ver-
    lies (Internal and external meaning in loss). *Streven,* November.
53 Dalai Lama and Desmond Tutu with Douglas Abrams (2016). *The Book of Joy:
    Lasting Happiness in a Changing World.* New York: Avery Publishing Group.
54 Liesbeth Rasker (2020). In conversation with her father Frans Rasker about the
    death of his wife and her mother in the podcast *Day by Day.*

9. The Key to Real Change is in Your Pocket

 1 Robert Neimeyer (2006). Bereavement And The Quest For Meaning: Rewriting
    Stories Of Loss And Grief. *Hellenic Journal of Psychology, 3;* Robert Neimeyer
    (2019). Meaning reconstruction in bereavement: Development of a research pro-
    gram. *Death Studies* Vol. 43(2); Roy Baumeister (1992). *Meanings of Life.* New
    York: Guilford Publications.
 2 Viktor Frankl (1984). *Man's Search for Meaning: An Introduction to Logotherapy.*
    New York: Simon & Schuster.
 3 Jim Collins (2010). *Good to Great: Why Some Companies Make the Leap . . .
    and Others Don't.* London: Random House; Thomas Peters and Robert Waterman
    (2004); *In Search of Excellence: Lessons from America's Best-Run Companies.* New
    York: HarperCollins Publishers.
 4 Martin Antony and Richard Swinson (2019). *When Perfect Isn't Good Enough:
    Strategies for Coping with Perfectionism.* Oakland: New Harbinger Publications.
 5 Brené Brown (2020). *The Gifts of Imperfection.* London: Ebury Publishing. The
    metaphor of the inner theater comes from Manfred Kets de Vries (2007). *The Lead-
    ership Mystique: Leading Behavior in the Human Enterprise.* London: Pearson.
 6 Margareth Robinson Ferguson (2019). *Perfectly Hidden Depression: How to Break
    Free from the Perfectionism That Masks Your Depression.* Oakland: New Harbin-
    ger Publications.
 7 George Kohlrieser (2006). *Hostage At The Table: How Leaders Can Overcome Con-
    flict, Influence Others, and Raise Performance.* New Jersey: John Wiley & Sons Inc.
 8 See also Stephan Poulter (2019). *The Shame Factor: Heal Your Deepest Fears and
    Set Yourself Free.* Buffalo: Prometheus; John Bradshaw (2005). *Healing The Shame
    That Binds You.* Deerfield Beach: Health Communications.
 9 Peter Senge (2006). *The Fifth Discipline: The Art & Practice of The Learning
    Organization.* New York: Bantam Doubleday Dell Publishing Group.
10 Michaela Driver (2007). Meaning and suffering in organizations. *Journal of
    Organizational Change Management,* Vol. 20(5).
11 Edith Eger (2018). *The Choice: Embrace the Possible.* New York: Scribner Book
    Company.
12 Emily Esfahani Smith (2019). *The Power of Meaning: The true route to happiness.*
    London: Ebury Publishing.
13 Brené Brown (2013). *The Power of Vulnerability: Teachings on Authenticity,
    Connection and Courage.* Louisville: Sounds True Inc.
14 Donald Hebb (2002). *The Organization of Behavior: A Neuropsychological The-
    ory.* London: Psychology Press.
15 Julianne Holt–Lunstad, Timothy Smith, Mark Baker, Tyler Harris and David Ste-
    phenson (2015). Loneliness and Social Isolation as Risk Factors for Mortality:
    A Meta-Analytic Review. *Perspectives on Psychological Science,* Vol. 10(2).
16 Victor Strecher (2016). *Life on Purpose: How Living for What Matters Most Changes
    Everything.* San Francisco: Harperone.
17 Klaartje van Gasteren, Marnix Reijmerink and Jakob van Wielink (2020). Het is de
    film die telt, niet de titel (It's the film that counts, not the title). In conversation with

Nick Craig on leadership and purpose. *Tijdschrift voor Coaching*, June; Nick Craig (2018). *Leading from Purpose. Clarity and the Confidence to Act When It Matters Most*. New York: Hachette Books.

18 Viktor Frankl (1984). *Man's Search for Meaning: An Introduction to Logotherapy*. New York: Simon & Schuster.

19 Klaartje van Gasteren, Marnix Reijmerink and Jakob van Wielink (2019). Ik heb Auschwitz in een klaslokaal veranderd (I turned Auschwitz into a classroom). In conversation with Dr. Edith Eva Eger. *Tijdschrift voor Coaching*, March.

20 Klaartje van Gasteren, Marnix Reijmerink, and Jakob van Wielink (2019). Er waren slachtoffers aan beide zijden van het geweer (There were victims on both sides of the gun). In conversation with Azim Khamisa on the power of forgiveness. *Tijdschrift voor Coaching*, June; Azim Khamisa (2020). Leadership for the Greater Good: A Guide for Truth to Power Champions. Cardiff: Waterside Productions.

21 Alex Pattakos and Elaine Dundon (2017). Discovering Meaning Through the Lens of Work. *Journal of Constructivist Psychology*, 30(1); Evgenia Lysova, Blake Allan, Bryan Dik, Ryan Duffy and Michael Steger (2019). Fostering meaningful work in organizations: A multi–level review and integration. *Journal of Vocational Behavior*, 110.

22 Edith Eger (2018). *The Choice: Embrace the Possible*. New York: Scribner Book Company.

23 Richard Leider and David Shapiro (2016). *Work Reimagined: Uncover Your Calling*. San Francisco: Berrett-Koehler Publishers.

24 Compare also Lenette Schuijt (2004). Op het kruispunt van beroep en roeping (At the crossroads of profession and calling). In: Henk Hoefman and Lenette Schuijt (ed.). *Het menselijke gezicht van werk. De integratie van professionaliteit en spiritualiteit (The Human Face of Work. The Integration of professionalism and spirituality)*. Rotterdam: Asoka.

25 James Hollis (2018). *Living an Examined Life: Wisdom for the Second Half of the Journey*. New York: Sounds True.

26 Jakob van Wielink and Leo Wilhelm (2020). (Re)discovering Calling in the Wake. Of Loss through Secure Bases. *AI Practitioner*, May.

27 Compare Marcus Buckingham (2005). *The One Thing You Need to Know: . . . About Great Managing, Great Leading, and Sustained Individual Success*. New York: Free Press.

28 Andreas Hirschi, Anita Keller and Daniel Spurk (2018). Living one's calling: Job resources as a link between having and living a calling. *Journal of Vocational Behavior*, 106.

29 Francesc Miralles and Héctor García (2017). *Ikigai: The Japanese Secret to a Long and Happy Life*. London: Penguin Life.

30 Mihaly Csikszentmihalyi (2008). *Flow: The Psychology of the Optimal Experience*. New York: Harper Perennial Modern Classics. Csikszentmihalyi describes flow as the optimal state of mind of intrinsic motivation, in which a person is completely absorbed in what he is doing.

31 Gill Corkindale (2008). Overcoming Imposter Syndrome. *Harvard Business Review*, May; Joe Langford and Pauline Rose Clance (1993). The impostor phenomenon: recent research findings regarding dynamics, personality and family patterns and their implications for treatment. *Psychotherapy: Theory, Research, Practice, Training*, Vol. 30(3); Pauline Clance and Suzanne Imes (1978). The imposter phenomenon in high achieving women: Dynamics and therapeutic intervention. *Psychotherapy: Theory, Research & Practice*, Vol. 15(3).

32 Miguel de Cervantes Saavedra (2018). *The Ingenious Nobleman Don Quixote of La Mancha*. Andover: Gale Ecco, Print Editions.

33 C.P. Cavafy (2008). *The Collected Poems*. Oxford: Oxford University Press.

34 Compare also Morten Hjort, Wibe Veenbaas, Mirjam Broekhuizen, Jane Coerts and Joke Goudswaard (2017). *De tekens verstaan. Over plek en ordening als bron in verbindend leiderschap (Understanding the Signs. On place and order as a resource in connecting leadership)*. Utrecht: Phoenix Opleidingen.

35 Thomas Lee and Angela Duckworth (2018). Organizational Grit: Turning passion and perseverance into performance: the view from the health care industry. *Harvard Business Review*, September/October; Thomas Malnight, Ivy Buche and Charles Dhanaraj (2019). Put Purpose at the CORE of Your Strategy. *Harvard Business Review*, September/October.

36 David Brooks (2019). *The Second Mountain: The search for a moral life*. London: Penguin Books.

37 Susanne Kruys (2020). *De biografie als medicijn. De zin van levensverhalen in de zorg (Biography as Medicine. The meaning of life stories in healthcare)*. Tielt: LannooCampus.

38 Bart Assies (2019). Eerst Philips-techneut, nu therapeut (First Philips Technician, Now Therapist). *Eindhovens Dagblad*.

39 Nick Craig (2018). *Leading from Purpose. Clarity and the Confidence to Act When It Matters Most*. New York: Hachette Books; Mark Savickas (2018). *Career Counseling*. Washington: American Psychological Association.

40 Jakob van Wielink, Leo Wilhelm and Denise van Geelen–Merks (2019). *Loss, Grief, and Attachment in Life Transitions. A Clinician's Guide to Secure Base Counseling*. New York: Routledge.

41 Jerry Fletcher (1995). *Patterns of High Performance: Discovering the Ways People Work Best*. San Francisco: Berett-Koehler Publishers.

42 Elizabeth Day (2019). *How to Fail: Everything I've Ever Learned From Things Going Wrong*. London: Fourth Estate; Miloe van Beek (2017). *Yes! I screwed up. 13 fouten die je bedrijf beter maken (Yes! I screwed up. 13 mistakes that make your business better)*. Zaltbommel: Thema.

43 Frederic Laloux (2014). *Reinventing Organizations: A Guide to Creating Organizations Inspired by the Next Stage of Human Consciousness*. St. Millis: Parker-Nelson Publishing.

44 Brian Robertson (2015). *Holacracy: The New Management System for a Rapidly Changing World*. New York: Henry Holt & Company.

45 Freek van Looveren (2018). *De kleine Laloux. Het inventieve boek samengevat (The Little Laloux. The inventive book summarized)*. Amsterdam: Business Contact.

46 Brian Robertson and Frederic Laloux (2014). *Reinventing Organizations: A Guide to Creating Organizations Inspired by the Next Stage of Human Consciousness*. St. Millis: Parker-Nelson Publishing.

47 Janis Forman (2013). *Storytelling in Business: The Authentic and Fluent Organization*. Redwood City: Stanford Business Books.

48 Simon Sinek (2019). *Start With Why: How Great Leaders Inspire Everyone to Take Action*. New York: Ballantine Books.

49 Klaus Horn and Regine Brick (2005). *Invisible Dynamics. Systemic Constellations in Organisations and in Business*. Heidelberg: Carl Auer International.

50 Richard Maxwell and Robert Dickman (2007). *The Elements of Persuasion: Use Storytelling to Pitch Better, Sell Faster and Win More Business*. New York: Harper Business.

51 Peter Scholters (2020). Dela opnieuw 'Best Workplace', Freo op tiende plek (Dela again 'Best Workplace', Freo in tenth spot). *ED*, June 16; Marloe van der Schrier (2019). Winnaars 'Best Workplaces 2019' zorgen dat mensen baas zijn over hun eigen werk (Winners 'Best Workplaces 2019' concerns. That people are masters of their own work). *AD*, March 26.

52 William Bridges (2001). *The Way of Transition: Embracing Life's Most Difficult Moments*. Cambridge: Da Capo Press.
53 Emma Freud (2017). What is your biggest regret?: Here are people's devastatingly honest answers. *The Guardian*, October 31.
54 Bronnie Ware (2012). *The Top Five Regrets of the Dying: A Life Transformed by the Dearly Departing*. Carlsbad (CA): Hay House Inc.
55 This famous dictum is attributed to Socrates who supposedly spoke these words at his trial for impiety and corrupting youth, for which he was subsequently sentenced to death.
56 Henri Nouwen (2012). *Can You Drink the Cup?* Notre Dame: Ave Maria Press.
57 Henri Nouwen (2011). *The Return of the Prodigal Son: A Story of Homecoming*. Veghel: Image Books; Lieuwe Koopmans (2012). *Dit ben ik! Worden wie je bent met Transactionele Analyse (This is me! Becoming who you are with Transactional Analysis)*. Zaltbommel: Thema.
58 Alice Miller (2015). *The Drama of the Gifted Child: The Search for the True Self*. New York: Basic Books; Dominique Haijtema (2019). *Nooit meer een zelfhulp-boek: Raw food for the mind (Never a self-help book again. Raw food for the mind)*. Amsterdam/Antwerp: Volt.
59 Warren Bennis and Patricia Ward Biederman (2010). *Still Surprised: A Memoir of a Life in Leadership*. San Francisco: Jossey-Bass.

The Shoulders On Which We Stand

1 Nick Craig (2018). *Leading from Purpose: Clarity and the Confidence to Act When It Matters Most*. New York: Hachette Books. Klaartje van Gasteren, Marnix Reijmerink and Jakob van Wielink (2020). Het is de film die telt, niet de titel (It's the film that counts, not the title). In conversation with Nick Craig on leadership and purpose. *Tijdschrift voor Coaching*, June.

Index

References to figures appear in *italic* type; those in **bold** type refer to tables

abandonment 52, 149
ability to listen 26 *see also* listening
acknowledging losses 118
acquired attachment 55, 75
activation 66
active listening 93, 94–5
addictive behaviors 117–18
adequate-to-substandard performers 21
adrenaline 156
adult attachment 52
Ainsworth, Marry 52–3
Alexander the Great 99
Am I valued? 36
"Am I welcome?" 36
amygdala 72
amygdala hijack 25, 72–3
'anesthetics' 71
anniversaries 126
anticipated losses 119
Any Given Sunday (film) 169
Aristotle 87
Aristotle Project (Google) 48
asking questions 48–9
attaching (embracing) 109, **110**
attachment 8–9, 52–79, 110; basis
        for life and work 68–71; and
        the brain 62–4; and grief 140;
        insecure attachment 53–7, 68–9,
        139–40; resilience 153; secure
        attachment 53, 55, 139, 159;
        secure bases 57–62; unconscious
        behavior 53 *see also* resilience
attachment history 54
attachment patterns 68, 75
attention to transition 15
attuned responses 63
Auschwitz xiv–xv, 5, 168, 170

authentic meaning 2
autobiographical memory 71
autonomy 15–16
avoidance 147, 150
avoiding attachment 140
avoiding bonding and intimacy 148–9
avoiding conflict 3–4, 101
avoiding pain and loss 101–2, *102*
avoiding painful feelings 120, 147–57
        see also stress
awareness 151
awe 83

babies of anxious mothers 34
Bailleur, Philippe 109, **110**, 112
Bakker, Siets 36
Barsoux, Jean-Louis 21
baseline of calm and quiet 77
becoming aware 44
behavioral patterns 43–4
being and doing energies 173
being born 33, 35
being calm 75–8
being safe and *feeling secure* 58
belonging 36–7
blaming others 21
Bommel, Floris van 17, 23–4
Bommel, Pepijn van 38
Bommel, Reynier van 23–4, 38
bonding 82–107, 169; active listening
        95; and calling 176; and
        dialogues 90–3; and intimacy
        9–10, 70, 82–4; keystones 90–9;
        leadership approaches 99–105;
        paraphrasing 95–7; saying
        goodbye 120–6; and stress 155;
        vulnerability 84–5

bonding conversations 57–8
boundaries 10, 69–71
Bowlby, John 8, 52–3
the brain 27; and attachment 62–4;
    growth 63; higher brain
    (neocortex) 63, 157; left
    hemisphere 63, 158–9; lower
    brain 63, 67, 158; plasticity 27;
    programmed 71; rewiring 55;
    right brain communication 63,
    65, 159; right brain to right brain
    communication 76, 159; right
    hemisphere 158–9; upper brain
    67, 157–8
brain building 62
brain development 62, 157–8
'brain triggers' 25
Braun, Daniëlle 128
Bridges, William 21–2, 185, 198–9
Brood, Herman 56
Brooks, David 178
brothers and sisters 38
Brown, Brené 140, 160, 169
bypassing discomfort 131–2

calling 3, 7, 172–5, 185–6; finding and
    formulating 179–80; influences
    183–4; Jakob *189*, 190–1;
    journey of adventure 17–19;
    journey to second mountain
    178–9; Leo *195*, 196–7; living
    your calling 4, 175; making
    visible 19; and meaning 175–8;
    organizations 184–5; resistance
    to 177; Riet *192*, 193–4; window
    of leadership and calling 2,
    174–5 *see also* meaning
calming the brain 75–7, 159–60
Campbell, Joseph 17
career moves 113
caring 9, 27
Carle, Eric 102
causing damage and pain 100
celebrating successes 29
Chabot, Bart 55–6
chair-switch 121
changes 20–3, 28, 58
Chasing Mavericks (film) 91
check-ins 128–9
children: activating attachment system
    63; attachment period 68;
    attachment styles 52–3; as
    budding researcher 66; family

system 39; insecure attachment
    styles 53–7; internalizing
    messages 34; parents calming 65;
    secure attachment 53; sensitivity
    to *type* of compliments 78 *see
    also* parents
The Choice (Eger) 35, 168, 198
clinging survival strategies 148
cognitive brain *see* higher brain
    (neocortex)
cognitive filters 97
cognitive neuroscience 115
Colbert, Steven 41
collaboration 82 *see also* bonding
collateral damage 100
collective farewells 129–30
collective unconscious 17
comfort zones 20, 29–30
commemoration 131
communication 87
compassion 88–90, 102–3
compulsory redundancies 130
conducting 3
conflict: avoiding 3–4, 101; dialogue 93;
    fight 97–9; harmony 3–4
confronting colleagues 1
conscious desires 9–10
conscious leaving ceremonies 133
contact and welcome 8, *8*, 33–50;
    behavioral patterns 43–6;
    leadership and organizational
    systems 36–43; psychological
    safety 9, 46–50, *102*
containment 65
contract 45–6
coping by fragmenting 152
co-regulation 66
corporate storytelling 184–5
Covid-19 pandemic (coronavirus crisis)
    3, 25, 43, 169
Craig, Nick 5, 199
creation and emergence life cycles 112
crucibles of leadership 19
culpable leadership 104
cultural differences 5
cutting ties 125–6
Cycle of Stalled Transition 148, *149*
cynicism 25, 117, 149–52

Dalai Lama 162
daring 9
deaths: of parents 41; rituals 126; of
    spouses 108

Deelder, Jules 56
deferring judgment 98–9
de Haan, Erik 85
Dekkers, Midas 69, 70
"DELA – for each other" (funeral
    organization) 185
delayed gratification 17
delaying judgment/responses 88–90, 98
demarcation 53–4, 71
denial of loss 116–17, 149
destiny 184
detaching (letting go) 109, **110**, 148
developing resilience 77
developing talents 4
developmental journey 5
dialogue model 90–1, *90*
dialogues 19, 90–3
disagreement ("I disagree") 95
discipline 4, 17
disconnection 67, 69–70
disruption 44
distance and invulnerability 70
"Do I belong?" 36
doing energy 173
dominating leadership 83, 101, *102*
Don Quixote 177
'downstairs brain' (Siegel) 63n25
drama triangle (Karpman triangle) 87n6
Dual Process Model (Stroebe and Schut)
    147

Edmondson, Amy 47, 48
Eger, Edith Eva xiv–xvi, 5, 151, 152, 160;
    The Choice 35, 168, 198; finding
    freedom 172; and Viktor Frankl
    169–70
Eger, Martha 168
embracing (attaching) 109, **110**
embracing by letting go 109–12
emotionally available leaders 55
emotional pain 88
emotional regulation 64–7, 72, 77
emotions 86–90
empathy 102–3
employee responsibilities 15
Enden, Geert van den 104–5
"entertainment" (Nouwen) 71
epigenetic research 34–5
Ericsson, Anders 79
Esfahani Smith, Emily 168, 169, 172
etiquette (social and cultural codes) 86
everyday problems 21
"evolving purpose" (Robertson) 184

excelling style of life and leadership
    100, 101, *102*
exclusion 36–7
exercises 180–4
expected and unexpected losses
    118–19, 152
experiencing stress 155
experiencing transcendence 171–2

facing new realities 120
failure 140
false sense of security 59–60
families 35, 37–41
family business 15
family of origin 33
farewell rituals 129, 131
fault lines 23, 24
fear 83
"fearful procrastination" 1
feedback 26
feeling secure and *being safe* 58
Ferriss, Tim 16–17
Fiddelaers-Jaspers, Maria Josina Martina
    (Riet) 150, 192–4, *192*
first mountain (*competence, happiness
    and competition*) 178–9
first year of life 62
forgiveness 161–3, 170–1, 172
fragmentation 152, *153*
Frankl, Viktor 169–70
freedom and running from the past 151
Full License (Dekkers) 70
future expectations 120

Galton, Francis 46
Gandhi 161
Gantt, Horsley 25n18
García, Héctor 175
Gasteren, Klaartje van *102*, 198, 199
genetic expression 35
gentleness 88
"getting your hands dirty" 104
giving and receiving 43
giving up and staying alive 169
goodbyes 109–14, **110**
good emotional regulation 77
"good enough" parents 35
good-to-excellent performers 21
Google 48
Gordian knot 99, 103–4
Grant, Adam 108
grief and grieving 10–11, 136–65;
        act of leadership 142–3; and

attachment 139–44; and awareness 151; and forgiveness 161–3; as a new reality 141–2; relief from 163; and resilience 153; social support 143–4; and transition 145–7; and work 137–9 *see also* loss and separation
grit factor 4
'group conscience' 86
groupthink 46–7, 91
growing beyond unwanted patterns 44
growth after loss 109
growth as a leader 25
growth mindset 78–9
Grün, Anselm 128

Haan, Erik de 85
handshakes 129
hard work 71, 150, 193
harmony 3–4
health and stress 157
healthy functioning 152, *153*
Hebb, Donald 74
Hedgehog Effect 68–9
Hellinger, Bert 36n8
Henley, William Ernest 161
Hero's Journey (Campbell) 17–18, 19–20
hidden grief 114–18
hidden loss 125
hidden pain 151
hierarchies 94
higher brain (neocortex) 63, 157
history line (Bailleur) 112
Holacracy (Robertson) 184
holidays 126
hostage state of mind 73
hugs 129
human contact 25
human kindness (*owed respect*) 59
Hunger Winter (1944–1945) 34

identity: and calling 172–3; of organizations and family systems 39
ikigai ("happiness of always being busy") 175
impact: and calling 173; as a leader 18; of words 71–2
impactful experiences 13
'implicit memory' 115
impostor syndrome 176
indecisive leaders 83

individual farewells 129
influence of circumstances 34
inner resistance 177–8
inner theater 73
innovative work 49
insecure attachment 53–7, 68–9, 139–40 *see also* attachment; secure attachment
instilling fear 49
integration 136–65; avoiding loss 146; and forgiveness 162–3; and grief 10–11, 160; and mental health 157–60; setbacks and disappointments into life 78
internal boundaries 10
internalized messages 35
internalized secure bases 58–9
interpersonal relationships 148
intimacy (proximity) 10, 69–70
intrinsic values and goals 18
Invictus (film) 162
Invictus (Henley) 161
isolation 70
isolation survival strategies 148

Jakob (Joost Peter Jakob van Wielink) *102*, 189–91, *189*
job changes 113
job losses 119
Johnson, Sue 77
Jordan, Michael 140
journeys as hero 17–20
joyful childhood experiences 180–1
joys of life 186
judgments 88, 97

Kahneman, Daniel 133
Karpman triangle (drama triangle) 87n6
Kasozi, Anthony 85
Kentie, Anita 72
Kessler, David 121, 138
Kets de Vries, Manfred 63, 68, 73, 160
Khamisa, Azim 170–1, 172
Khamisa, Tariq 170
Kintsugi ("golden connection"/"golden repair") 167–8
Klasen, Tijsse 44
knowing the past 7
knowledge-intensive work 49
Kohlrieser, George 59, *90*, 160, 198
Kolk, Bessel van der 65, 158
Kortie, Jan 60–1
Kosteljk, Ton 179

Kotter, John 21
Kramer, Jitske 128
Kübler-Ross, Elisabeth 90, *90*, 109, 121

leadership 1–6; approaches to 99–105;
    being trapped 144–5; defining
    16; instilling fear 49; and
    learning 85; lifeline 11–13;
    organizational systems 36–43;
    person effect 24–9; respect for
    employees 59; secure bases
    59–61; walking uncharted paths
    13–14
leading change 1–2
leading from your calling 19, 178
leading transition 20–4, 46
learning: and leadership 85; and
    meaning 167; and psychological
    safety 49–50
learning-oriented mindset 49
left hemisphere of the brain 63, 158–9
Leo (Leonard Wilhelm) 195–7, *195*
letting go (detaching) 109, **110**
Lewis, C.S. 140
the lifeline 11–13
life stories 171
listening 26, 93–7
listening without judgment 97
living in a community 175
living with a purpose 169–70
living your calling 4, 175 *see also* calling
logotherapy 170
loneliness 37, 52, 103–5, 149, 169
long-term relationships 169
losing commitment 133
loss and separation 10, 108–33, 140;
    abandonment and loneliness
    149; engaging in recovery 146;
    expected and unexpected losses
    118–19, 152; experiences of 68;
    forms of loss 109; and healthy
    functioning 152; leaving the old
    behind 146; and restoration 186;
    rituals 126–31; saying goodbye
    113–14, 120–6; separation
    108, 110–11 *see also* grief and
    grieving
loss of control, pain and discomfort 20
loss orientation *147*
loving 82–4
lower brain 63, 67, 158
loyalty to system of origin 87
Lynch, James 25

Maitlis, Sally 142
Mandela, Nelson 161, 162
man of control 18
Manzoni, Jean-François 21
mapping lives 11–12
Marquet, David 24
meaning 11, 167–72, 175–8 *see also*
    calling
meaningfulness 149–52, 167–8
memory reconsolidation 121–4
mending 100–3
mental health 157–60
mergers 130
merit (*earned respect*) 59
mindsets 78–9, 155–6
mind's eye 9
Miralles, Francesc 175
mismatches 121
mistakes 140
mountain of *competence, happiness
    and competition* (first mountain)
    178–9
mountain of *calling, joy and service*
    (second mountain) 179
Mr. Nice Guy/Woman 83–4
murder 170
myths and legends 17

Nazi concentration camps 169 *see also*
    Auschwitz
'Neanderthals' 158
need-for-attachment switch 66
needs 86–8
negative emotions 70–1
negative judgments 88
negative memory 121
negative messages 71–2
negative thoughts 71
negativity and cynicism 25
Neijenhuis, Joyce 143–4
Neimeyer, Robert 198
neocortex (higher brain) 63, 157
neural connections/pathways 74–5
neural networks 74
neurogenesis 74
neurons 74
neuroplasticity 74, 121
new beginning rituals 127
nostalgic longings 3
Nouwen, Henri 71, 186

Okinawa, Japan 175
Ollongren, Kajsa 39–40, 125

optimal stress levels 154, *154*
Option B (Sandberg and Grant) 108
organizational changes 20, 131
organizational functions 38
organizational roles 2, *174*; Jakob *189*;
        Leo *195*; Riet *192*
organizations: calling 184–5; creation
        and emergence life cycle 112;
        identity 39
'otherness' of the other 5
Ottens, Peter 56–7
'over-caring' behavior 41–2
overidentification with roles 174
Oxytocin 63

painful emotions 124
painful feedback 27
painful feelings *153*
paraphrasing 94, 95–6
Paraphrasing 1.0 94
Paraphrasing 2.0 94
parent-child alignment 36
parentification 41
parents 33–6; attuned responses with
        children 63; *brain-building*
        62; calming children's brains
        65; death of 41; giving and
        receiving 43; leader-employee
        relationships 61; secure bases 41
        see also children
patterns of families and organizations 39
patterns of leadership 182–3
Pavlov, Ivan 25n18
peak-end rule 133
people (*tribes*) 128
perfectionism 167
perfect parenting 35
performance 59
Perry, Bruce 67, 75
personal changes 20
personal growth 78
personal influences 12–13
personal loss 156
personal mastery of the leader (Senge) 167
personal nature of leadership 16
personal responsibility (autonomy)
        15–16
personal roles 2, *174*; Jakob *189*; Leo
        195; Riet *192*
the person effect 24–9
person effect 24–9
Petriglieri, Gianpiero 142
physical pain 88

Porges, Stephen 140
positive people 25
positive person effect 27–8
powerlessness 83
power of focus 169
predictable stress 154
primal sources 4
processing 143
professional milestones 126
professional roles 2, *174*; Jakob *189*; Leo
        195; Riet *192*
profound loss 128, 170
projection 44–5
protest behaviors 53
psychological contract 45–6
psychological safety 9, 46–50, *102*
puberty 157–8
purpose 170, 184
putting the fish on the table (Kohlrieser)
        59

quality interaction 169

Rasker, Frans 163
reactions to situations/people
        (transference reactions) 44–5
real change 15 *see also* transition
Reason (strategy for disconnection) 67
receivers (people who listen) 70
Regulate (strategy for disconnection) 67
Reijmerink, Marnix *102*, 198, 199
Relate (strategy for disconnection) 67
relating to people 7
remembering and commemorating 131
reorganizations 130
reptilian brain 63
rescuing behavior 71
resentment and revenge 149–50
resilience 8–9, 75–8, *153 see also*
        attachment
resistance: to calling 177; to change
        144–5; to pain of change 132–3;
        as protective mechanism 149
respect 59
restoration orientation *147*
restoring broken contacts 76
rewiring the brain 55
Rhenen, Rachel Naomi 113
Riet (Maria Josina Martina Fiddelaers-
        Jaspers) 150, 192–4, *192*
right brain communication 63, 65, 159
right brain to right brain communication
        76, 159

right hemisphere 158–9
rigidity 153 *see also* resilience
risks 58
rituals 126–31
Robertson, Brian 184
roles 3
Roosevelt, Theodore 140
roots 5
Route Planner (Transition Cycle) 148
running from the past 151

safety/insecurity lens 61
Sancho Panza (*Don Quixote*) 177
Sandberg, Sheryl 108
Santayana, George 7
saying goodbye 21–2, 109, 113–14,
    120–8
Schopenhauer, Arthur 68–9
Schut, Henk *147*
Schwarzenegger, Arnold 16–17
seat switching 124
second mountain (*calling, joy and
    service*) 179
secure attachment 53, 55, 139, 159
    see also attachment; insecure
    attachment
secure bases 9; adults 56; and
    attachment 57–62; calming
    nervous system 156; impact of
    words 71–2; leadership 59–60;
    loss of 10; resilience 77–8; as
    support and inspiration 178;
    survival strategies 160
self-chosen career moves 113
self-control 17
self-fulfilling prophecies 9
self-made leaders 16
self-made men 16–17
self-regulation 65–6, 69–70, 159
Senge, Peter 167
sense-making 167
sense of belonging 29
sensitivity to compliments 78
separation 108, 110–11 *see also* loss
    and separation
separation anxiety 53, 110
set-up-to-fail syndrome 21, 46
shaking hands 129
shaping change 113–14
shaping transition 28, *147*
shaping your calling 11
shared experiences 47
sharing lifelines 12

sharing life stories 171
sharing losses 109
Shortcutting the Transition Cycle *131*
shutting out vulnerability 140 *see also*
    attachment
Siegel, Daniel 63n25, 75, 159
'slow questions' 23
Smith, Emily Esfahani 168, 169, 172
social and cultural codes (etiquette) 86
social involvement system (Porges) 140
social pain (discomfort) 88
social rejection and isolation 88
social roles 2, *174*; Jakob *189*; Leo *195*;
    Riet *192*
social support 143–4 *see also* grief and
    grieving
Socrates 186
Soeters, Michiel 199
'solidified grief' 23
sources of inspiration 181
spiritual growth 109, **110**
staying alive and giving up 169
staying calm 75–8
Steeghs, Leanne 36
Strecher, Victor 169
stress 153–9; listening 94; mindsets
    and effects of 155–6; optimal
    stress 154, *154*; reverting to
    'Neanderthals' 158; and secure
    bases 58; stretched levels 154–6,
    155; unhealthy stress 156–7, *157*
Stroebe, Margareth *147*
suffering 170
suppressing feelings 149 *see also*
    resistance
'surface current' changes 20
survival strategies 148–52, *153*, 160
"survivor syndrome" and "survivor guilt"
    127
sword of Damocles 99
systemic work (Hellinger) 36n8

tabula rasa 33
talking about experiences 76–8
talking to yourself 66
Tariq Khamisa Foundation 170–1
team as secure base 113, 137–9
team performance 46
teams and teamwork 46–50, 59
temporary farewells 125
tension 156
"10,000 hours guideline" (Ericsson) 79
therapeutic interactions 75

thinking about stress 155
threatening person effect 26
Throw the Helm (Marquet) 24
'tilting at windmills' (*Don Quixote*) 177
Tony (gang member) 170–1
Tools of Titans (Ferriss) 16–17
transcendent experiences 171–2
transference 26, 61
transference reactions (reactions to situations/people) 44–5
transformational leadership 18
transformations 19
transient losses 125
transition 2, 15–30; and change 15–16, 21; emotional language 71–4; and grief 145–6; importance 15–20; layers 22–3; and leadership 20–3; leading 23–30; and learning 29–30; secure base leaders 60; shaping in everyday life *147*; stages 22
transitional objects 58
Transition Cycle 4–5, 186, 199; and rituals 128; Route Planner 7–14, 148; shortcutting *131*; themes 7–11, *8*
transition moments 181–2
transmitters (people who talk) 70
trouble shared is a trouble halved 76–8
trust 20–1, 47, 55, 59
Tutu, Desmond 162

uncomfortable emotions 103
unconscious behavior 8, 53
unconscious blocking behavior 115–16
unconscious family patterns 39
unconscious memories 64
unexamined life 186
unexpected effects of loss 118–20
unexpected losses 118–20, 152
unfinished business 163
unhealthy stress levels 156–7, *157*
uninvolved person effect 26

unraveling 44
unspoken expectations 62
upper brain 67, 157–8
'upstairs brain' (Siegel) 63n25

Van Bommel Shoes 23–4, 38
The Very Hungry Caterpillar (Carle) 102
virtue 87
VUCA (Volatility, Uncertainty, Complexity and Ambiguity) 28n26
vulnerability: beliefs about scarcity 101–2; and bonding 84–5; boundaries 160; and courage 140; getting hurt 70; and intimacy 10

well-organized farewells 127
Wersch, Marcel, van 199
wielding the axe 100
Wielink, Joost Peter Jakob van (Jakob) *102*, 189–91, *189*
Wilhelm, Leonard (Leo) 195–7, *195*
willingness to change 15
willpower 4
Window of Excellence (Gasteren, Reijmerink and Wielink) *102*
window of leadership and calling 2, 174–5, *174*; Jakob *189*; Leo *195*; Riet *192 see also* calling
window of stress tolerance: optimal stress levels 154, *154*; stretched stress levels 154–6, *155*; unhealthy stress levels 156–7, *157 see also* stress
wisdom of the group 46, 91
withdrawing styles of life and leadership 101, *102*
words spoken in attachment 71–2
work and grief 137–9
working hard 71, 150, 193

Yalom, Irvin 10
YETS Foundation 56–7

Taylor & Francis eBooks

www.taylorfrancis.com

A single destination for eBooks from Taylor & Francis with increased functionality and an improved user experience to meet the needs of our customers.

90,000+ eBooks of award-winning academic content in Humanities, Social Science, Science, Technology, Engineering, and Medical written by a global network of editors and authors.

TAYLOR & FRANCIS EBOOKS OFFERS:

A streamlined experience for our library customers

A single point of discovery for all of our eBook content

Improved search and discovery of content at both book and chapter level

REQUEST A FREE TRIAL
support@taylorfrancis.com